Customized excerpts from:

Microsoft® Official Academic Course

Windows Server® 2008 Administrator Lab Manual

Microsoft Certified IT Professional Exam 70-646

Microsoft® Official Academic Course

Windows Server® 2008 Network Infrastructure Configuration Lab Manual

Microsoft Certified Technology Specialist Exam 70-642

Microsoft® Official Academic Course

Windows Server® 2008 Active Directory Configuration Lab Manual

Microsoft Certified Technology Specialist Exam 70-640

Customized by Amado K. Figueroa

WILEY *Custom*
LEARNING SOLUTIONS

To order books or for customer service, please call 1(800)-CALL-WILEY (225-5945).

Printed in the United States of America.

ISBN 978-1-118-29757-5
Printed and bound by Bind Rite.

10 9 8 7 6 5 4 3

The content of this lab manual contains customized excerpts from:

Microsoft® Official Academic Course
Windows Server® 2008 Administrator Lab Manual Microsoft Certified IT
Professional Exam 70-646

Microsoft® Official Academic Course
Windows Server® 2008 Network Infrastructure Configuration Lab Manual
Microsoft Certified Technology Specialist Exam 70-642

And

Microsoft® Official Academic Course
Windows Server® 2008 Active Directory® Configuration Lab Manual
Microsoft Certified Technology Specialist Exam 70-640

Since this custom lab manual is based on customized excerpts of the full Microsoft® Official Academic Course lab manuals for 70-646, 70-642, and 70-640, it is not intended to cover the entire objective domain for the Microsoft® certification exams. In that way, this custom lab manual is not meant to be a preparatory lab manual for the Microsoft® 70-646, 70-642 or 70-640 certification exams.

CUSTOM CONTENTS

PART 1: CUSTOMIZED EXCERPTS FROM WINDOWS SERVER® 2008 ADMINISTRATOR MICROSOFT CERTIFIED IT PROFESSIONAL EXAM 70-646 LAB

PART 2: CUSTOMIZED EXCERPTS FROM WINDOWS SERVER® 2008 ADMINISTRATOR MICROSOFT CERTIFIED IT PROFESSIONAL EXAM 70-646 LAB AND WINDOWS SERVER® 2008 NETWORK INFRASTRUCTURE CONFIGURATION MICROSOFT CERTIFIED TECHNOLOGY SPECIALIST EXAM 70-642 LAB

PART 3: CUSTOMIZED EXCERPTS FROM WINDOWS SERVER® 2008 ACTIVE DIRECTORY® CONFIGURATION MICROSOFT CERTIFIED TECHNOLOGY SPECIALIST EXAM 70-640 LABS

PART 1: CUSTOMIZED EXCERPTS FROM:

WINDOWS SERVER® 2008 ADMINISTRATOR MICROSOFT CERTIFIED IT PROFESSIONAL EXAM 70-646 LAB

LAB 1
PREPARING A SECOND VIRTUAL SERVER IMAGE

This lab contains the following exercises:

Exercise 1.1   Creating a Windows Server 2008 Virtual Appliance

Exercise 1.2   Performing Initial Configuration Tasks

Exercise 1.3   Testing Network Connectivity

Exercise 1.4   Installing the DNS Server Role

Exercise 1.5   Installing the DHCP Server Role

Estimated lab time: 95 minutes

Exercise 1.1	Creating A Windows Server 2008 Virtual Appliance
Overview	This lab assumes that you have the Active Directory Domain Controller and Windows 7 Machines you created in NT1230 (Server##) stored on your hard drive. You are creating a new computer virtual appliance with Windows Server 2008 using VMware Player. Your first task is to create a new Virtual Machine and install Windows Server 2008 Standard 32bit with appropriate settings for the test lab network. This server will become a replica Domain Controller for your test network.
Completion time	30 minutes

1. Start VMWare Player and create a new Virtual Machine. Make sure that you have your Windows Server 2008 32 bit installation disk in the DVD player.

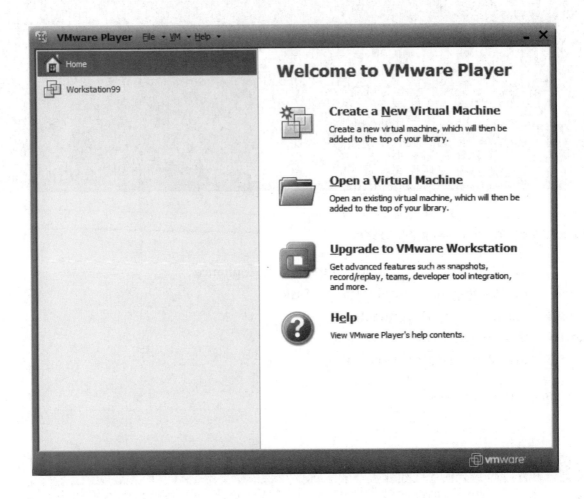

*Note	Depending on the version of VMWare Player you are using some screens will be slightly different.

2. Select the installation disk and click next.

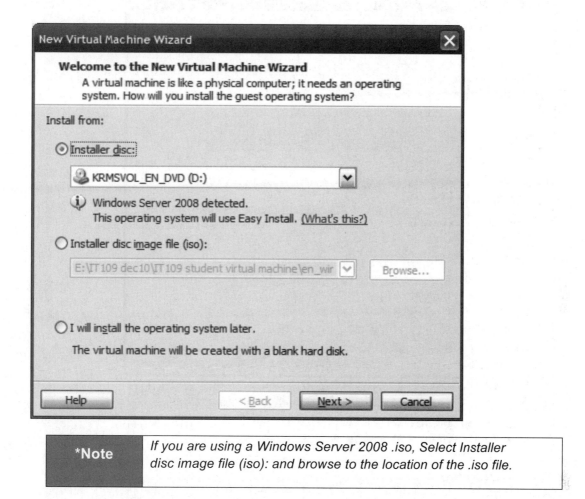

*Note	If you are using a Windows Server 2008 .iso, Select Installer disc image file (iso): and browse to the location of the .iso file.

3. Skip the Product key and use "Student ## "where ## is the number provided by your instructor as the full name, and P@ssw0rd as password.

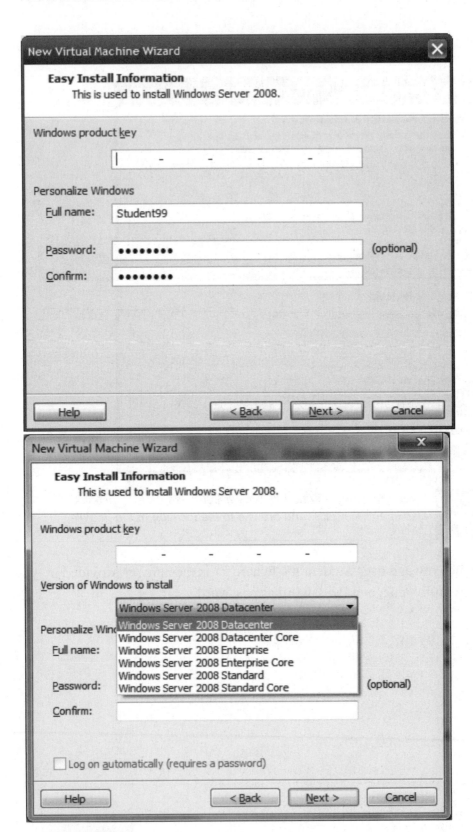

| *Note | Depending on the version of VMWare Player you are using you may need to choose Windows Server 2008 Standard as the Operating System to install during this step. Please ensure Windows Server 2008 Standard is the version chosen. |

*Note	Online students can use Student01 as the name of their student account.

4. You would like to continue. Click Yes.

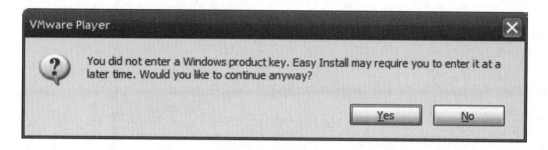

5. Name your VM Appliance Server##A where ## is the number assigned by your instructor. And store the new Appliance in a newly created Windows Server 2008 Replica folder in you're my Virtual Machines folder on your removable USB hard disk.

*Note	Online students can use Server01A as their Virtual Machine Name.

6. Click next and choose the default disk size of 40GB, and click next.

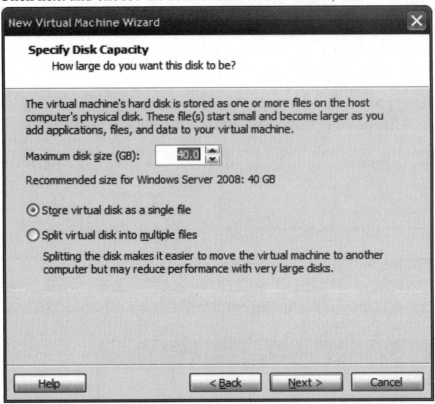

7. Remember to customize Hardware and select Advance and "legacy systems" for the CD/DVD drive. Also change the Network Adapter Settings to Host Only.

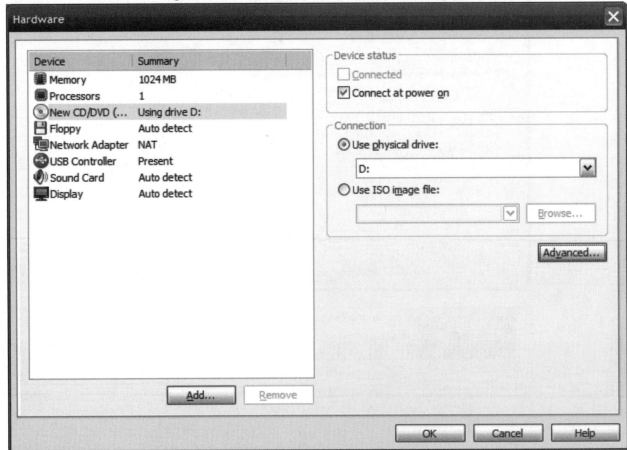

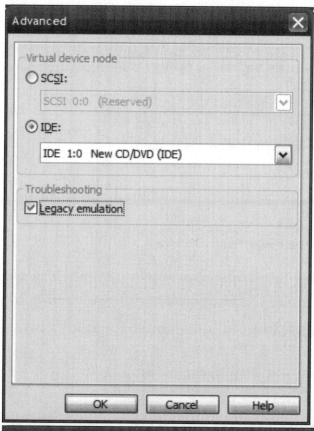

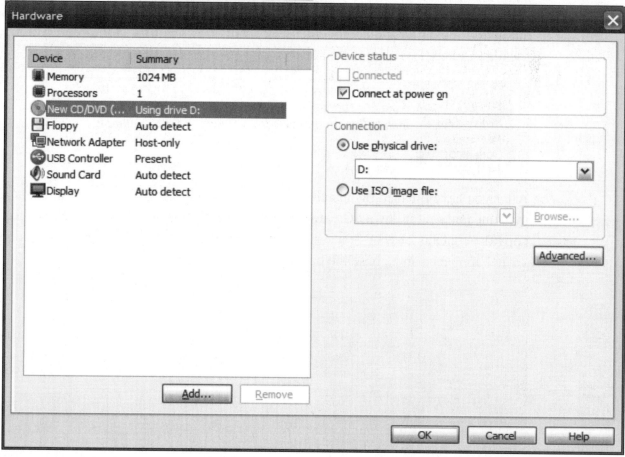

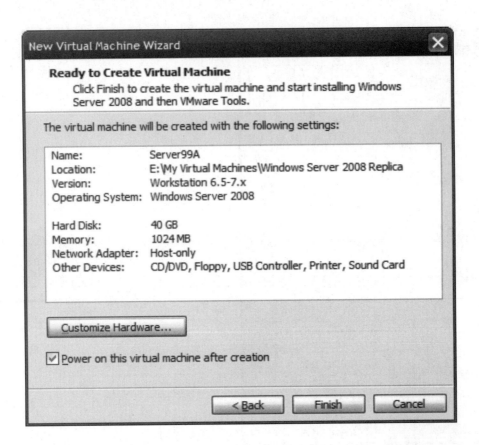

8. Click finish and install Windows Server 2008 Standard (32bit). Remember uncheck the automatic activation and do not enter a key. Shut down your VM in order to proceed to the next exercise.

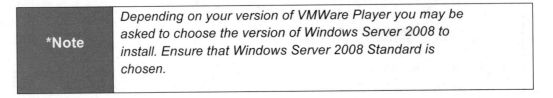

*Note	Depending on your version of VMWare Player you may be asked to choose the version of Windows Server 2008 to install. Ensure that Windows Server 2008 Standard is chosen.

9. After you have finished the installation of your Windows Server 2008 Standard (32bit) machine and shut it down. Create a second folder in the My Virtual Machines folder and copy the contents of your first server folder to this new folder, giving you a second virtual appliance and a baseline backup.

192.168.1.1 - win
192.168.?.2 - servcore
192.168.?.3 . servA
192.168.1.4 - web serv
192.168.1.5 - FTP
192.168.1.6 - Email
192.168.107 - Router
192.168.108-9 - Excluded

Preparing a Second Virtual Server Image   9

Exercise 1.2	Performing Initial Configuration Tasks
Overview	Now that you have installed Windows Server 2008 you must configure the computer with appropriate settings in order for it to communicate with the computers on your test network.
Completion time	30 minutes

1. Turn on the Server##A computer and log on using your Student## account and the password P@ssw0rd. The Initial Configuration Tasks window appears.

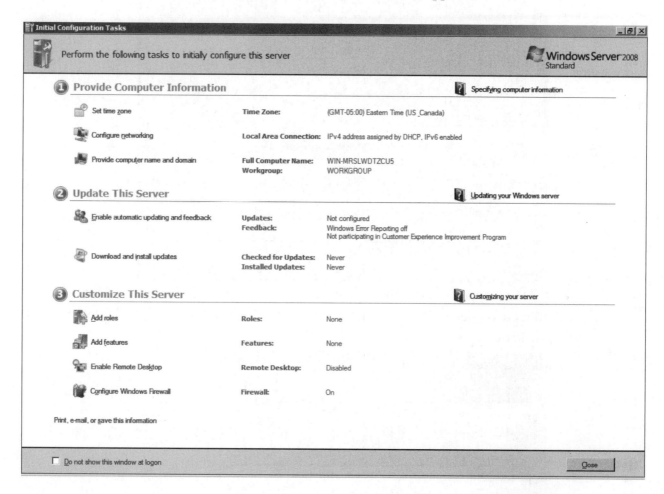

2. Take a screen shot showing the Initial Configuration Tasks window by pressing Alt+ Prt Scr, and then paste the resulting image into the Lab01_worksheet file in the page provided by pressing Ctrl + V.
3. Click Provide Computer Name And Domain. The System Properties dialog box appears with the Computer Name tab selected.

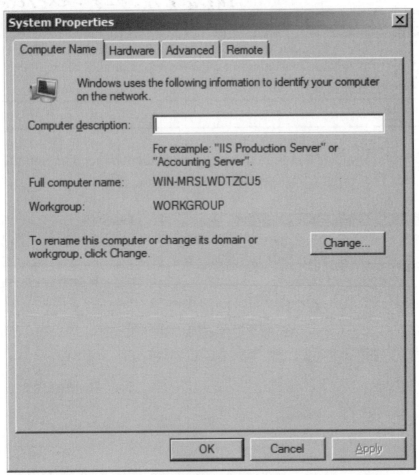

4. Click Change. The Computer Name/Domain Changes dialog box appears.

5. In the Computer Name text box, key Server##A where ##, supplied by your instructor, identifies your computer and click OK.

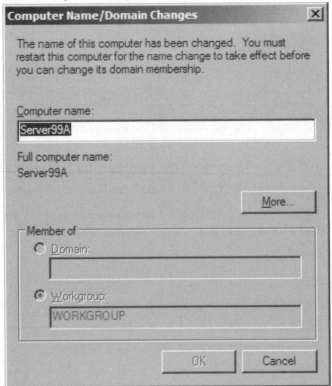

6. You will be prompted to restart the machine. Click OK. Then click close to close the Systems Properties sheet. A Microsoft Windows message box appears, reminding you again to restart the computer.

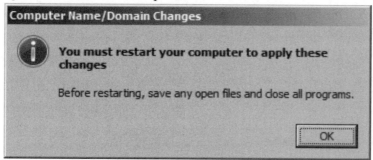

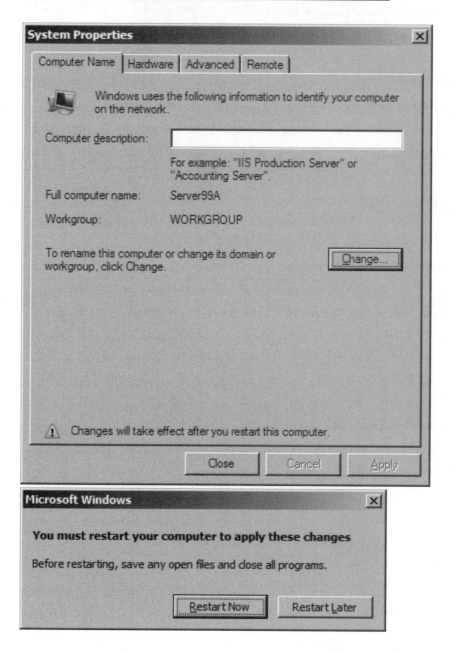

7. Click Restart Now. The computer restarts.
8. Log on to the Server##A computer using your Student## account and the password P@ssw0rd. The Initial Configuration Tasks window appears.

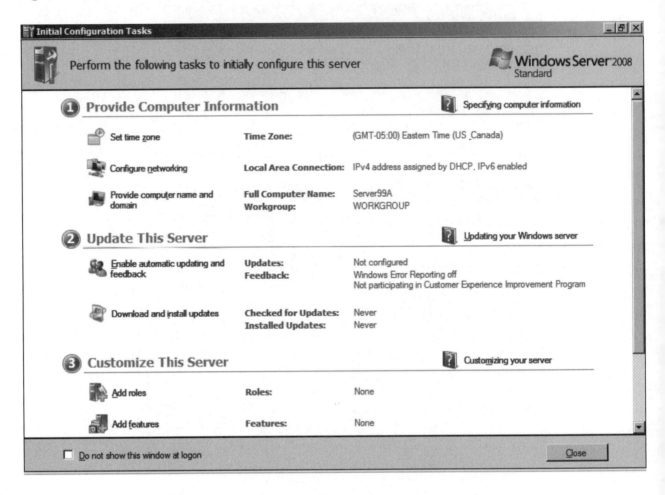

9. Click Configure Networking. The Network Connections window appears.

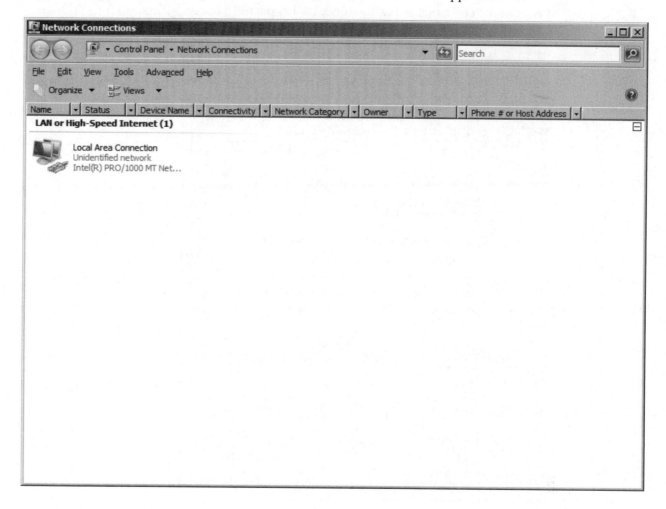

10. Right-click the Local Area Connection icon and, from the context menu, select Properties. The Local Area Connection Properties sheet appears.

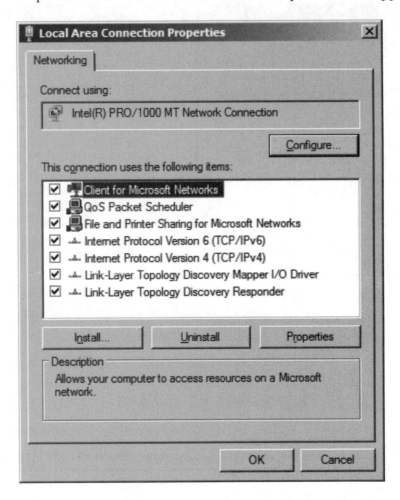

11. Clear the Internet Protocol Version 6 (TCP/IPv6) checkbox.

12. Select Internet Protocol Version 4 (TCP/IPv4) and click Properties. The Internet Protocol Version 4 (TCP/IPv4) Properties sheet appears.

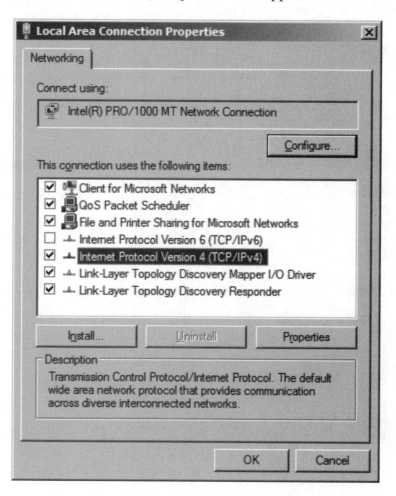

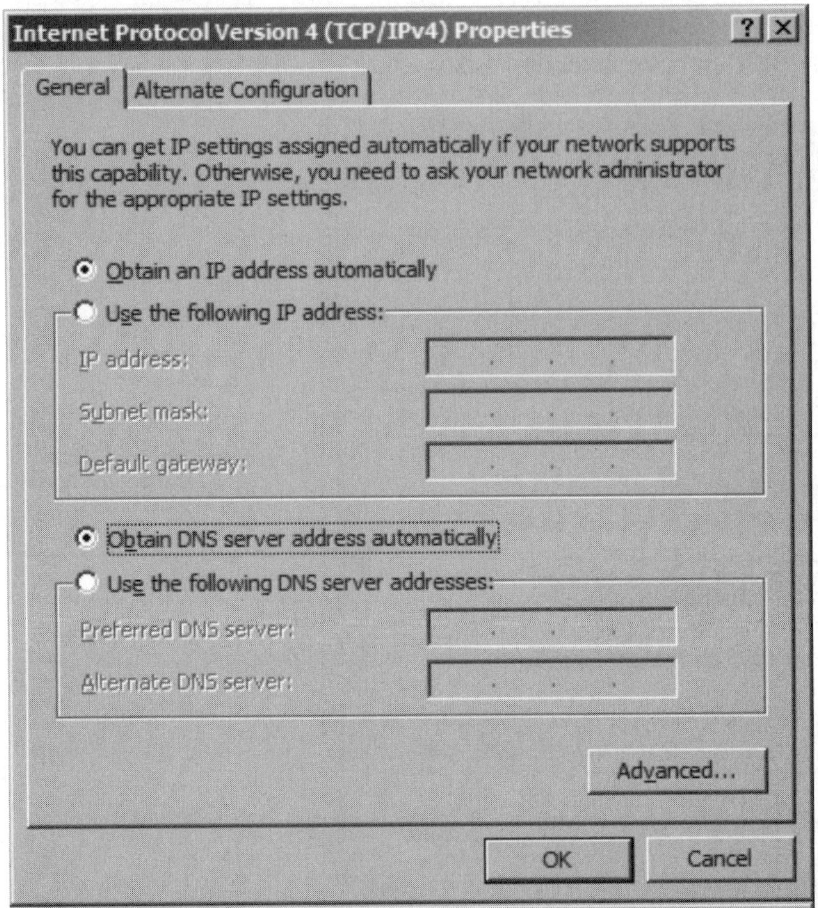
Internet Protocol Version 4 (TCP/IPv4) Properties
General
Alternate Configuration
You can get IP settings assigned automatically if your network supports this capability. Otherwise, you need to ask your network administrator for the appropriate IP settings.
Obtain an IP address automatically
Use the following IP address:
IP address:
Subnet mask:
Default gateway:
Obtain DNS server address automatically
Use the following DNS server addresses:
Preferred DNS server:
Alternate DNS server:
Advanced...
OK
Cancel

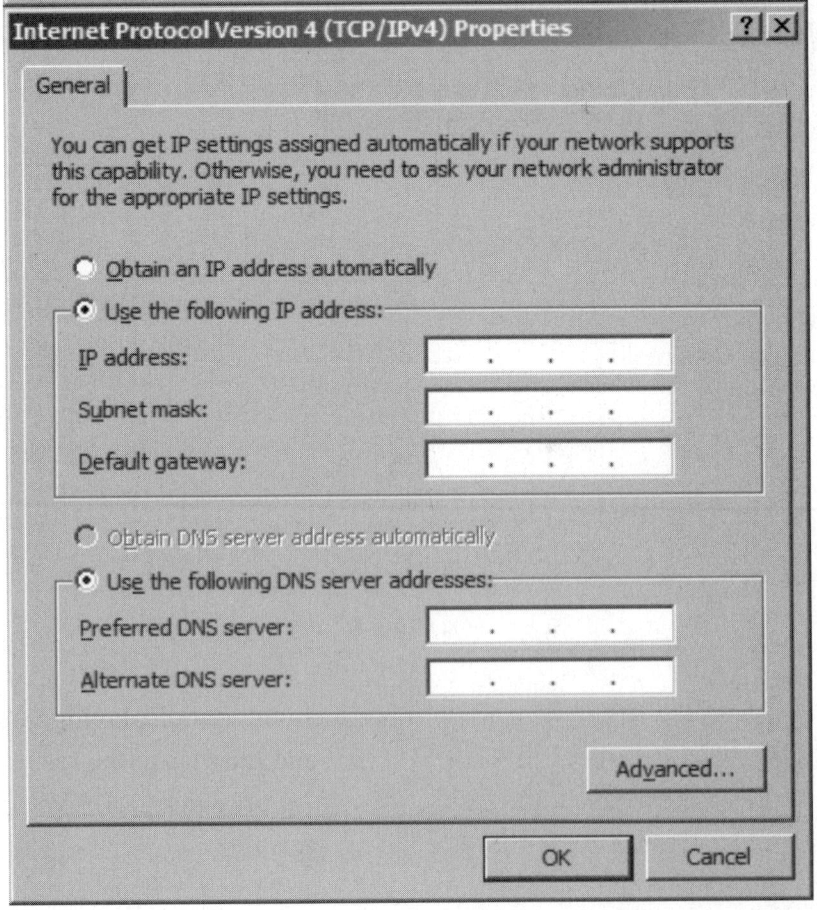
Internet Protocol Version 4 (TCP/IPv4) Properties
General
You can get IP settings assigned automatically if your network supports this capability. Otherwise, you need to ask your network administrator for the appropriate IP settings.
Obtain an IP address automatically
Use the following IP address:
IP address:
Subnet mask:
Default gateway:
Obtain DNS server address automatically
Use the following DNS server addresses:
Preferred DNS server:
Alternate DNS server:
Advanced...
OK
Cancel

13. Select the Use the following IP address and the Use the following DNS server addresses radio buttons and enter the following information:

      • IP Address: 172.16.##.3 (Where ## is the number assigned by your instructor)

      • Subnet Mask: 255.255.255.0

      • Preferred DNS Server: 172.16.##.1 (This is the IP address of your Server## machine)

*Note	The IP addresses supplied in this setup document and in the lab manual are suggestions. You can use any IP addresses for the computers in your classroom, as long as all of the systems are located on the same subnet. If the classroom network is connected to a school network or the Internet, you can specify the address of the router providing the network connection in the Default Gateway field. Otherwise, leave it blank.

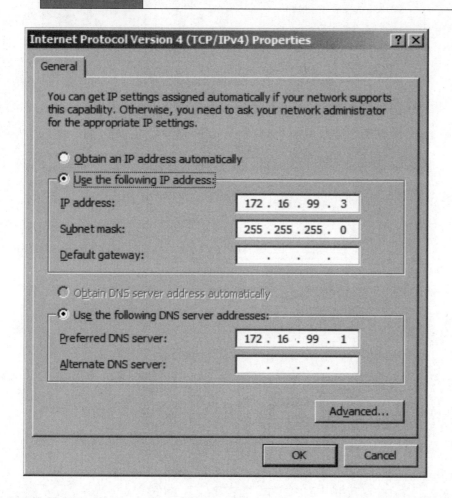

14. Click OK twice to close the two Properties sheets. Close the Network Connections window.
15. Take a screen shot showing the Initial Configuration Tasks window displaying your new Computer Name and IP address by pressing Alt+ Prt Scr, and then paste the resulting image into the Lab01_worksheet file in the page provided by pressing Ctrl + V.
16. Leave the Server##A computer logged on for the next exercise.

Exercise 1.3	Testing Network Connectivity
Overview	Now that you have configured Windows Server 2008 you will test network connectivity between Server##A and Server## using the ping command.
Completion time	10 minutes

1. Turn on the Server## computer and log on using your Student## account and the password P@ssw0rd.

2. On Server##A Click Start. Then All Programs > Accessories > Command Prompt. A Command Prompt window appears.

3. In the Command Prompt window, type ping 172.16.##.1 and press Enter.

4. Type ping Server## and press enter.

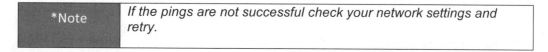

```
Command Prompt                                                    _ □ X
Pinging 172.16.99.1 with 32 bytes of data:
Reply from 172.16.99.1: bytes=32 time=1ms TTL=128
Reply from 172.16.99.1: bytes=32 time=1ms TTL=128
Reply from 172.16.99.1: bytes=32 time=1ms TTL=128
Reply from 172.16.99.1: bytes=32 time=20ms TTL=128

Ping statistics for 172.16.99.1:
    Packets: Sent = 4, Received = 4, Lost = 0 (0% loss),
Approximate round trip times in milli-seconds:
    Minimum = 1ms, Maximum = 20ms, Average = 5ms

C:\Users\Student99>ping server99

Pinging server99 [172.16.99.1] with 32 bytes of data:
Reply from 172.16.99.1: bytes=32 time=5ms TTL=128
Reply from 172.16.99.1: bytes=32 time=1ms TTL=128
Reply from 172.16.99.1: bytes=32 time<1ms TTL=128
Reply from 172.16.99.1: bytes=32 time<1ms TTL=128

Ping statistics for 172.16.99.1:
    Packets: Sent = 4, Received = 4, Lost = 0 (0% loss),
Approximate round trip times in milli-seconds:
    Minimum = 0ms, Maximum = 5ms, Average = 1ms

C:\Users\Student99>
```

Question 1	*What service is necessary in order to ping Server## by name?*

5. Take a screen shot showing the successful pings by pressing Alt+ Prt Scr, and then paste the resulting image into the Lab01_worksheet file in the page provided by pressing Ctrl + V.

*Note	*If the pings are not successful check your network settings and retry.*

6. Log off of Server## and leave Server##A logged on for the next exercise.

Exercise 1.4	Installing the DNS Server Role
Overview	Now that the server is configured and network connectivity has been confirmed you will install the DNS Server Role in preparation for future testing.
Completion time	10 minutes

1. On Server##A click Start > Administrative Tools > Server Manager. Click Continue in the User Account Control message box, and the Server Manager console appears.

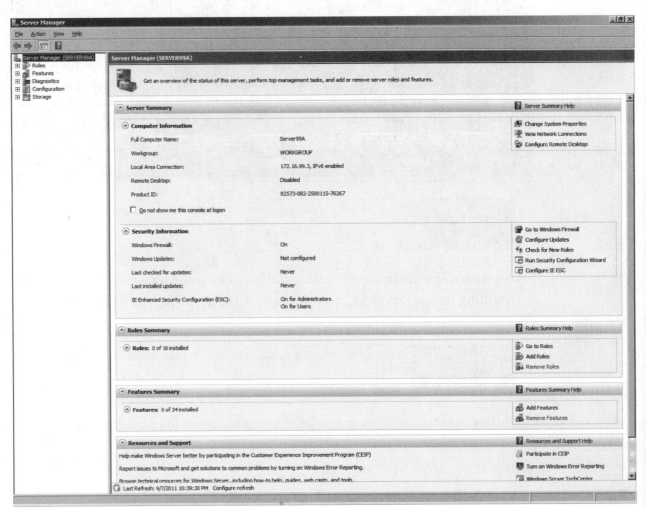

2. Select the Roles node, and click Add Roles. The Add Roles Wizard appears, displaying the Before You Begin page.

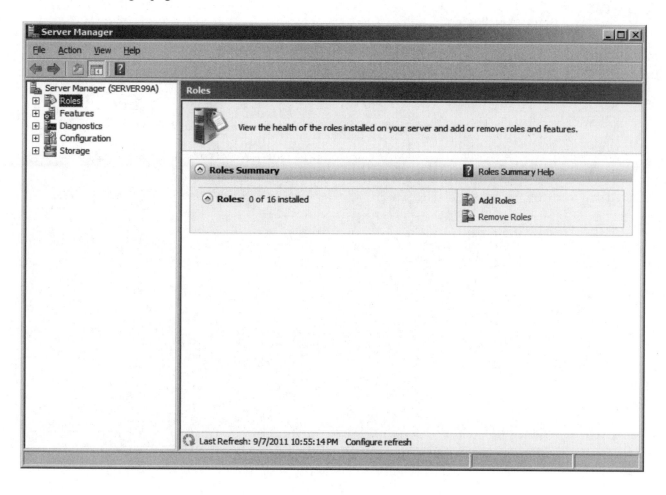

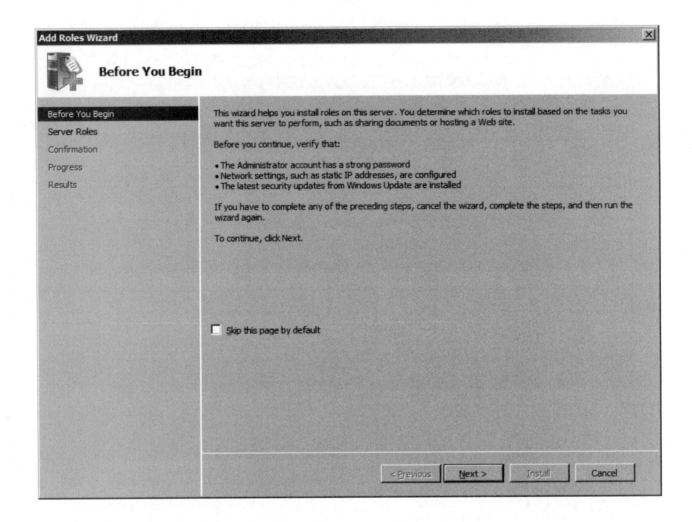

3. Click Next to continue. The Select Server Roles page appears.

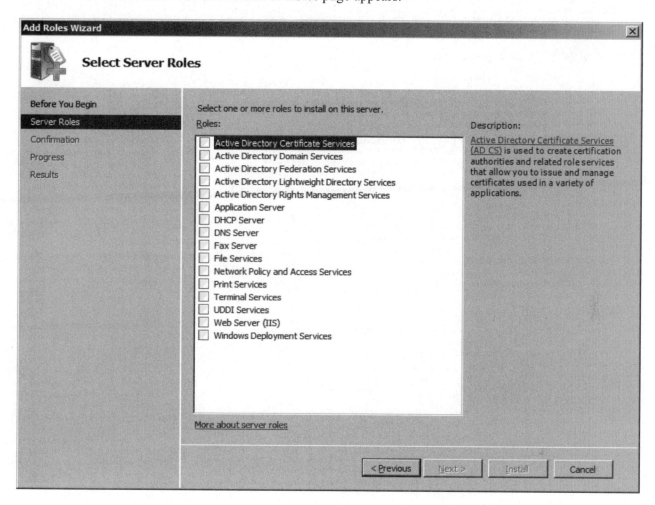

4. On the Select Server Roles page select the DNS Server role and then click Next.

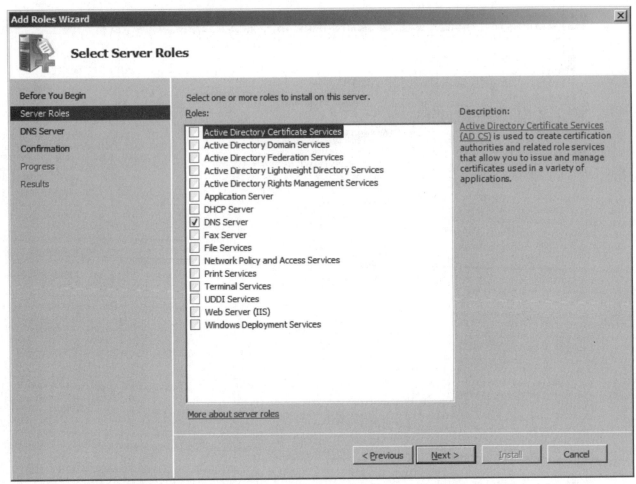

| *Note | If a message box appears, warning that the computer does not have a static IP address click Install DNS Server anyway. |

5. The DNS Server page appears. Click Next to continue.

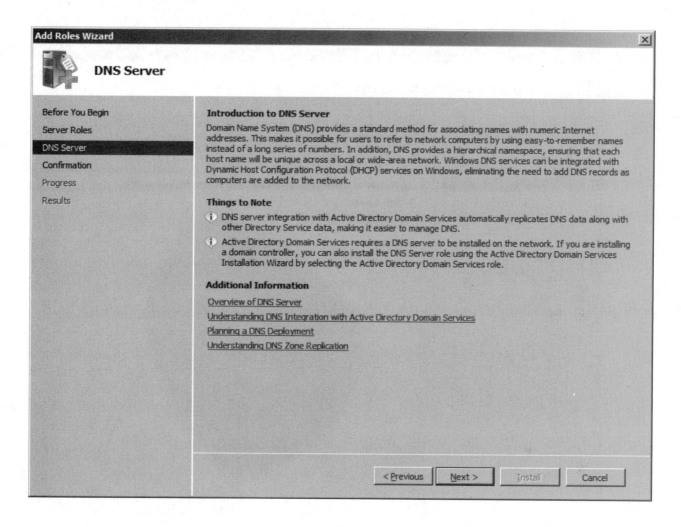

6. The Confirm Installation Selections page appears. Click Install. The wizard installs the DNS Server role.

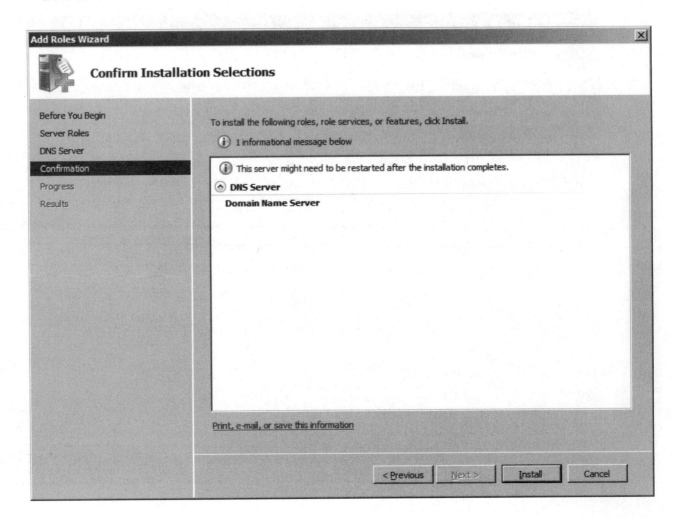

7. Click Close on the Installations Results screen.

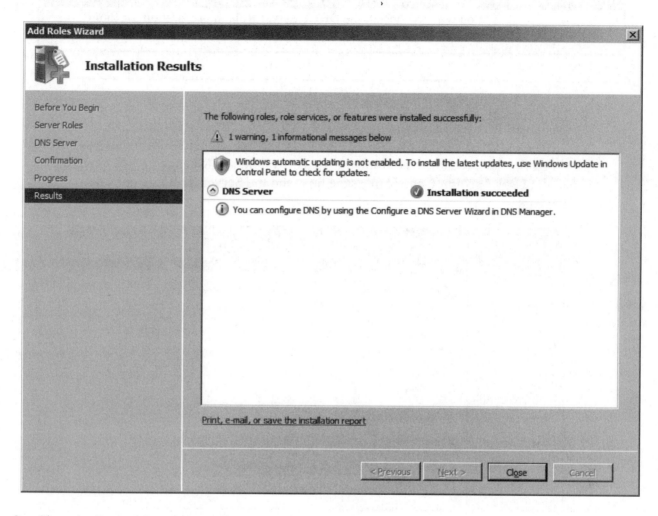

8. Close the Server Manager console.

9. Leave the computer logged on for the next exercise.

Exercise 1.5	Installing the DHCP Server Role
Overview	You will now install the DHCP Server Role in preparation for future testing.
Completion time	15 minutes

1. On the Server##A computer and log on using your Student## account and the password P@ssw0rd.

2. Click Start Click Start > Administrative Tools > Server Manager. Click Continue in the User Account Control message box, and the Server Manager console appears.

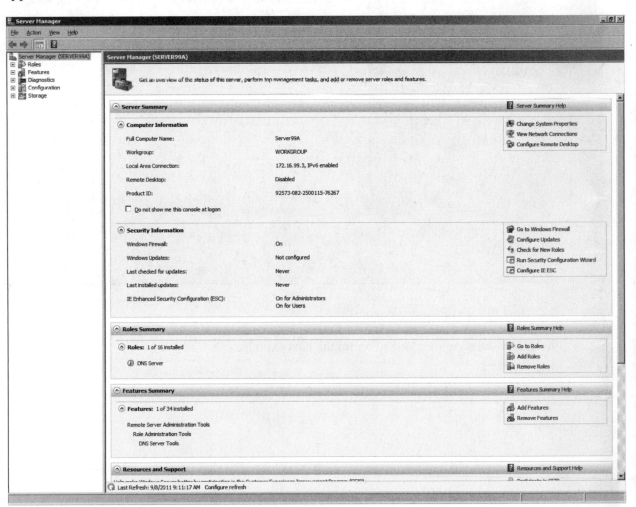

3. Select the Roles node, and click Add Roles. The Add Roles Wizard appears, displaying the *Before You Begin* page.

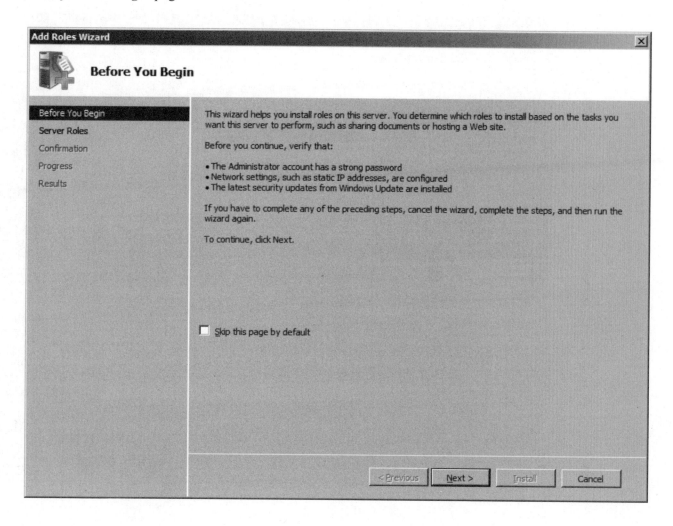

4. Click Next to continue. The *Select Server Roles* page appears.

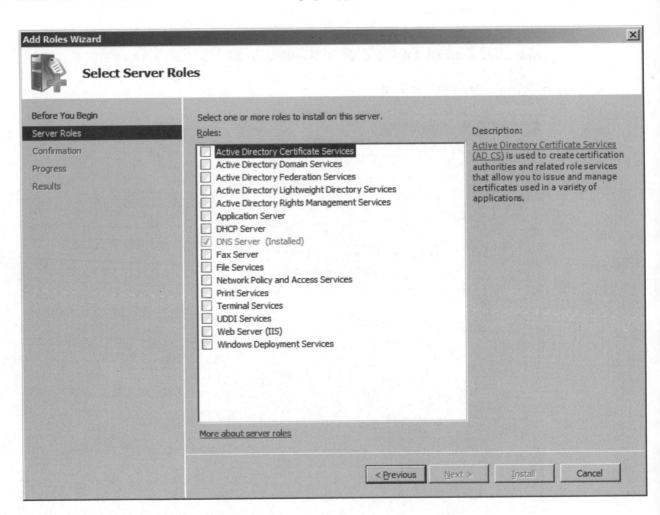

5. Select the DHCP Server role. Click Next to continue. The *DHCP Server* page appears.

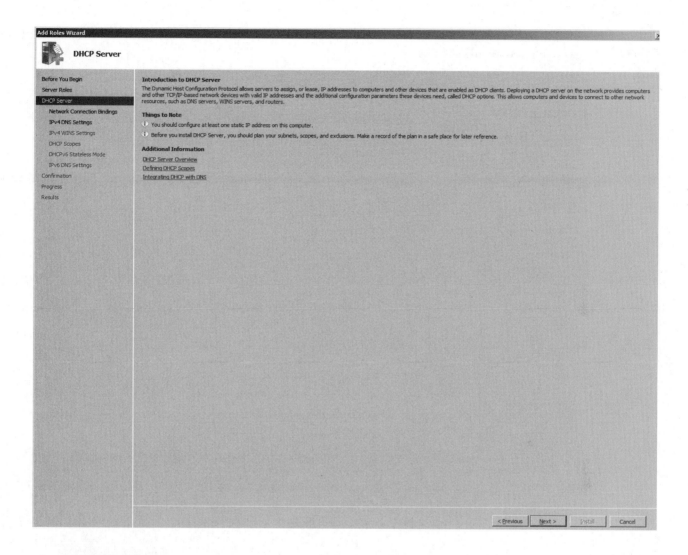

*Note	If a message box appears, warning that the computer does not have a static IP address click Install DHCP Server anyway.

6. Click Next. The *Select Network Connection Bindings* page appears.

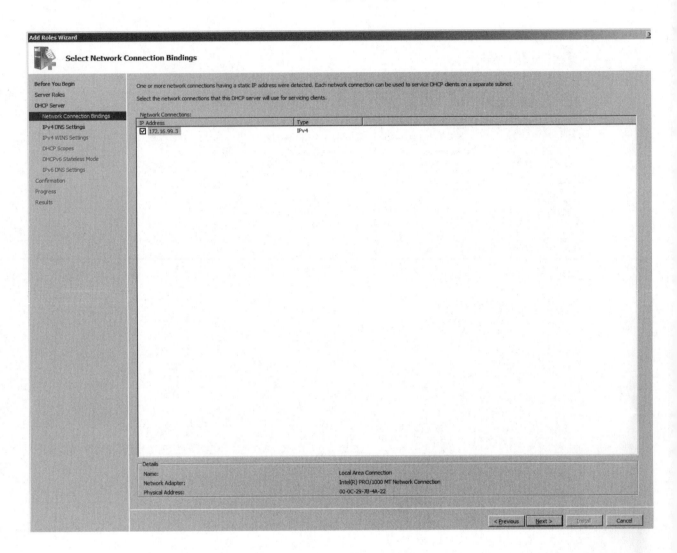

7. Click Next. The *Specify IPv4 DNS Server Settings* page appears.

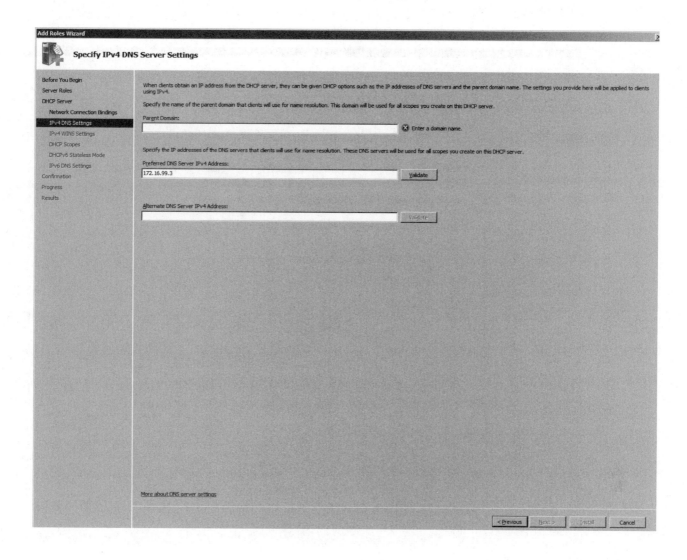

8. In the Parent Domain text box, key Contoso##.Local, where ## is the number provided by your instructor.

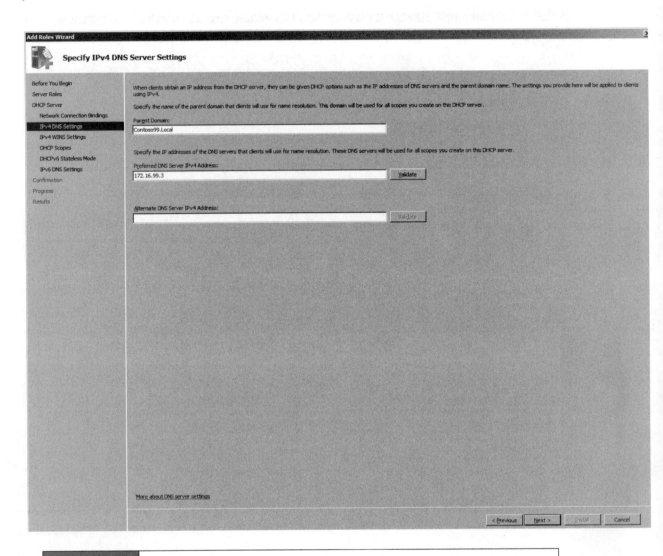

Question 2	*Where did the wizard obtain the IP address that appears in the Preferred DNS Server IPv4 Address text box by default?*

9. Click the Validate button.

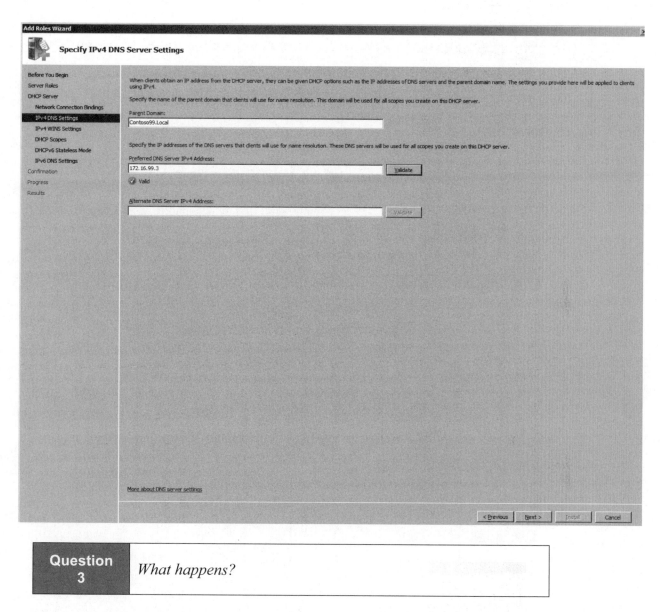

Question 3	*What happens?*

10. Press Ctrl+Prt Scr to take a screen shot of the Add Roles Wizard, showing the *Specify IPv4 DNS Server Settings* page, and then press Ctrl+V to paste the resulting image into the lab01_worksheet file in the page provided.

11. Click Next to continue. The *Specify IPv4 WINS Server Settings* page appears.

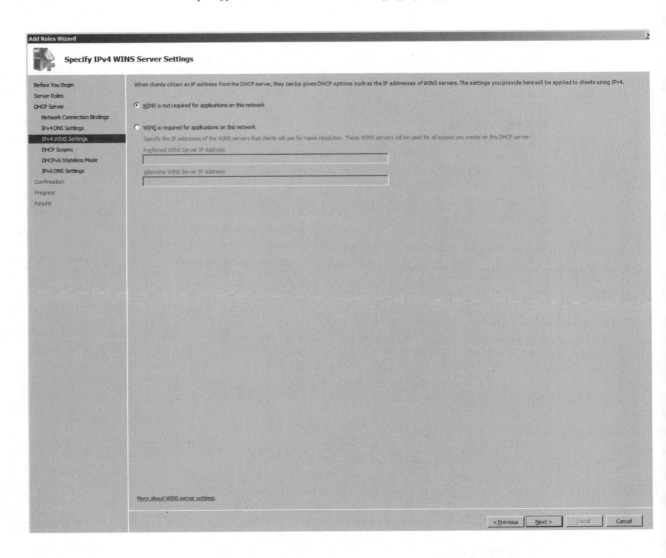

12. Click Next to accept the default settings. The *DHCP Scopes* page appears.

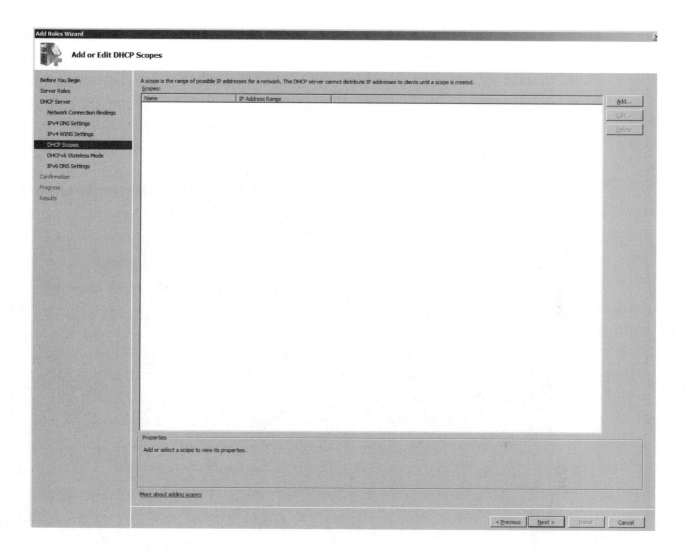

13. Click Next to continue. The *Configure DHCPv6 Stateless Mode* page appears.

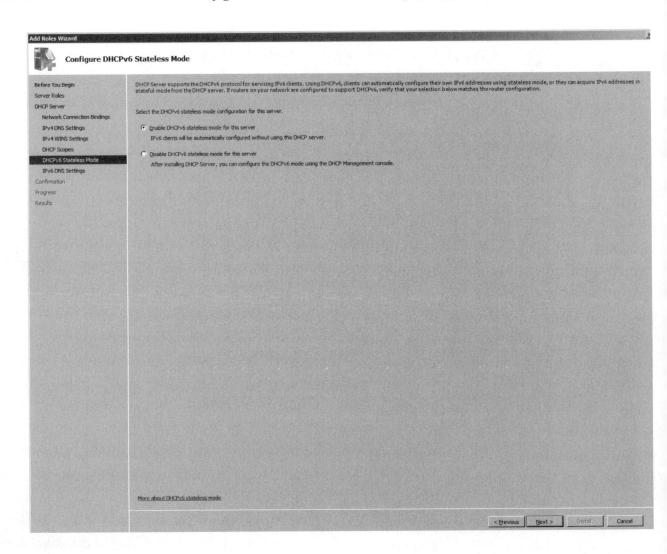

14. Select the Disable DHCPv6 stateless mode for the server option and click Next. The *Authorize DHCP Server* page appears.

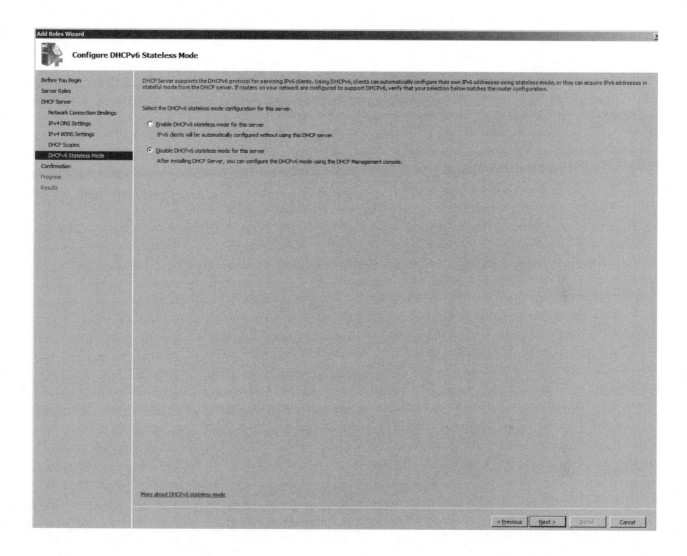

15. Select the Skip authorization of this DHCP server in AD DS option and click Next. The *Confirm Installation Selections* page appears.

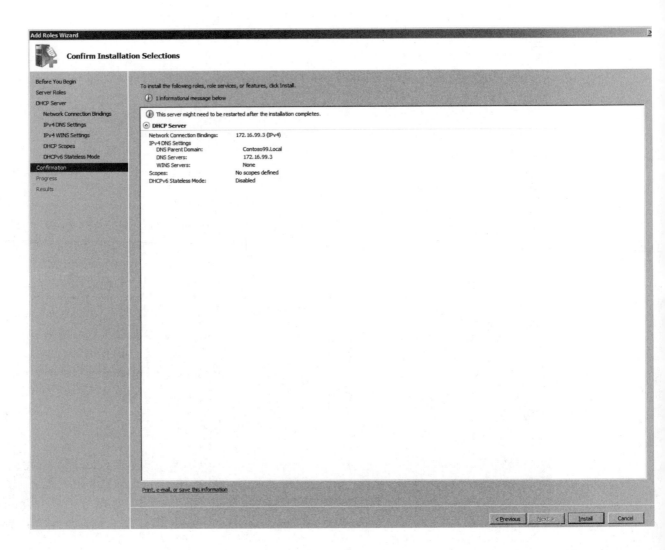

16. Click Install. The wizard installs the DHCP Server role.

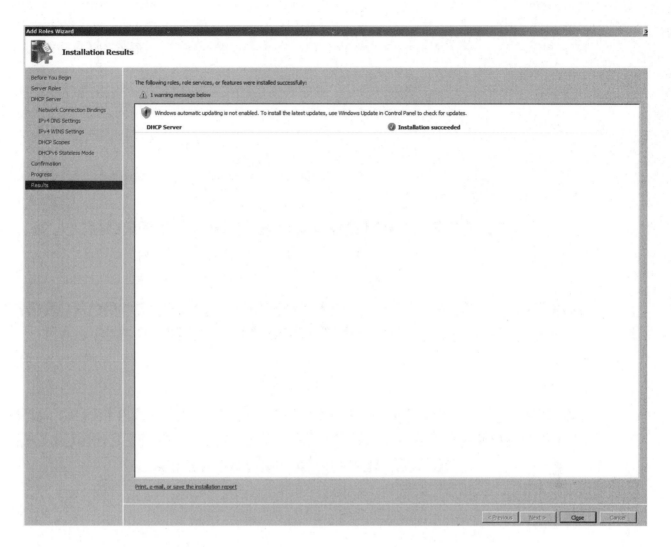

17. Click Close. The wizard closes.

18. Close the Server Manager console.

19. Log off of the computer.

PART 2: CUSTOMIZED EXCERPTS FROM:

WINDOWS SERVER® 2008 ADMINISTRATOR MICROSOFT CERTIFIED IT PROFESSIONAL EXAM 70-646 LAB

AND

WINDOWS SERVER® 2008 NETWORK INFRASTRUCTURE CONFIGURATION MICROSOFT CERTIFIED TECHNOLOGY SPECIALIST EXAM 70-642 LAB

LAB 2
CONFIGURING DNS AND DHCP

This lab contains the following exercises:

Exercise 2.1   Designing a DNS Namespace

Exercise 2.2   Creating a Zone

Exercise 2.3   Creating Domains

Exercise 2.4   Creating Resource Records

Exercise 2.5   Creating a Scope

Exercise 2.6   Confirming DHCP Server Functionality

Exercise 2.7   Configuring DHCP Reservations

Workstation Reset: Returning to Baseline

Estimated lab time: 100 minutes

Exercise 2.1	Designing a DNS Namespace
Overview	You have been tasked with creating a test DNS namespace structure for your organization. Your first task is to design that namespace by specifying appropriate domain and host names for the computers in the division.
Completion time	15 minutes

1. Design a DNS namespace for your organization that conforms to the following guidelines.

    a. The root domain name for the test DNS namespace is Contoso##.com, where ## is the number assigned to your computer by your instructor. All of the additional domains that you create must be subordinate to this domain.

    b. The internal network must be located in a different domain from the external network.

    c. The organization consists of three internal divisions: Sales, Human Resources, and Production. Each division must be represented by a separate subdomain in the namespace.

43

     d.   Each division has departmental servers performing various roles and as many as 200 workstations, only some of which are shown in the diagram. Your host names should identify the function of each computer.

     e.   Three servers on an external perimeter network host the company's Internet services: Web, FTP, and e-mail. These servers must be in the domain Contoso##.com.

2.   In the diagram provided in Figure 2-1, write both the domain names and the fully qualified domain names that you have selected for the computers in the appropriate spaces.

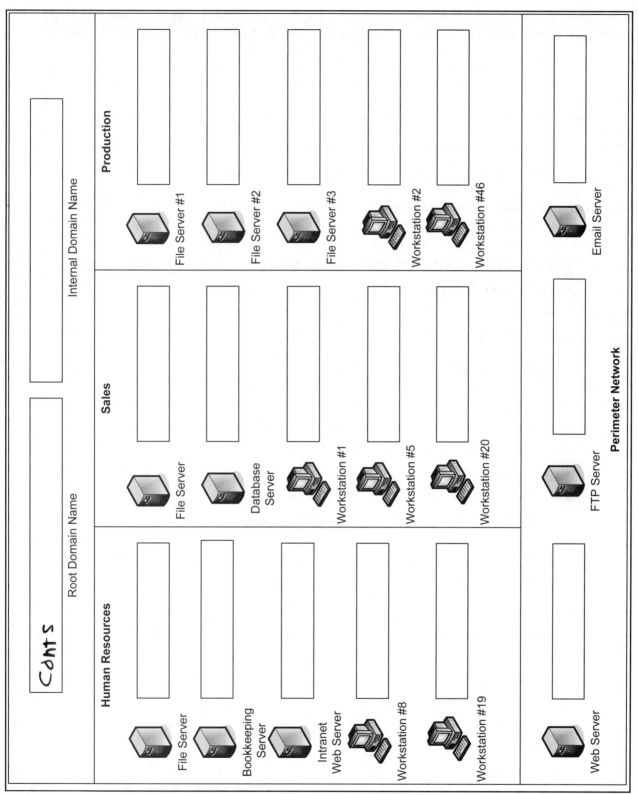

Figure 2-1

Exercise 2.2	Creating a Zone
Overview	You will now configure the DNS Server Role you installed in lab 1.4 by creating zones. A zone is the administrative division that DNS servers use to administer domains. The first step in implementing the DNS namespace that you designed is to create a zone representing your root domain.
Completion time	10 minutes

1. Turn on the Server##A computer and log on using your Student## account and the password P@ssw0rd.

2. If the Initial Configuration Tasks (ICT) screen window opens automatically, place a checkmark next to Do not show this window at logon, and click Close.

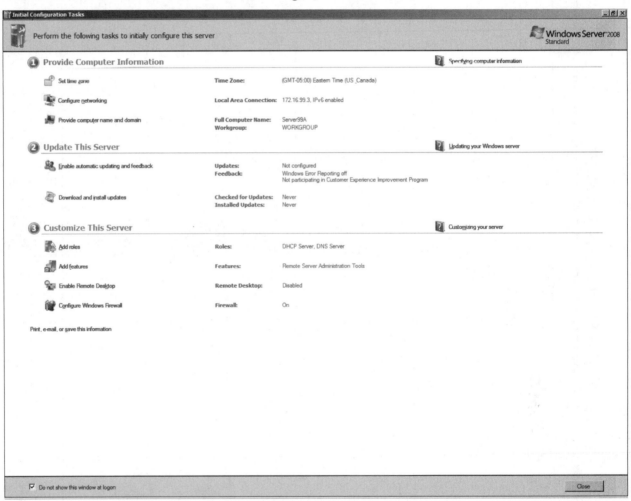

3. If the Server Manager window appears automatically, close it.

4. Click Start, and then click Administrative Tools > DNS. Click Continue in the User Account Control message box, and the DNS Manager console appears.

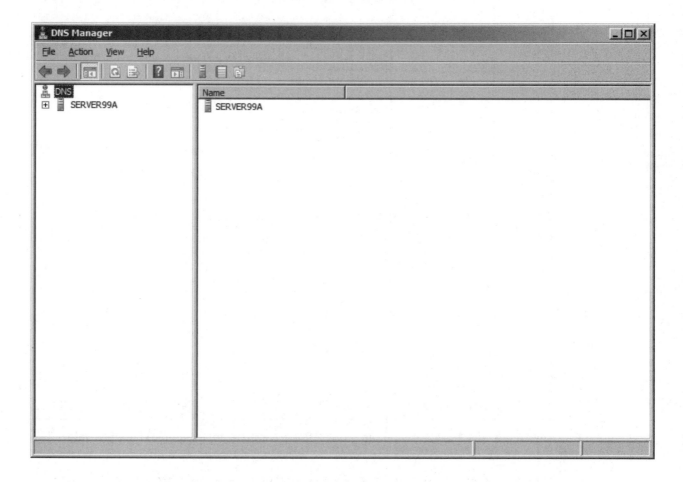

5. Expand the SERVER##A node in the DNS console.

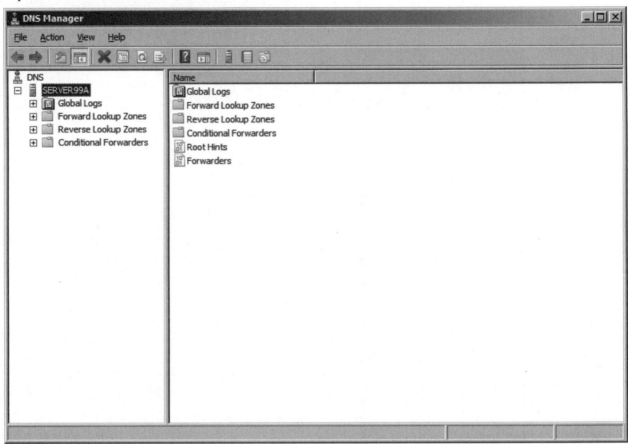

6. Right-click the Forward Lookup Zones folder and, from the context menu, select New Zone. The New Zone Wizard appears.

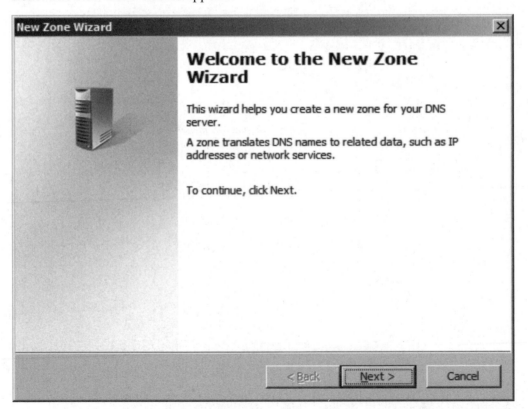

7. Click Next to bypass the Welcome page. The *Zone Type* page appears.

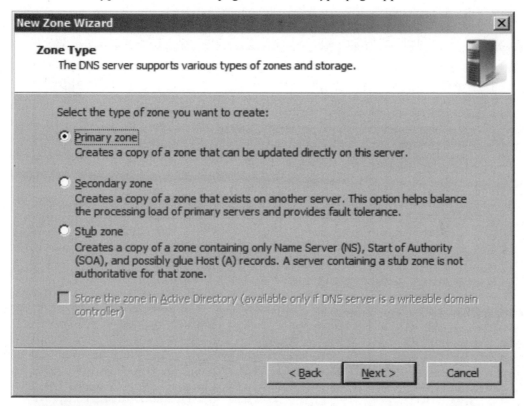

Question 1	*Why is the Store the zone in Active Directory checkbox grayed out?*

8. Leave the Primary Zone option selected, and click Next. The *Zone Name* page appears.

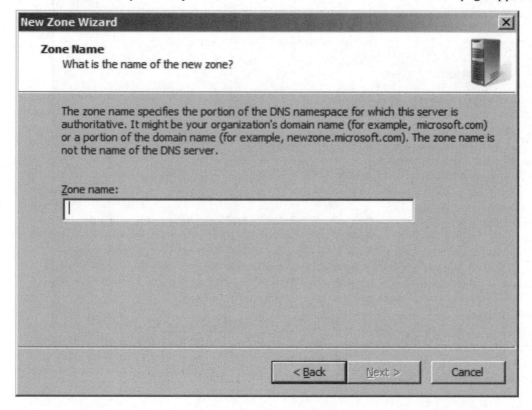

9. In the Zone name text box, key the root domain name from the diagram you created in Exercise 2.1, and click Next. The *Zone File* page appears.

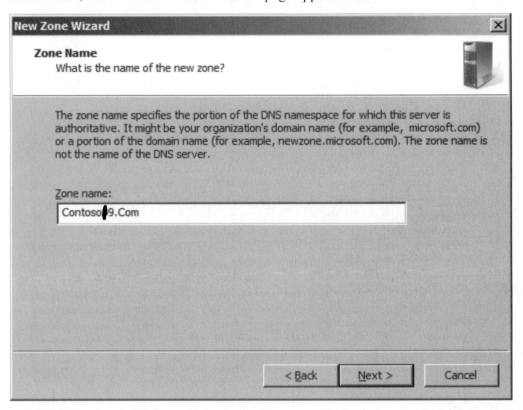

10. Click Next to accept the default zone file name. The *Dynamic Update* page appears.

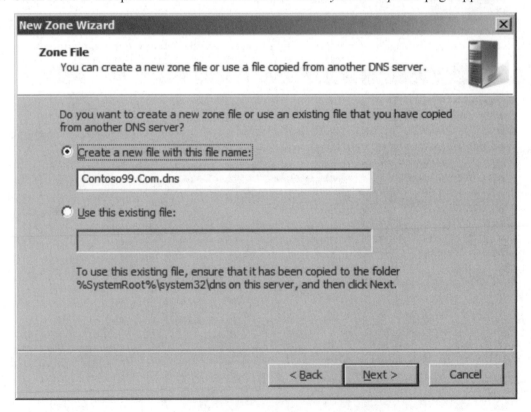

11. Select the Allow both nonsecure and secure dynamic updates option, and click Next. The *Completing the New Zone Wizard* page appears.

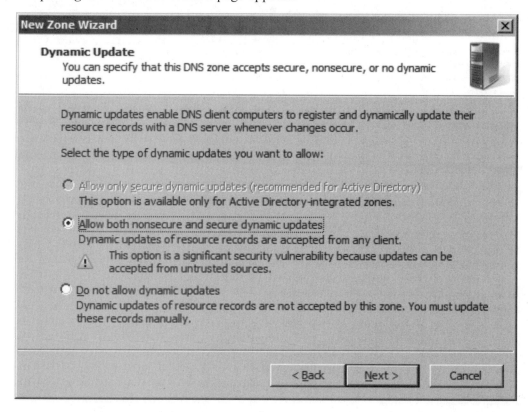

12. Click Finish. The new zone appears in the Forward Lookup Zones folder in the console.

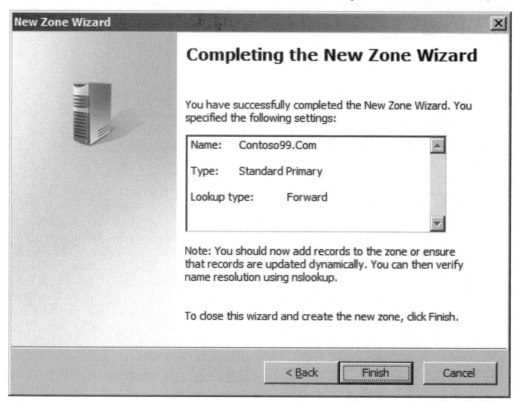

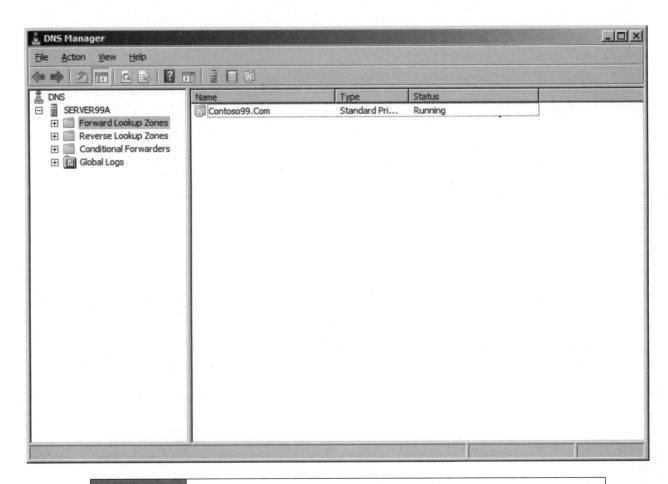

| Question 2 | *What resource records appear in the new zone you created by default?* |

13. Repeat steps 3 to 9 to create another zone by using the internal domain name you specified in the diagram in Exercise 2.1.

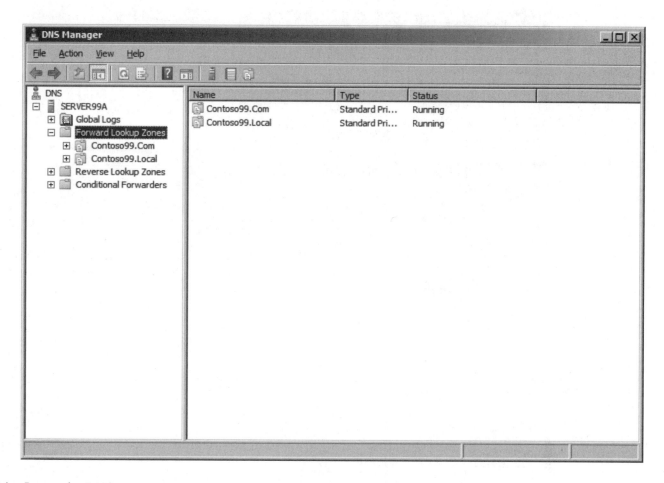

14. Leave the DNS Manager console open for the next exercise.

Exercise 2.3	Creating Domains
Overview	A single zone on a DNS server can encompass multiple domains as long as the domains are contiguous. In this exercise, you create the departmental domains you specified in your namespace design.
Completion time	10 minutes

1. In the DNS Manager console, right-click the zone you created using the internal domain name from your namespace in Exercise 2.3. From the context menu, select New Domain. The New DNS Domain dialog box appears.

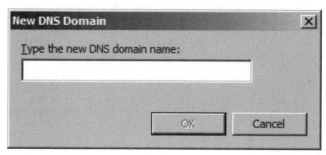

2. In the Type the new DNS domain name text box, key the name of the Human Resources domain you specified in your namespace design, and click OK.

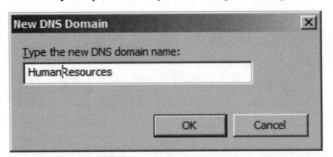

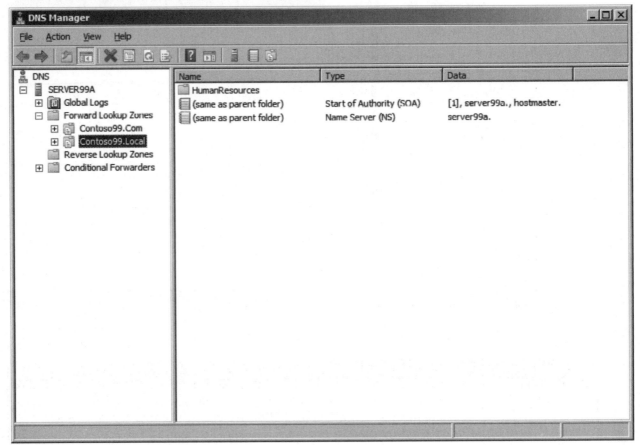

> **NOTE**
>
> *When you create a domain within a zone, you specify the name for the new domain relative to the zone name. For example, to create the qa.contoso.com domain in the contoso.com zone, you would specify only the qa name in the New DNS Domain dialog box.*

3. Repeat steps 1 to 2 to create the domains for the Sales and Production departments from your namespace design.

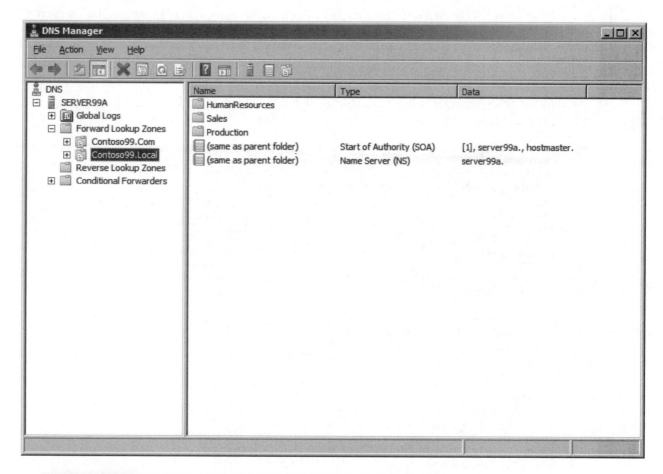

Question 3	*What resource records appear in the new domains you created by default?*

4. Leave the DNS Manager console open for the next exercise.

Exercise 2.4	Creating Resource Records
Overview	Now that you have created the zones and domains for your namespace, you can begin to populate them with the resource records that the DNS server uses to resolve host names into IP addresses.
Completion time	15 minutes

1. In the DNS Manager console, right-click the root domain zone you created in Exercise 2.3. From the context menu, select New Host (A or AAAA). The New Host dialog box appears.

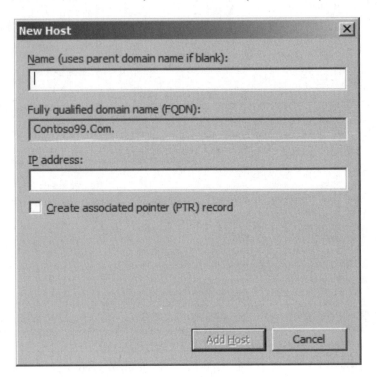

2. In the Name text box, key the host name of the Internet Web server you specified in your namespace design.

3. In the IP Address text box, key **172.17.xx.201**, where *xx* is the number assigned to your computer by your instructor.

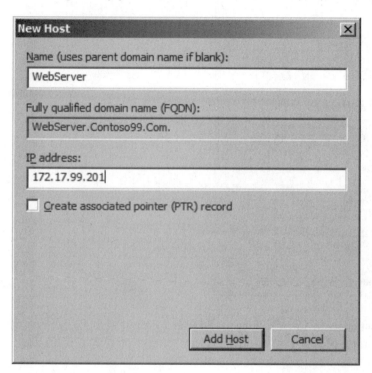

4. Click Add Host. A DNS message box appears, stating that the resource record was created.

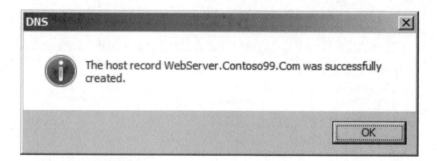

| Question 4 | *What must you do before you can select the Create associated pointer (PTR) record checkbox in the New Host dialog box?* |

5. Click OK. A new, blank Add Host dialog box appears.

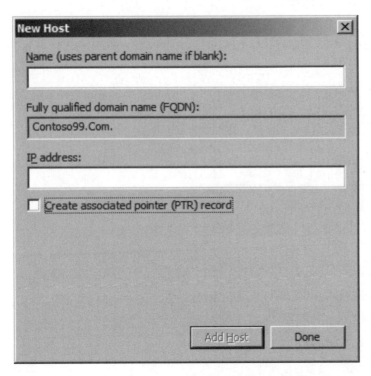

6. Repeat steps 2 to 4 to create Host records for the Internet FTP and e-mail servers in your namespace design. For each resource record, use a different IP address on the 172.17. *xx* subnet.

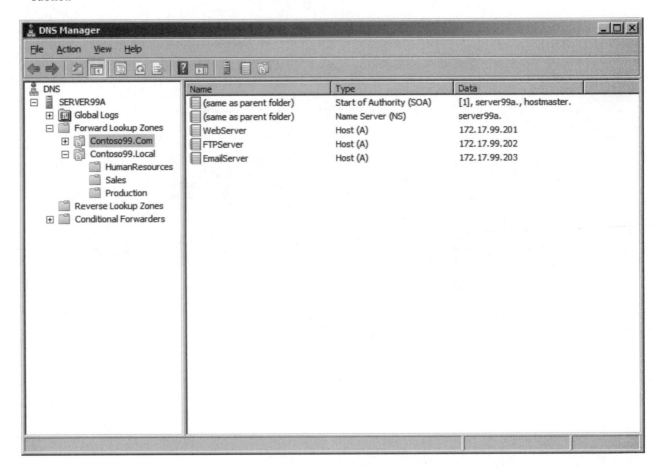

7. In the three domains you created in Exercise 2.3, create Host resource records for all of the remaining computers in your namespace design, using the names you specified in your diagram and a different IP address in the 172.16.*xx* (start from 172.16.##.9) subnet for each record.

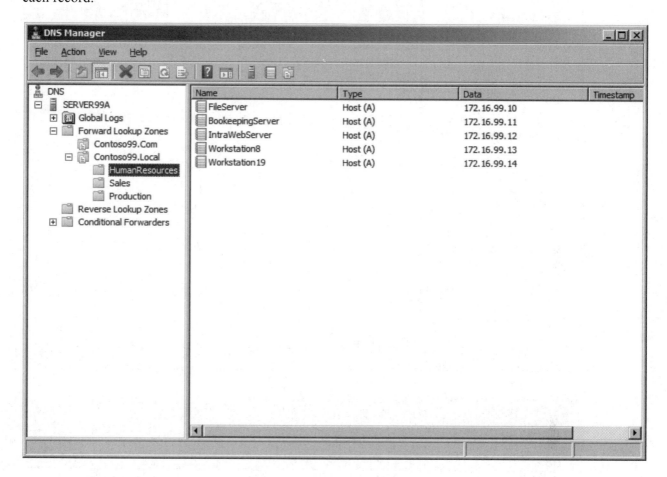

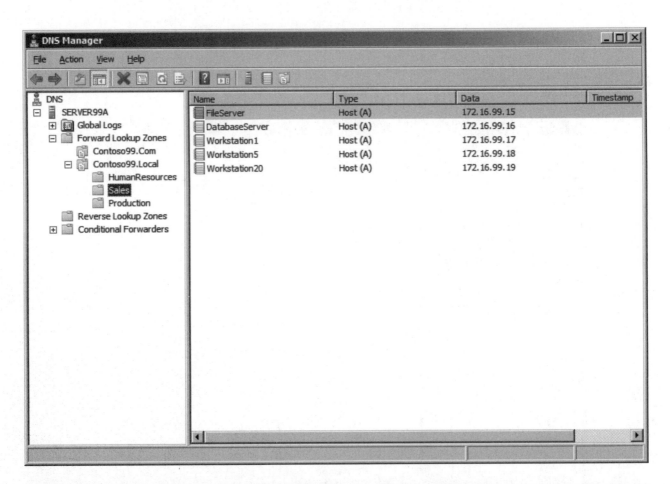

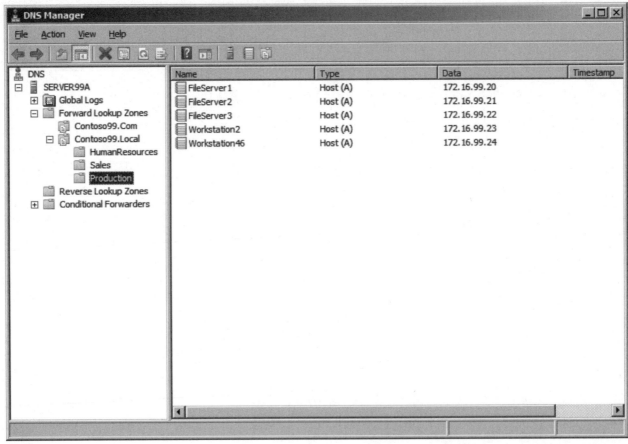

NOTE *For the purposes of this exercise, the actual IP addresses you use when creating your resource records do not matter. In an actual DNS deployment, you must either specify an appropriate IP address for each host, based on the subnet to which the computer is connected, or rely on DHCP to create the resource records for the computers.*

8.   Click Done to close the Add Host dialog box.

9.   Press Ctrl+Prt Scr to take a screen shot of the DNS Manager console, showing the resource records you created in the Human Resources domain, and then press Ctrl+V to paste the resulting image into the lab02_worksheet file in the page provided.

10.   Close the DNS Manager console.

Exercise 2.5	Creating a Scope
Overview	In this exercise you will configure the DHCP Server Role you installed in lab 1.5 by creating a scope. A scope is a range of IP addresses that a DHCP server uses to supply clients on a particular subnet with IP addresses. In this exercise, you create a scope on your DHCP server.
Completion time	15 minutes

NOTE

Ensure that your virtual machines network settings are set to Host-only before beginning this exercise.

1. On Server##A click Start, and then click Administrative Tools > DHCP. Click Continue in the User Account Control message box, and the DIICP console appears.

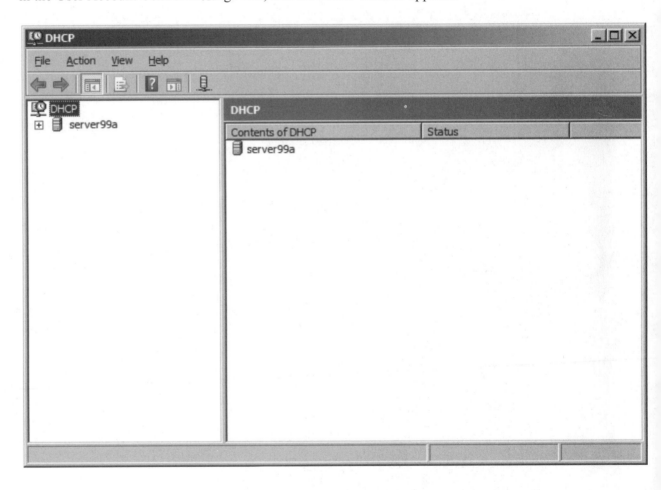

2. Expand the Server##*A* node.

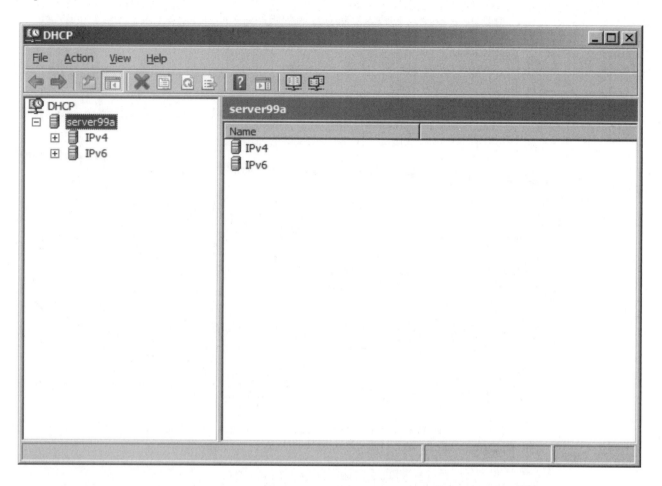

3. Right-click the IPv4 node and, from the context menu, select New Scope. The New Scope Wizard appears.

4. Click Next to bypass the Welcome page. The *Scope Name* page appears.

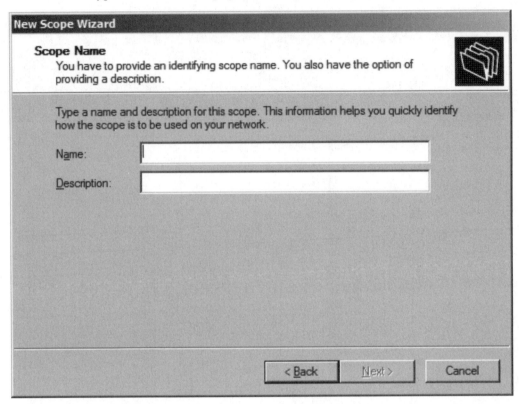

5. In the Name text box, key **Student## Scope**, where ## is the number provided by your instructor and click Next. The *IP Address Range* page appears.

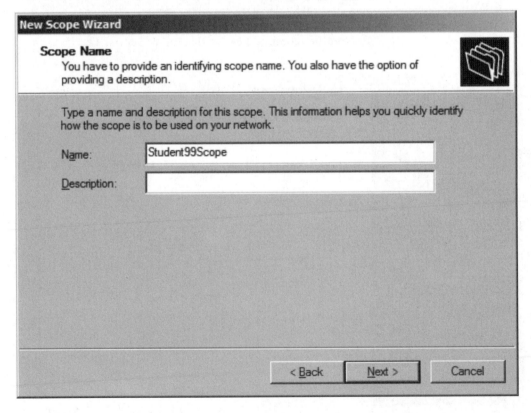

6. In the Start IP address text box, key **172.16.##.240**, where ## is the number assigned to your computer by your instructor.

7. In the End IP address text box, key **172.16.##.250**.

Question 5	*Notice that the wizard automatically adds a value to the Subnet mask text box. Where did this value come from?*

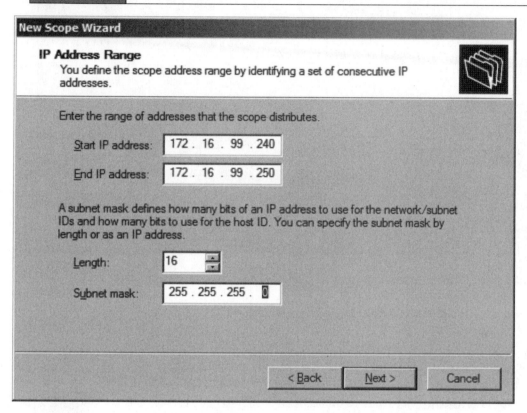

8. In the Subnet mask text box, key **255.255.255.0**, and then click Next. The *Add Exclusions* page appears.

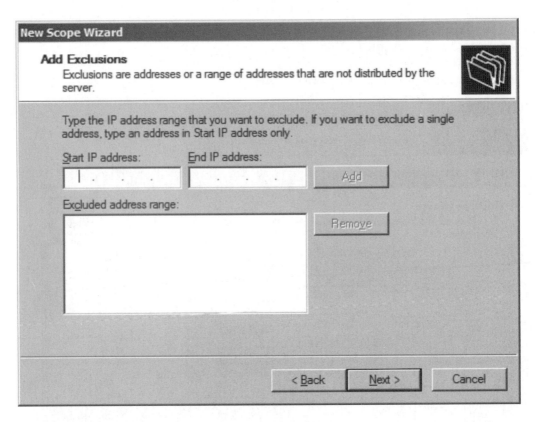

9.   In the Start IP address text box, key **172.16.##.245**.

10. In the End IP address text box, key **172.16.##.245.**

11. Click Add. The address appears in the Excluded address range list.

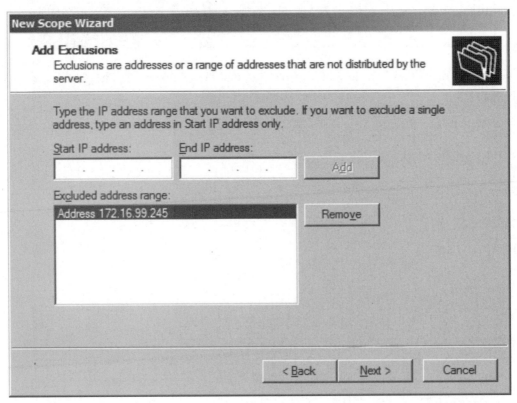

12. Click Next. The *Lease Duration* page appears.

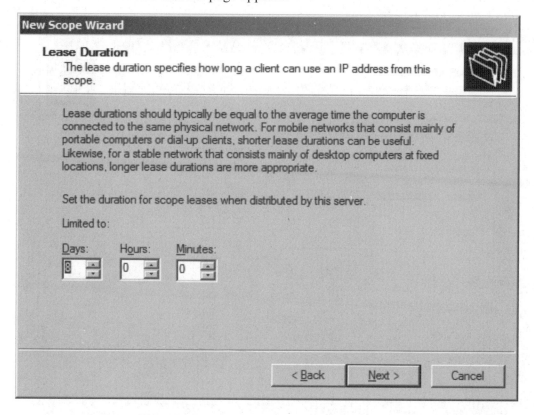

13. Click Next to accept the default value. The *Configure DHCP Options* page appears.

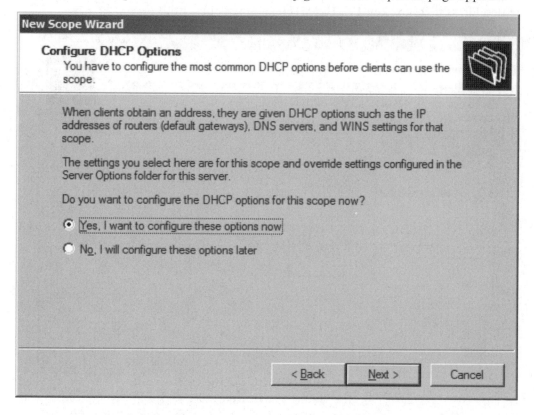

14. Click Next to accept the Yes, I want to configure these options now option. The *Router (Default Gateway)* page appears.

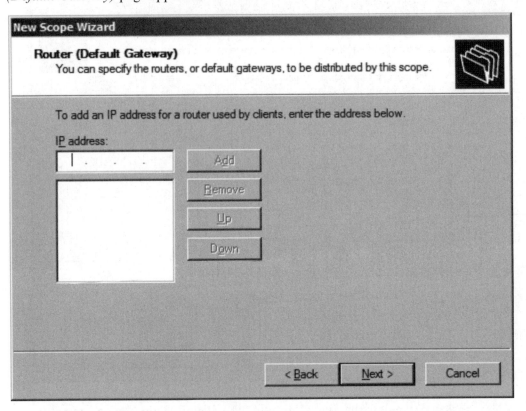

15. In the IP address text box, key **172.16.##.100** and then click Add.

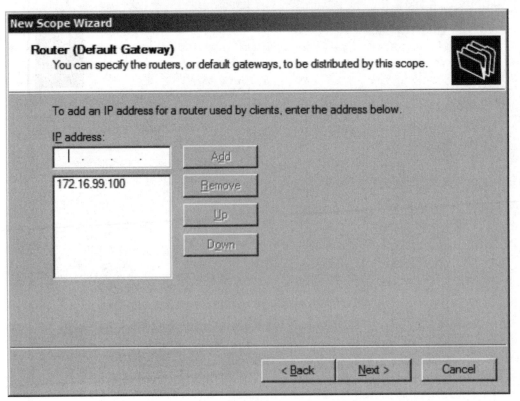

16. Click Next to continue. The *Domain Name and DNS Servers* page appears.

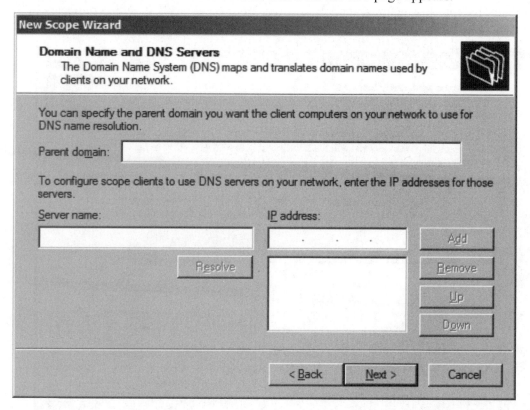

17. In the Parent domain text box, key the name of the internal domain you specified in your namespace design in Exercise 2.1.

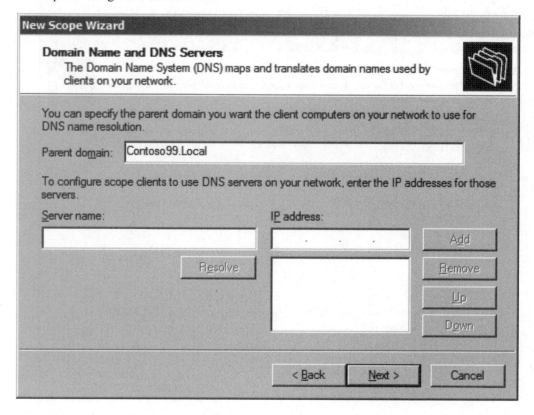

18. In the Server name text box, key **Server##A**, where ## is the number assigned to your computer by your instructor, and click Resolve. Your computer's IP address appears in the adjacent text box.

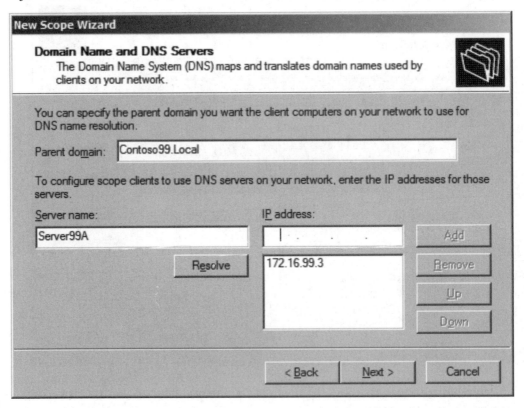

19. Click Add, and then click Next. The *WINS Servers* page appears.

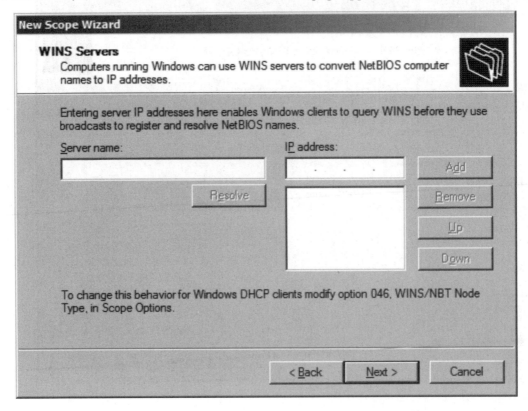

20. Click Next to bypass the page. The *Activate Scope* page appears.

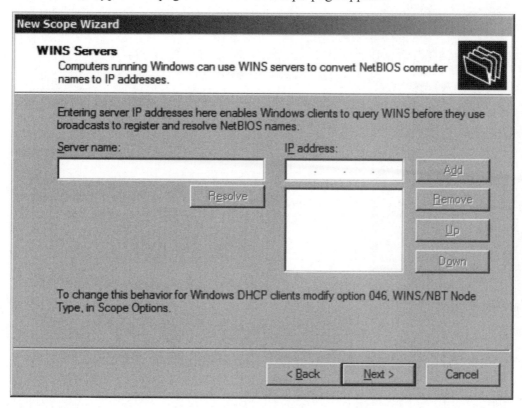

21. Click Next to accept the default Yes, I Want To Activate This Scope Now option. The *Completing the New Scope Wizard* page appears.

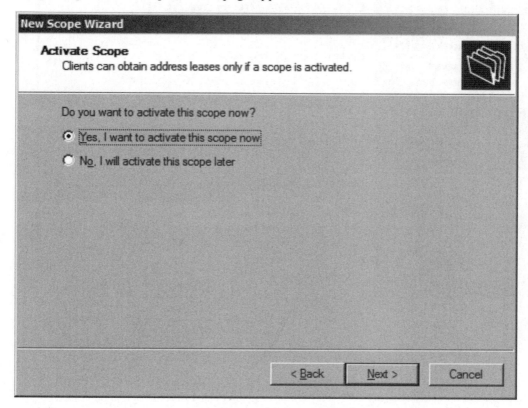

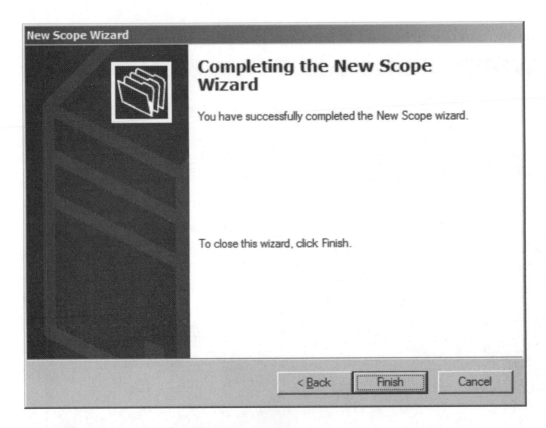

22. Click Finish. The scope is added to the console.

23. Expand the IPv4 node and the new scope, and then select the Address Pool folder.

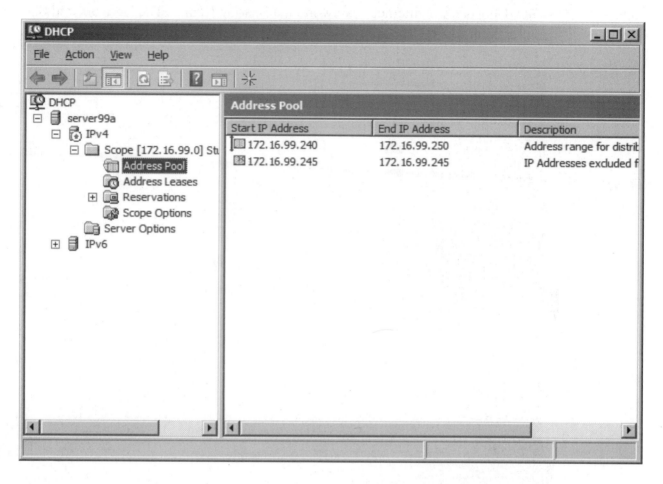

24. Press Ctrl+Prt Scr to take a screen shot of the DHCP console, showing the contents of the Address Pool folder, and then press Ctrl+V to paste the resulting image into the lab02_worksheet file in the page provided.

25. Close the DHCP Server console.

26. Leave the computer logged on for the next exercise.

Exercise 2.6	Confirming DHCP Server Functionality
Overview	In this exercise you will test the functionality of your DHCP Server using your Windows 7 virtual machine.
Completion time	10 minutes

1. Turn on the Workstation## computer and log on using your Student## account and the password P@ssw0rd.

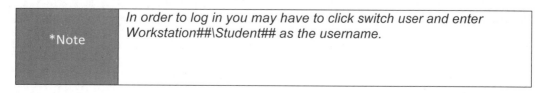

*Note	In order to log in you may have to click switch user and enter Workstation##\Student## as the username.

2. Click Start and then click Control Panel. The Control Panel window appears.

3. Click Network and Internet > Network and Sharing Center. The Network and Sharing Center control panel appears.

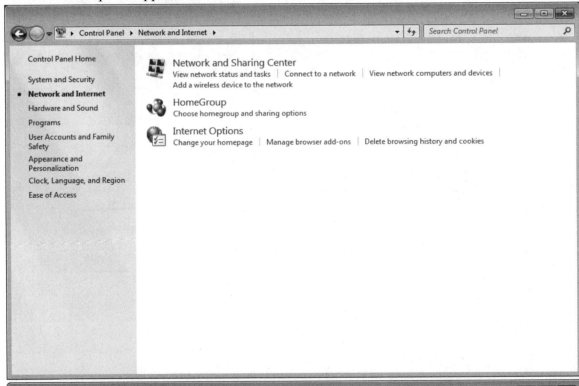

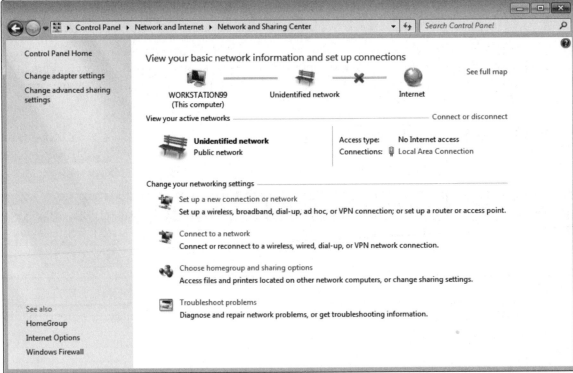

4. In the Network and Sharing Center control panel select Change Adapter Settings. The Network Connections window appears.

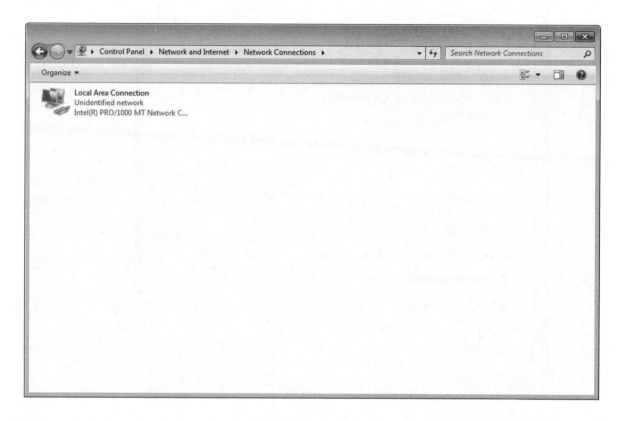

5. Right-click the Local Area Connection icon and, from the context menu, select Properties. The Local Area Connection Properties sheet appears.
6. Select Internet Protocol Version 4 (TCP/IPv4) and click Properties. The Internet Protocol Version 4 (TCP/IPv4) Properties sheet appears.

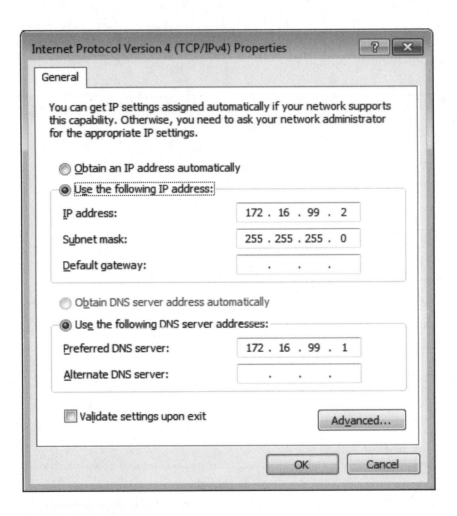

Question 6	*What IP addressing settings are currently configured?*

7. Select the Obtain an IP address automatically radio button.

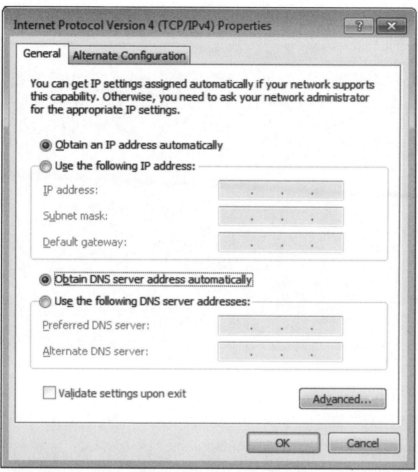

8. Click OK twice to close the two Properties sheets. Close the Network Connections window.

9. Click Start, key **cmd**, and press Enter.

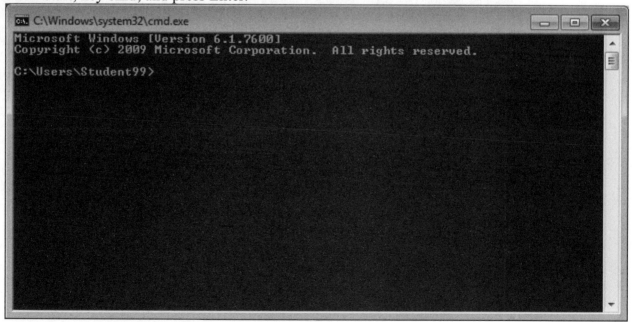

10. At the command prompt, key **ipconfig /release**.

11. At the command prompt, key **ipconfig /renew**.

12. At the command prompt, key **ipconfig /all**.

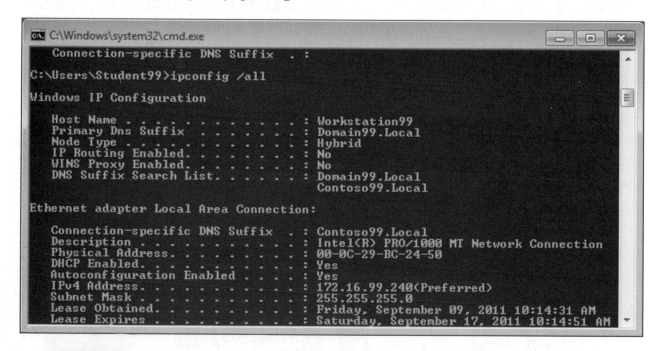

> **NOTE**
>
> *You may have to execute the ipconfig /release and /renew commands more than once in order for your client machine to obtain an IP Address from your DHCP server.*

Question 7	*Is the computer currently configured for DHCP? How can you tell?*

Question 8	*What is the IP address of the DHCP server from which Workstation## has obtained its IP address?*

Question 9	*If the answer to #8 was not the IP address of the Server##A computer, why might this have happened?*

Question 10	*What DNS Server address was Workstation XX assigned?*

13. Record the Physical address of WorkstationXX for use in the next exercise.

    192.68.1.1   00-0C-29-22-D1-FF

14. At the command prompt, key **exit**, and press Enter to close the command prompt window.

Exercise 2.7	Configuring DHCP Reservations
Overview	In this exercise you will configure a DHCP reservation for your Windows 7 virtual machine. A DHCP reservation enables the DHCP server to always assign a specific address to a client machine. You will test the DHCP reservation using your Windows 7 virtual machine.
Completion time	15 minutes

1. On Server ##A Click Start, and then click Administrative Tools > DHCP. Click Continue in the User Account Control message box, and the DHCP console appears.

2. Expand the Server##A node, followed by IPv4, followed by Scope [<address>].

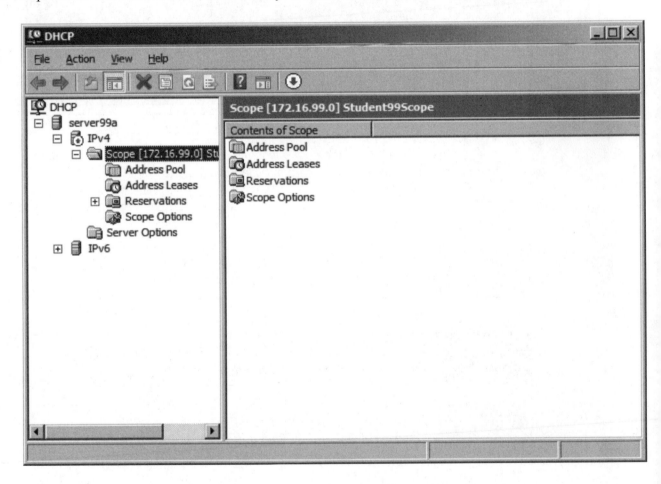

3. Click Reservations. Right-click Reservations, and select New Reservation.

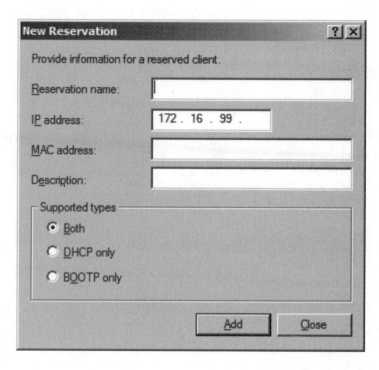

4. In the Reservation Name text box, enter Workstation##.

5. In the IP Address: field, enter an available IP address within the scope that you defined in exercise 2.5.

6. In the MAC address: field, enter the physical address of the even-numbered computer as indicated in the ipconfig /all output from Workstation##.

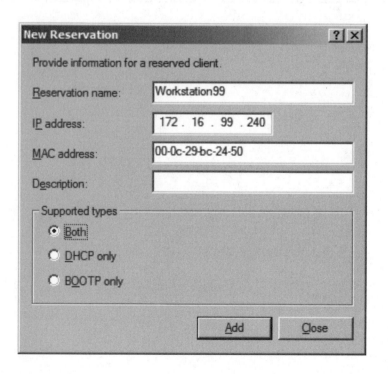

7. Click Add, and then Close.

8. Expand the Reservations node. Right-click the reservation you just created, and click Configure Options.

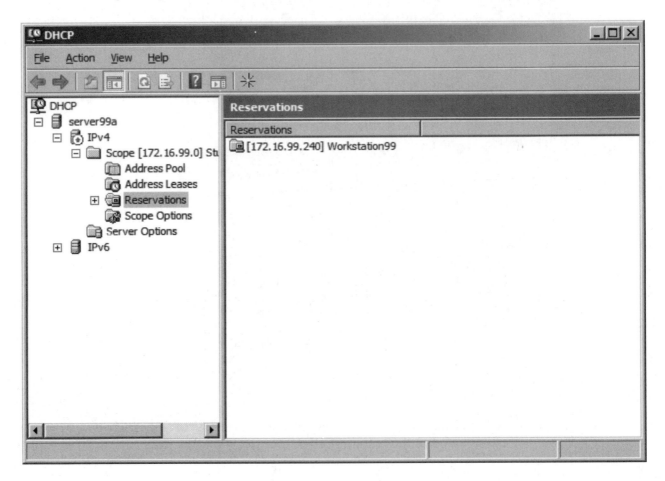

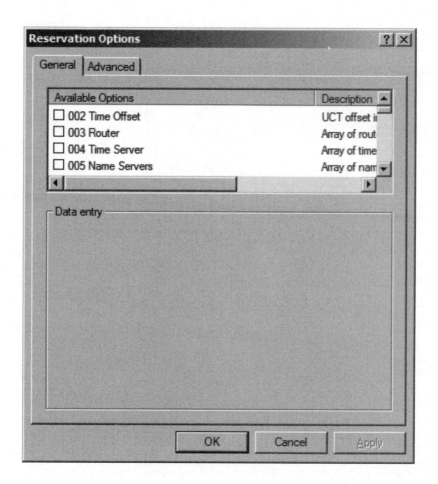

9. Place a checkmark next to 006 DNS Servers. Enter the IP address you assigned to Server##A.

10. Click Add, and then click OK.

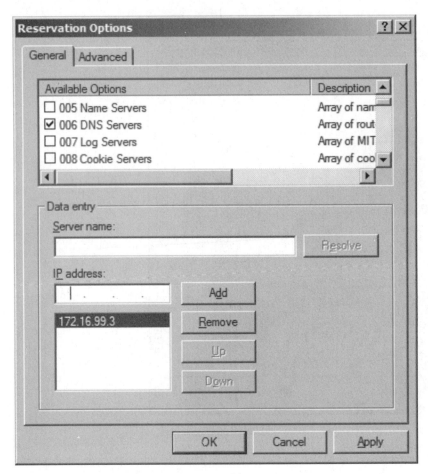

11. Close the DHCP MMC.

12. Log on to the Workstation## computer. Open a command prompt, key **ipconfig /release**, and press Enter.

13. At the command prompt, key **ipconfig /renew**, and press Enter.

> **NOTE**
>
> *You may have to execute the ipconfig /release and /renew commands more than once in order for your client machine to obtain an IP Address from your DHCP server.*

14. On Server##A open the DHCP Server console and click on the Address Leases node.

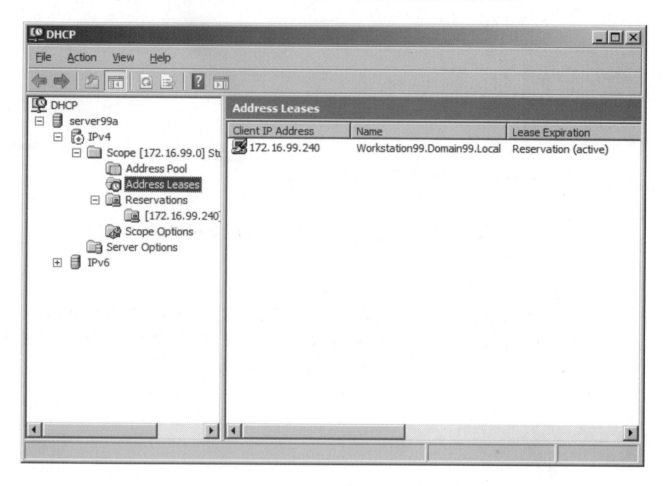

15. Press Ctrl+Prt Scr to take a screen shot of the DHCP Server console, showing the reservation you created is active, and then press Ctrl+V to paste the resulting image into the lab02_worksheet file in the page provided.

16. Log off of both machines.

WORKSTATION RESET: RETURNING TO BASELINE

Completion time	10 minutes

To return the computer to its baseline state, complete the following procedures.

1. Open the Server Manager console.

2. Remove the DNS Server and DHCP Server roles you installed during the course of the lab. Restart the computer.

PART 3: CUSTOMIZED EXCERPTS FROM:

WINDOWS SERVER® 2008 ACTIVE DIRECTORY® CONFIGURATION MICROSOFT CERTIFIED TECHNOLOGY SPECIALIST EXAM 70-640 LABS

LAB 3
CREATING A REPLICA DOMAIN CONTROLLER

This lab contains the following exercises:

Exercise 3.1   Installing the Active Directory Domain Services Role
Exercise 3.2   Creating a Replica Domain Controller
Exercise 3.3   Verifying Domain SRV Records
Exercise 3.4   Adding User Accounts to Administrative Groups

Estimated lab time: 55 minutes

Exercise 3.1	Installing the Active Directory Domain Services Role
Overview	Now that you have finished testing DNS and DHCP you will now configure the Windows Server 2008 machine as a replica Domain Controller. In this exercise you will install the Active Directory Domain Services Role on Server##A.
Completion time	10 minutes

1. Turn on the Server## computer and log on using your Administrator account and the password P@ssw0rd.
2. Turn on the Server##A computer and log on using your Student## account and the password P@ssw0rd.

3. If the Initial Configuration Tasks (ICT) screen window opens automatically, place a checkmark next to Do not show this window at logon, and click Close.

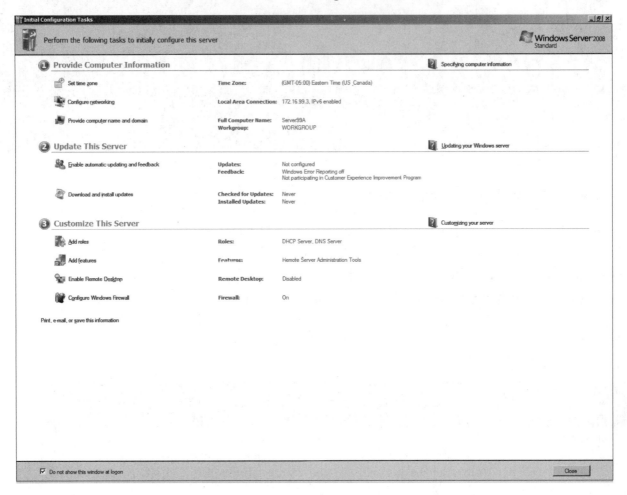

4. The Server Manager window will be displayed automatically. If the Server Manager window does not display automatically on Server##A Click Start > Administrative Tools > Server Manager. Click Continue in the User Account Control message box, and the Server Manager console appears.

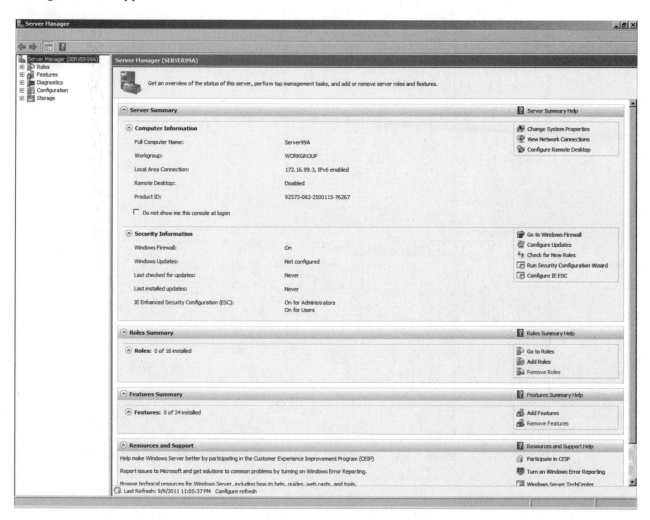

5. On Server##A in the left pane of Server Manager, click Roles.

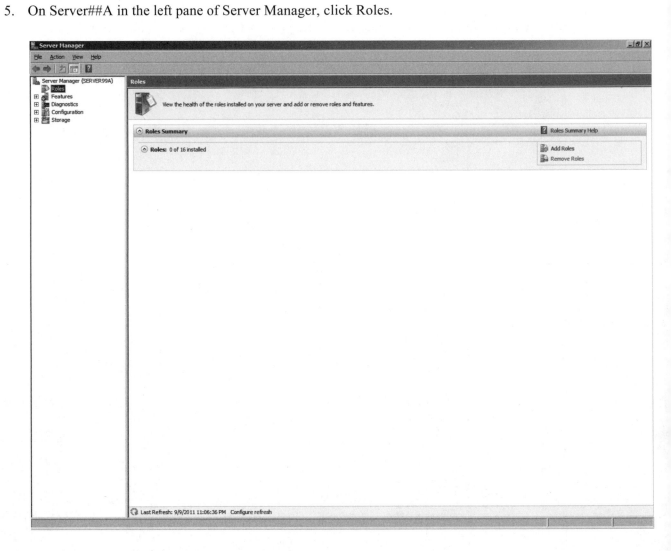

6. Click Add Role. Click Next to bypass the initial Welcome window. The Select Server Roles window is displayed.

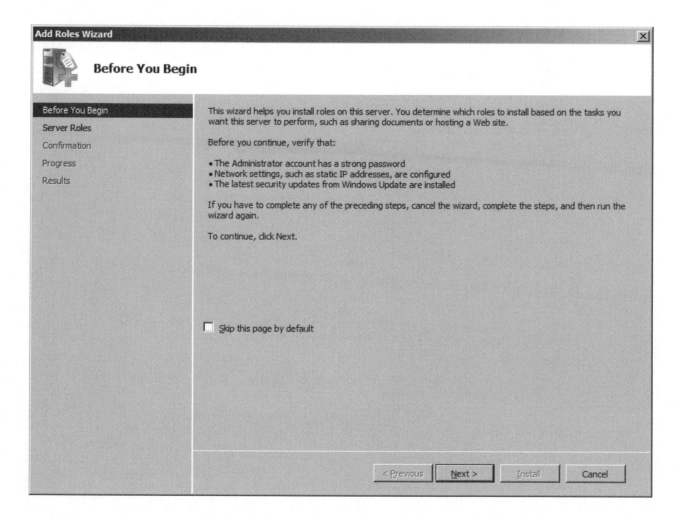

7. Place a checkmark next to Active Directory Domain Services. Click Next. The Active Directory Domain Services window is displayed.

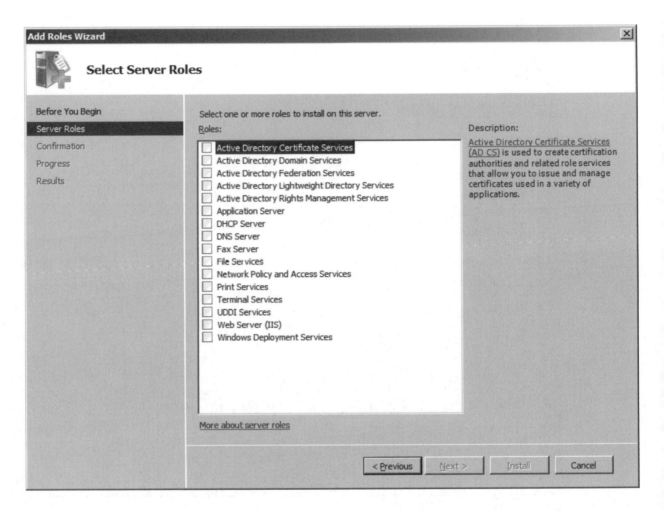

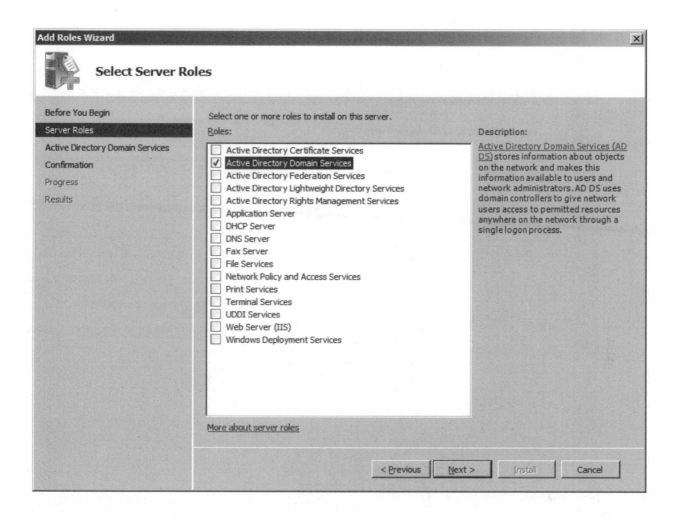

8. Read the introductory information about Active Directory Domain Services and click Next. The Confirm Installation Selections window is displayed.

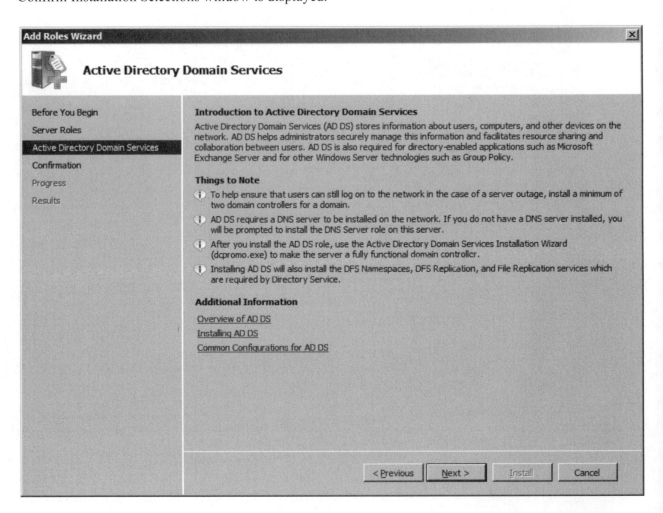

9. Read the confirmation information to prepare for the installation. Click Install to install the Active Directory Domain Services role. The Installation Results window is displayed.

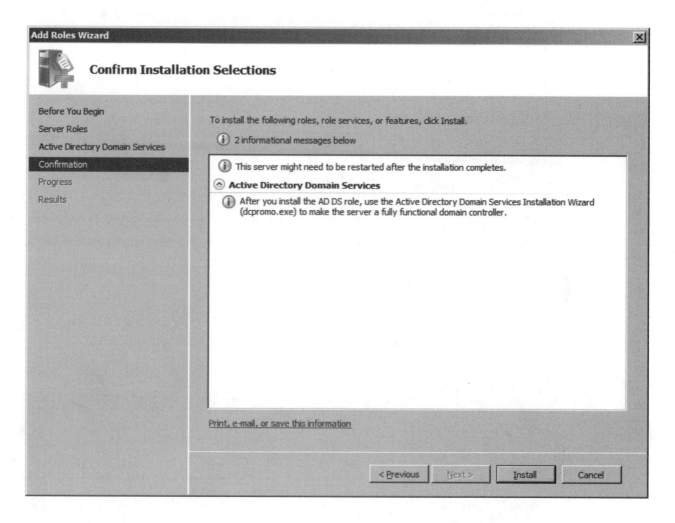

10. Read the information contained on this window and click Close.

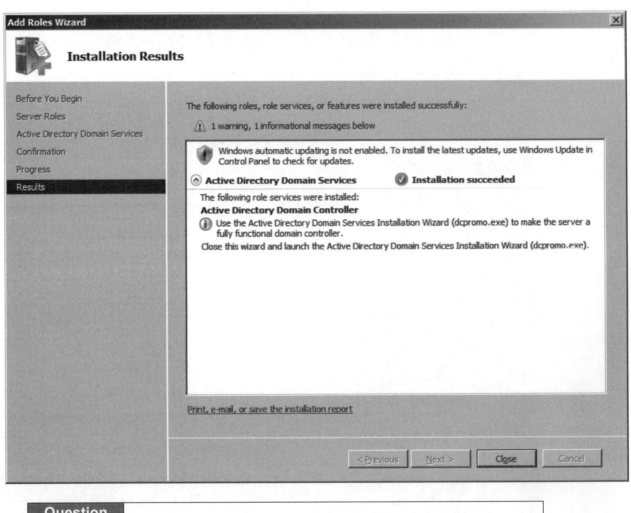

Question 1	*What does this window indicate must be done next?*

11. Leave the Server Manager window open and the computer logged on for the next exercise.

Exercise 3.2	Creating a Replica Domain Controller
Overview	You will now install Active Directory on the Server##A machine and make it a replica Domain Controller for the Domain##.Local domain. This will create a fault tolerant environment and a backup server in the event of a failure in Server##.
Completion time	25 minutes

1. In the left pane of Server Manager, click Roles. In the right pane, you will see the number of roles that are installed on this server and the names of those roles.

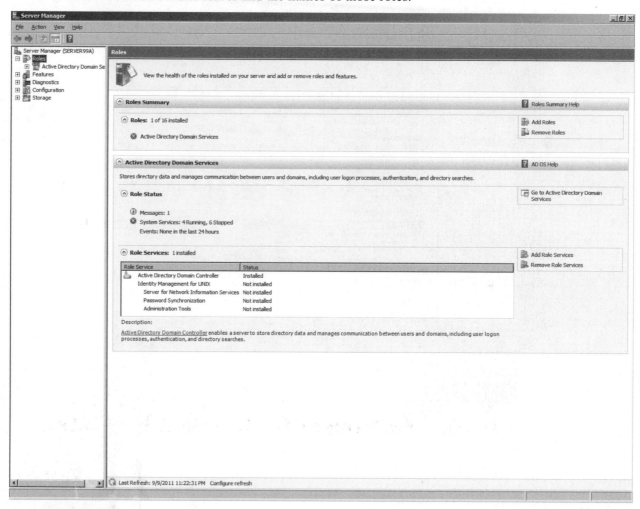

Question 2	What roles are currently installed?
	AD DS
Question 3	Why do you think this role has a red 'X' next to it?
	full version Not installed yet.

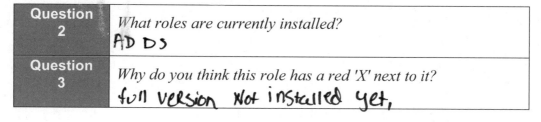

2. Click Active Directory Domain Services. The Active Directory Domain Services window is displayed.

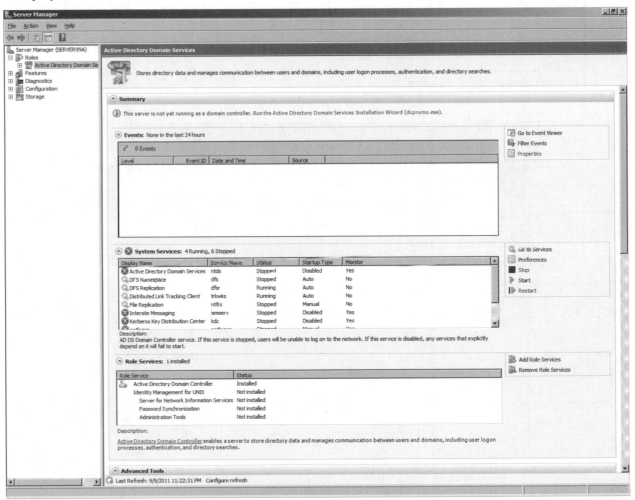

Question 4	*What warning do you see on the Summary window?*

Run DCPROmo.exe to install full version

3. Click Run The Active Directory Domain Services Installation Wizard (dcpromo.exe).

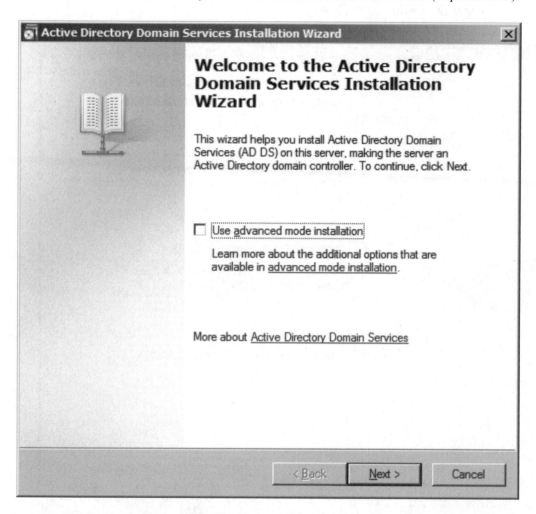

4. Place a checkmark next to Use Advanced Mode Installation and click Next. The Operating System Compatibility window is displayed.

5. Read the presented information and then click Next. The Choose A Deployment Configuration window is displayed.

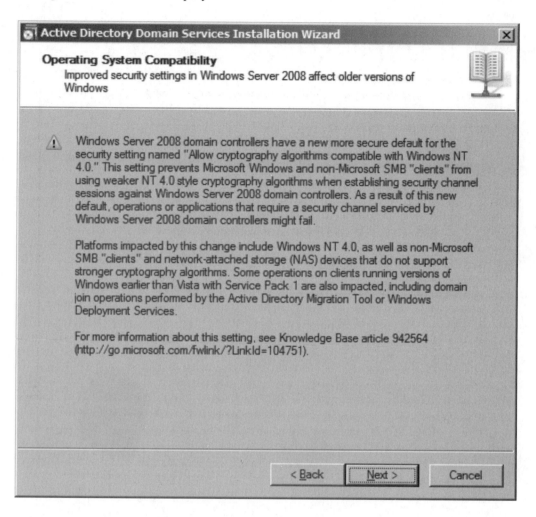

6. Click the Existing forest radio button, ensure the Add a domain controller to an existing domain radio button is clicked and click Next. The Network credentials window is displayed.

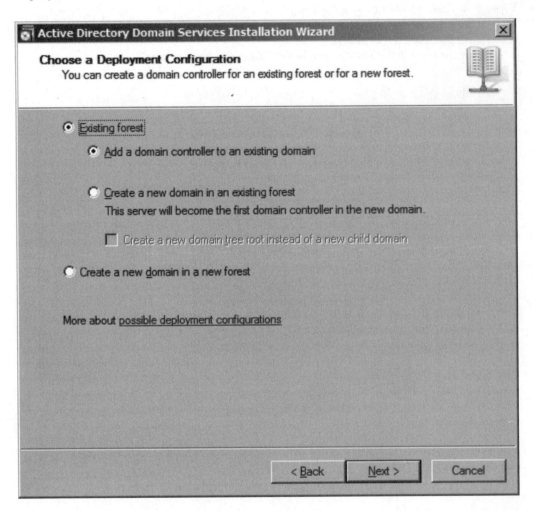

Tesserac.local

7. Key ~~Domain##.local~~ as the name of the forest where you plan to install this domain, where ## is the number provided by your instructor. Click the Set button to set alternate credentials and key Administrator for the username and the password P~~@ssw0rd~~ *H1shing0q* and click OK. Click Next to continue. The Select a domain window is displayed.

Network forrest
01

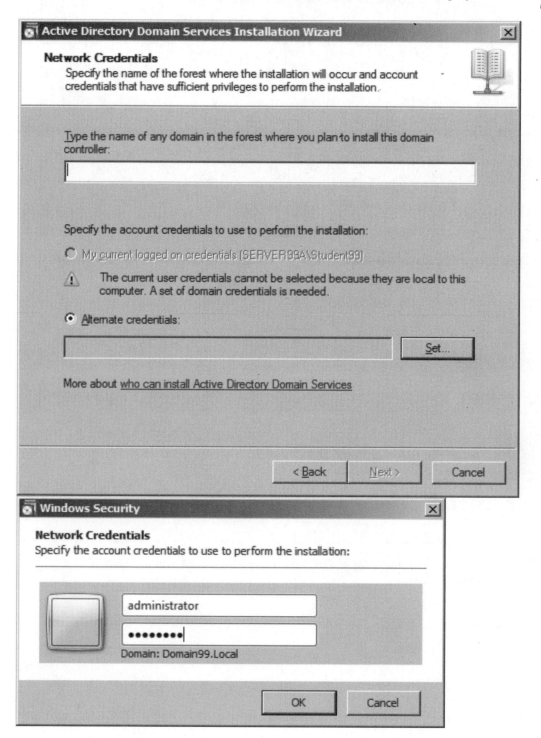

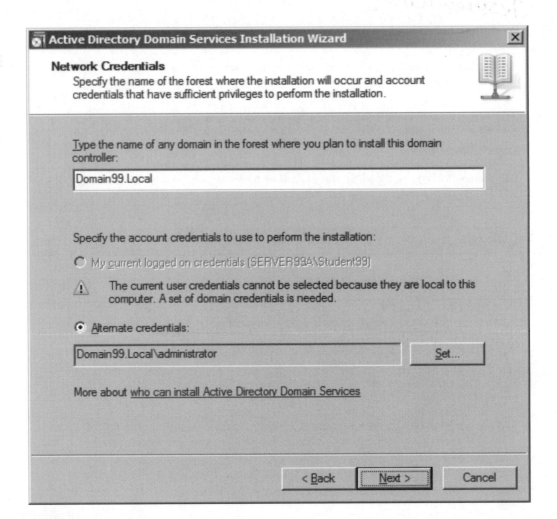

	The domain used in step 8 is the domain you created in your previous class.
NOTE	

	If you receive any DNS errors during this step check your network settings and retry.
NOTE	

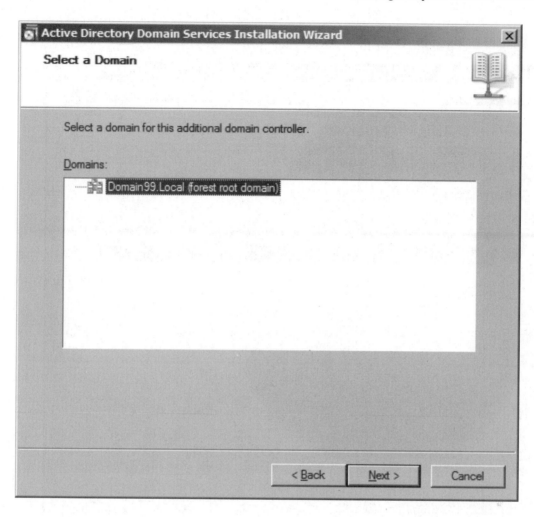

8. Click Next to accept the Domain99.Local domain. The Select a site window is displayed.

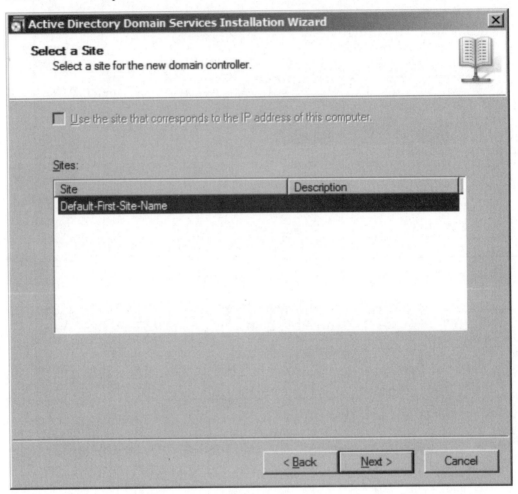

9. Click Next to accept the Default-First-Site-Name site. The Additional domain controllers options window is displayed.

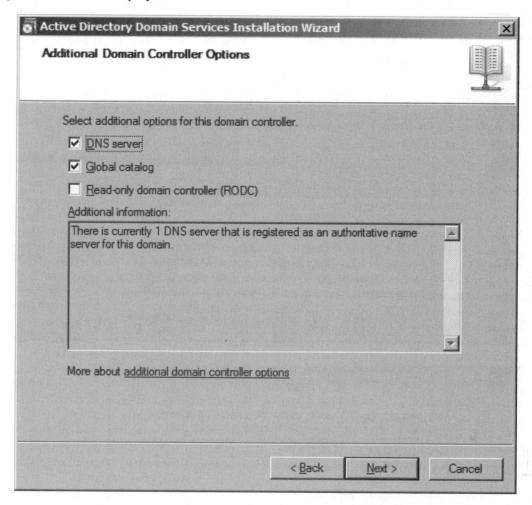

10. Accept the default selections and click Next. One or more Active Directory Domain Services Installation Wizard warning windows are displayed sequentially.

NOTE *If a Static IP assignment message appears click Yes, the computer will us a dynamically assigned IP address (not recommended).*

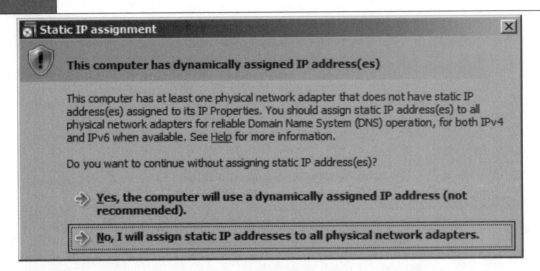

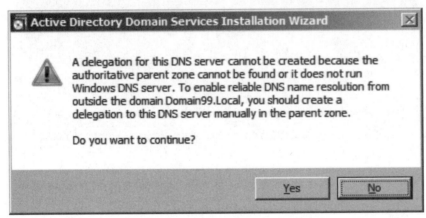

11. Read each warning and click Yes to continue. The Install from media window is displayed.

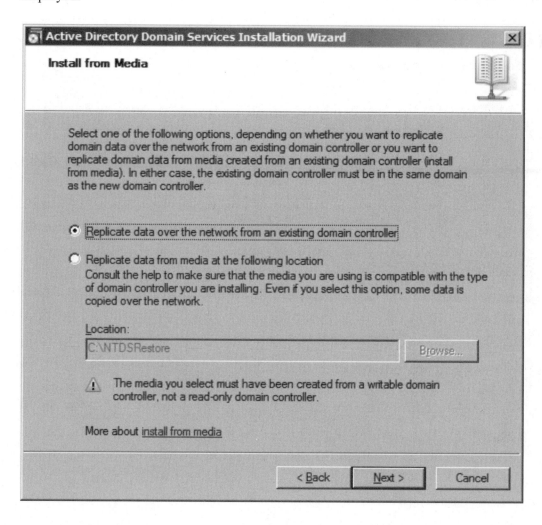

12. Click Next to accept the default selections and continue. The Source domain controller window is displayed.

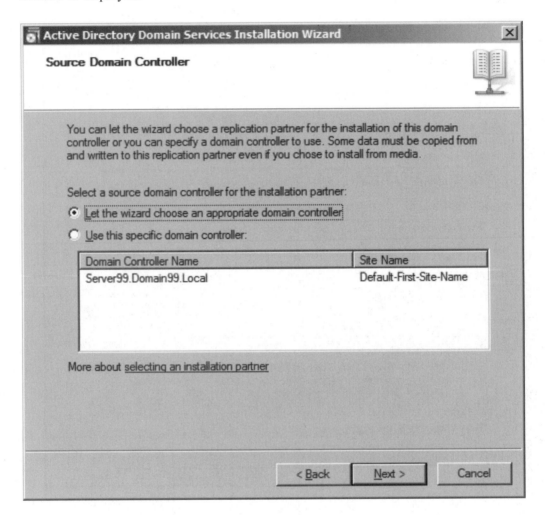

13. Click Next to accept the default selections and continue. The Location For Database, Log Files, And SYSVOL window is displayed.

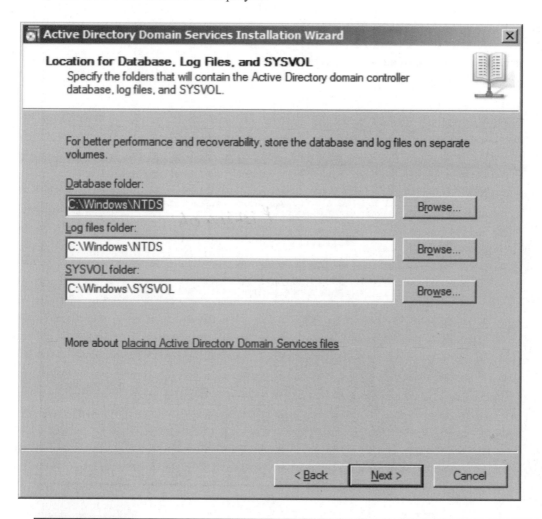

Question 5	What are the default locations for the Active Directory Domain Services files?

14. Click Next to accept the default selections and continue. The Directory Services Restore Mode Administrator Password window is displayed.

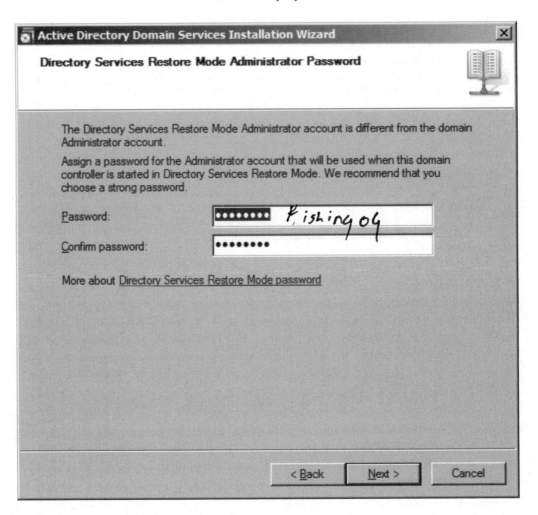

15. Key P@ssw0rd in the Password and Confirm Password text boxes and click Next. The Summary window is displayed.

Question 6	*What is the purpose of the Directory Services Restore Mode password?*

Active Directory Domain Services Installation Wizard ☒

Summary

Review your selections:

Configure this server as an additional Active Directory domain controller for the domain Domain99.Local.

Site: Default-First-Site-Name

Additional Options:
  Read-only domain controller: No
  Global catalog: Yes
  DNS Server: Yes

Update DNS Delegation: No

Source domain controller: any writable domain controller

To change an option, click Back. To begin the operation, click Next.

These settings can be exported to an answer file for use with other unattended operations.
More about using an answer file

[Export settings...]

[< Back] [Next >] [Cancel]

16. Review your installation choices and click Next to continue. The Active Directory Domain Services Installation Wizard window is displayed, indicating that the Active Directory Domain Services service is being installed. Then, the Completing The Active Directory Domain Services Installation Wizard is displayed.

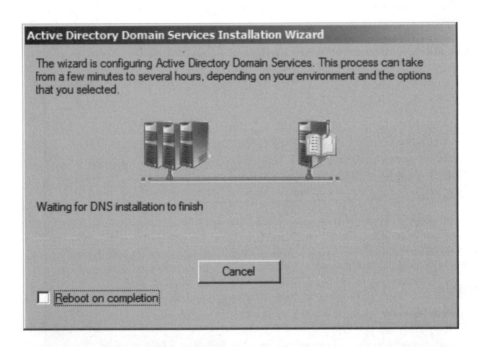

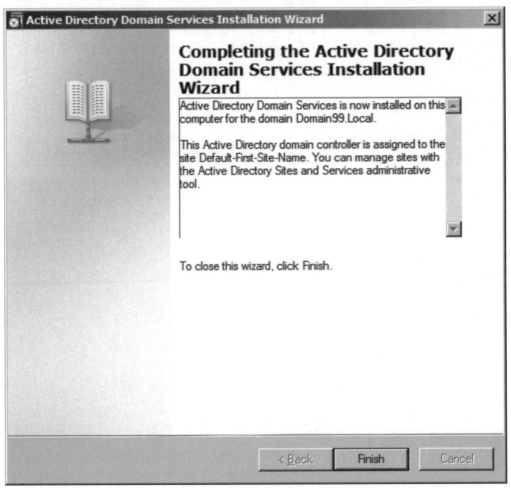

17. Press Ctrl+Prt Scr to take a screen shot of the Completing The Active Directory Domain Services Installation Wizard screen, and then press Ctrl+V to paste the resulting image into the lab03_worksheet file in the page provided.

18. Click Finish. When prompted, click Restart Now to restart the newly configured domain controller.

Exercise 3.3	Verifying Domain SRV Records
Overview	You have just completed the installation of a replica domain controller. Your colleague asks you to verify the Lightweight Directory Access Protocol (LDAP) service locations (SRV) resource record for the domain controller.
Completion time	10 minutes

1. Log on to Server##A using your Administrator account and the password P@ssw0rd.
2. On Server##A Click Start. Then All Programs > Accessories > Command Prompt. A Command Prompt window appears.

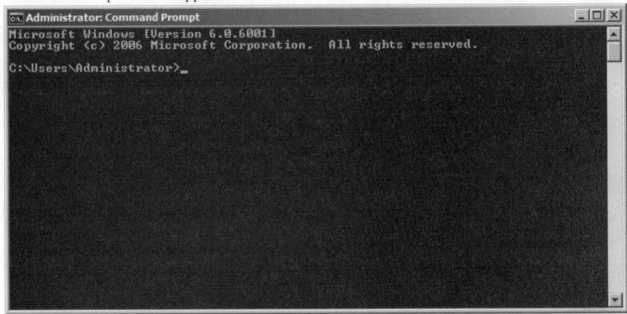

3. Key **nslookup** in the command-prompt window. Press Enter.

> **NOTE**
>
> *If you see an error message that says "Can't find server name for that address," followed by the IP address of your server, this means that your DNS server does not have a reverse lookup zone configured. You can disregard this error for now. For more information on reverse lookup zones, as well as about the format of SRV records, refer to Lesson 12 or search the Microsoft TechNet Website.*

4. Key **set type=srv** and press Enter.

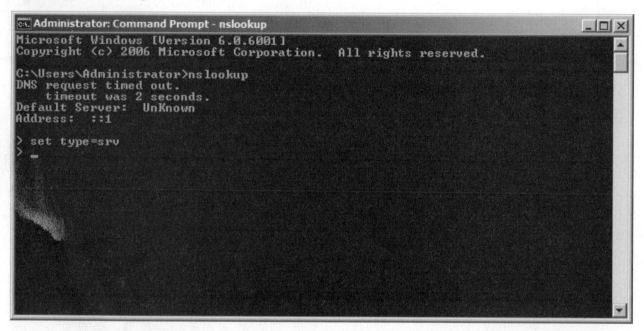

5. Key **_ldap._tcp.dc._msdcs.domain##.local** and press Enter.

```
C:\Users\Administrator>nslookup
DNS request timed out.
        timeout was 2 seconds.
Default Server:  UnKnown
Address:  ::1

> set type=srv
> _ldap._tcp.dc._msdcs.domain99.local
Server:  UnKnown
Address:  ::1

_ldap._tcp.dc._msdcs.domain99.local     SRV service location:
        priority       = 0
        weight         = 100
        port           = 389
        svr hostname   = server99a.domain99.local
_ldap._tcp.dc._msdcs.domain99.local     SRV service location:
        priority       = 0
        weight         = 100
        port           = 389
        svr hostname   = server99.domain99.local
server99a.domain99.local        internet address = 172.16.99.3
server99.domain99.local internet address = 172.16.99.1
>
```

6. Press Ctrl+Prt Scr to take a screen shot of the nslookup results, and then press Ctrl+V to paste the resulting image into the lab03_worksheet file in the page provided.

7. Key **exit** and press Enter.

8. Close the command-prompt window and leave the computer logged on for the next exercise.

Exercise 3.4	Adding User Accounts to Administrative Groups
Overview	You have just completed the installation of a replica domain controller. Now, you will add your Student## to administrative groups for future labs.
Completion time	10 minutes

1. Click the Start button, click Administrative Tools, and then click Active Directory Users And Computers. Maximize the Active Directory Users And Computers window, if necessary.

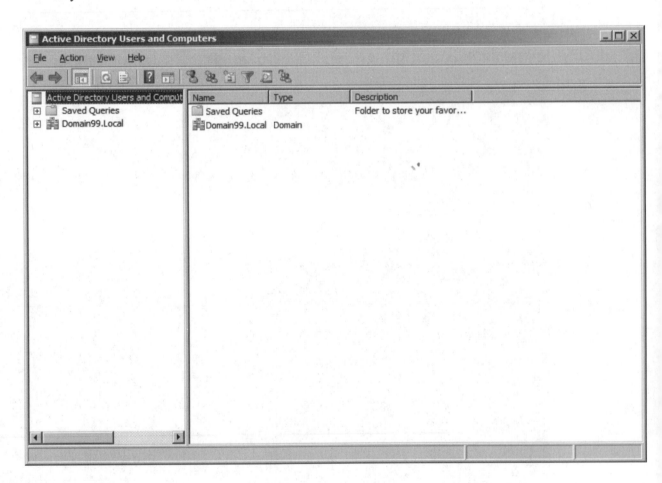

2. Click the plus sign (+) next to domain##.local. Click the Users container.

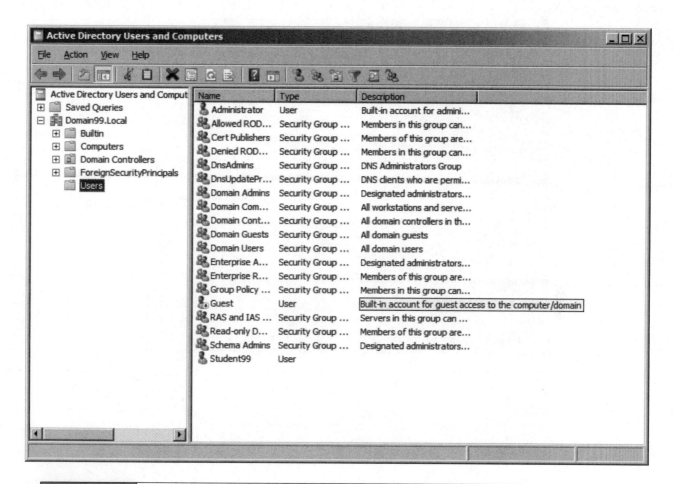

| Question 7 | What objects have been created in this container automatically by the Active Directory Domain Services Installation Wizard? |

3. Right-click Enterprise Admins and select Properties.

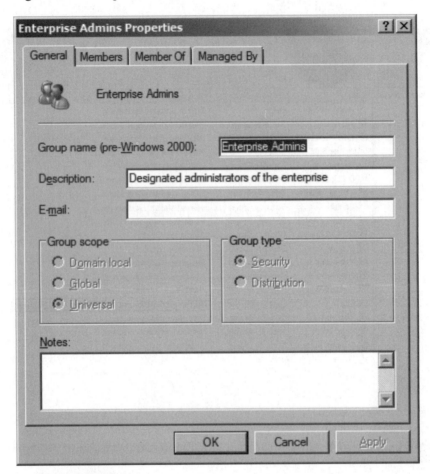

Question 8	*What is the group scope and group type of the Enterprise Admins group? Can you change either of these settings?*

4. Click the Members tab.

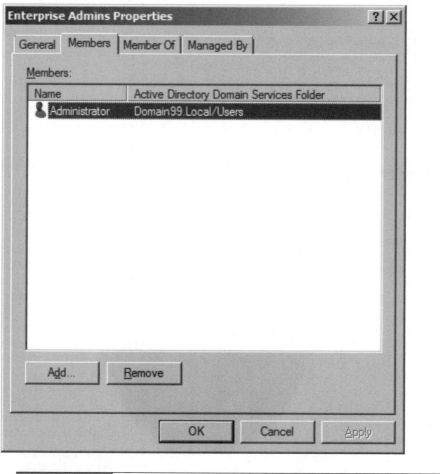

Question 9	*What object(s) belong to the Enterprise Admins group by default?*

5. Click Add. The Select Users, Contacts, Computers, Or Groups window is displayed.

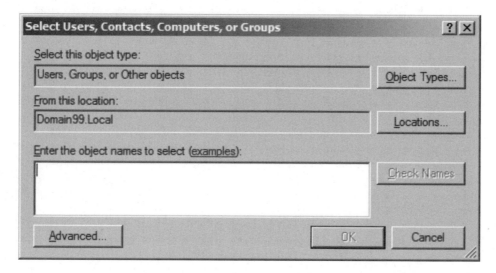

6. Key **student##** and click OK.

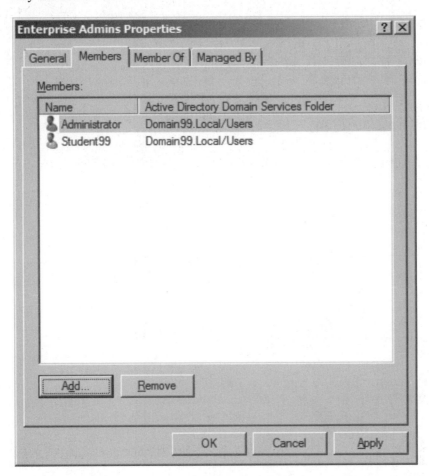

7. Press Ctrl+Prt Scr to take a screen shot of the Enterprise Admins properties sheet, displaying the members tab with student## as a member, and then press Ctrl+V to paste the resulting image into the lab03_worksheet file in the page provided.

8. Click OK and close the Active Directory Users And Computers window.

9. Log off of both machines.

LAB 4
WORKING WITH ACTIVE DIRECTORY SITES

This lab contains the following exercises:

Exercise 4.1   Replication Management

Exercise 4.2   Preparing Your Infrastructure

Exercise 4.3   Configuring a Site

Exercise 4.4   Configuring a New Subnet

Exercise 4.5   Moving Computers and Creating Site Links

Post-Lab Cleanup

Estimated lab time: 100 minutes

Exercise 4.1	Replication Management
Overview	Now that you have added a new domain controller to the Domain99.Local domain, you want to ensure replication is occurring properly. You have reviewed the replication error messages in the Event Viewer Directory Service log and identified some errors that you are anxious to resolve. First, you plan to force replication. Then, you plan to create a manual connection object. Finally, you will use repadmin to troubleshoot any further problems.
Completion time	60 minutes

- **PART A: Forcing Replication**

1. Turn on the Server## computer and log on using your Administrator account and the password P@ssw0rd.
2. Turn on the Server##A computer and log on using your Administrator account and the password P@ssw0rd.

> NOTE
>
> *You can perform the following tasks from eitherWindows Server 2008 machine.*

NOTE *Remember to use your domain adminstrator account and not the local administrator account.*

3. To open the Active Directory Sites And Services MMC snap-in, click Start, click Administrative Tools, and then click Active Directory Sites And Services.

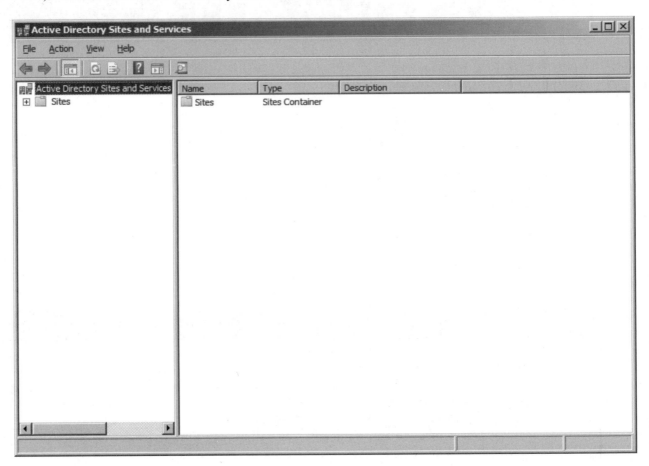

4.   In the left pane, expand the Sites folder.

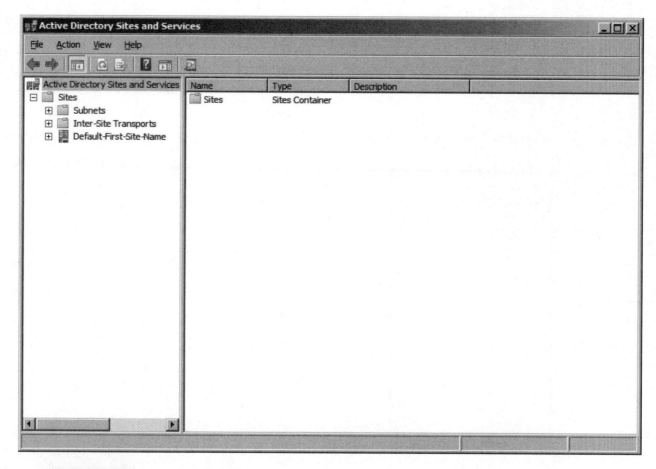

Question 1	*What is the name of the site that was created by default when you installed the Active Directory Domain Services role?*

Default _ first _ Site _ Name

5. Expand the Default-First-Site-Name site. Click the Servers folder.

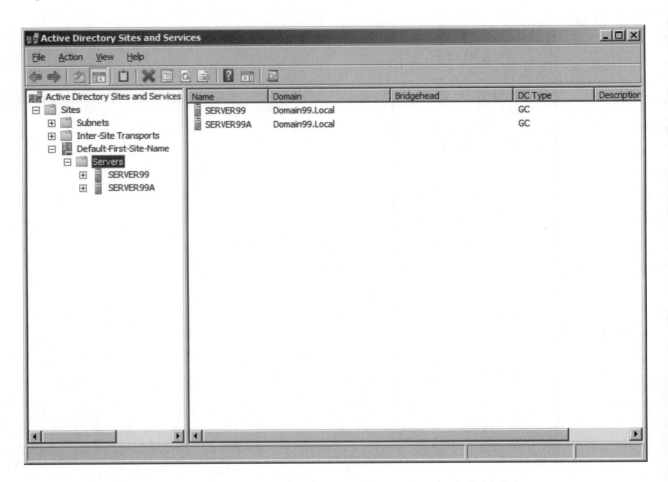

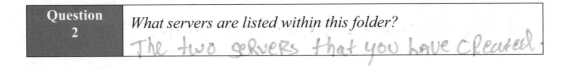

Question 2	*What servers are listed within this folder?*
	The two servers that you have created.

6. Expand the icon for the server that you are using. In the left pane, click NTDS Settings.

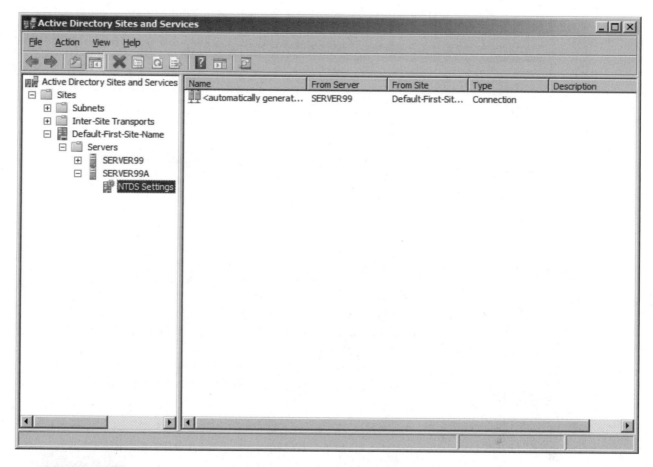

Question 3	What connection objects are configured in this folder?
	automatically generated.

7. In the right pane, select the replication connection that has been configured for your server. Right-click the connection and then click Replicate Now. A Replicate Now message box is displayed, indicating that Active Directory has replicated the connection.

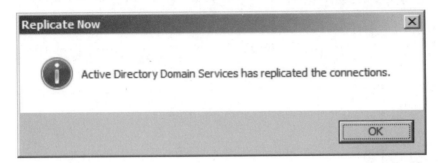

NOTE	*You may see the following error message when you select Replicate Now: "The following error occurred during the attempt to synchronize naming context Configuration from domain controller Server## to domain controller Server##A. The naming context is in the process of being removed or is not replicated from the specified server. The operation will not continue." If you receive this error, wait a few minutes for the domain controllers to synchronize and then try again to force a replication. You can also try to open the command prompt and run the repadmin /syncall command.*

8. Click OK. Leave the Active Directory Sites And Services console open for the next exercise.

- ### PART B: Managing Connection Objects

Suppose that your attempt to force replication did not work. In this case, you could check the Event Viewer's Directory Service log to learn what occurred. Let's say that you decide there may be a problem with the connections objects and decide to create one manually as a temporary troubleshooting measure. (It is not a best practice to configure manual connection objects for everyday replication, because they can become stale or out-of-date. This project is designed to illustrate creating a manual connection object for troubleshooting purposes only.)

> **NOTE**
> *You can perform the following tasks from eitherWindows Server 2008 machine.*

1. Right-click NTDS Settings, and then click New Active Directory Domain Services Connection. The Find Domain Controllers dialog box is displayed.

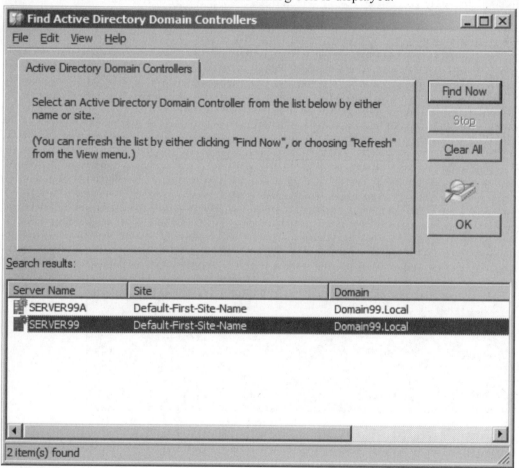

2. Select the name of your partner computer. For example, if you are using Server##, select Server##A from the list of computer names displayed in the Search Results window pane; if you are using Server##A, select Server## from the list of computer names displayed in the Search Results window pane. Click OK. An Active Directory message box is displayed, indicating that there is already a connection and asking you if you want to create another connection.

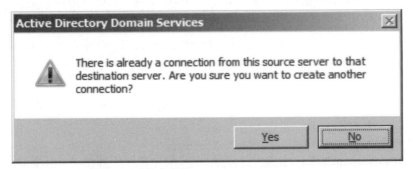

3. Click Yes. A New Object-Connection dialog box is displayed.

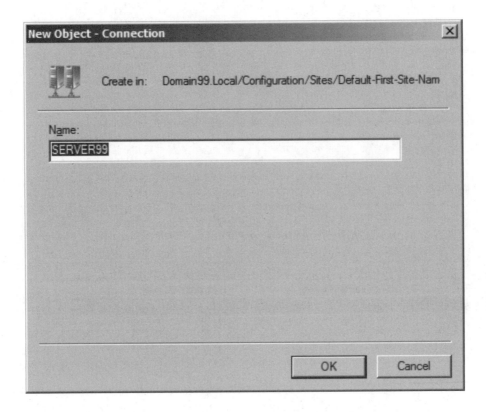

4. To accept the default settings, click OK. The new connection is created. Two connections should be displayed: the automatically generated connection and the manually generated connection.

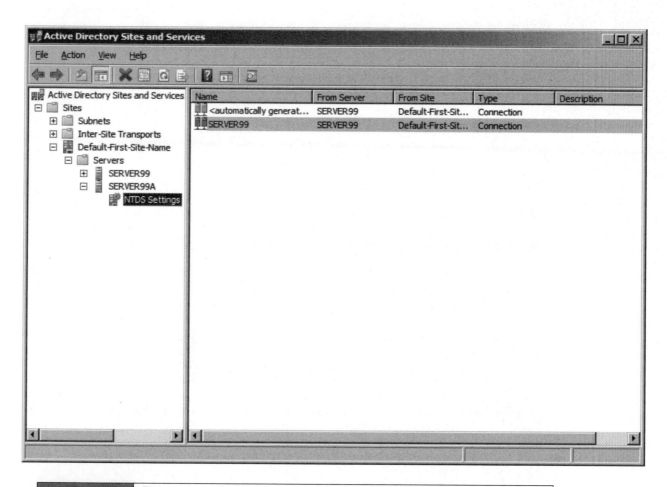

| | | Question 4 | Forcing replication on the new connection object was described in the previous section. How can you tell which connections are the automatically generated connections and which ones have been created manually? |

The automatically one is told to you.

5. In the right pane, select the replication connection that you just created. Right-click the connection and then click Replicate Now. A Replicate Now message box is displayed, indicating that Active Directory has replicated the connection.

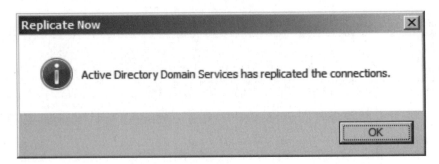

6. Click OK. In the right pane, right-click the manually created connection and click Delete. An Active Directory message box is displayed.

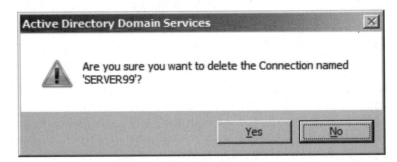

7. Click Yes to confirm that you want to delete the connection object. The object is deleted.

- **PART C: Identifying the Global Catalog**

    While performing your replication checks, you learn that certain users are unable to log on to the network. You begin to wonder if the global catalog server is functional. You need to verify which server is functioning as the global catalog server.

NOTE	*You can perform the following tasks from eitherWindows Server 2008 machine.*

1. In the Active Directory Sites And Services console's left pane, right-click NTDS Settings and then click Properties. The NTDS Settings Properties dialog box is displayed.

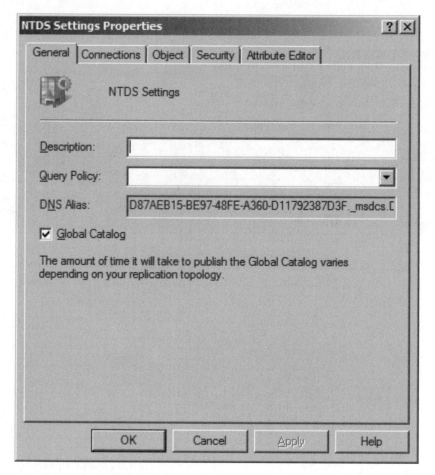

2. On the General tab, you can see that the Global Catalog checkbox is selected. Click Cancel.

Question 5	*What does it mean when the Global Catalog checkbox is selected?*

3. Close the Active Directory Sites And Services console.

- **PART D: Using repadmin**

  You decide to force replication with repadmin this time. You also want to verify your replication partner connections.

  1. On Server## and Server##A Open a command-prompt window.

  2. In the command-prompt window on the Server## computer, key **repadmin /syncall**. In the command-prompt window on the Server##A computer, key **repadmin /syncall**.

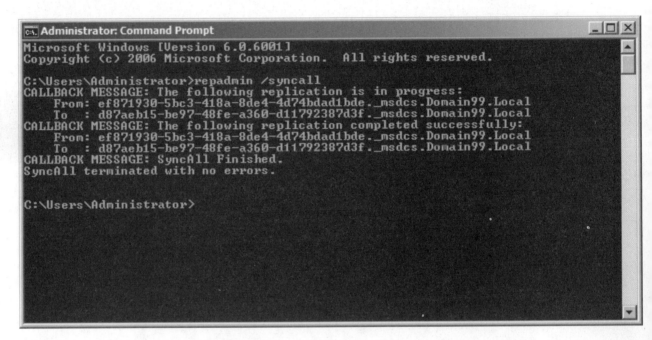

  3. Read all of the repadmin command output. Confirm that the repadmin output includes an indication that "The following replication completed successfully." All domain controllers are now synchronized.

4. On the Server##, key **repadmin /showrepl**. On the Server##A computer, key **repadmin /showrepl**.

Question 6	*Who are your inbound neighbors?*

5.   Key **cls** and press Enter to clear the window.

6.   On the Server## computer, key **repadmin /showconn**. On the Server##A computer, key **repadmin /showconn**.

Question 7	*How many connections were found?*
	5

7.   Close the command-prompt window.

Exercise 4.2	Preparing Your Infrastructure
Overview	You want to configure your existing network to support a new site so that you can run some tests to see how a custom application will perform. However, you are unable to locate a router or additional network cards. You decide that you can create a logical Internet Protocol (IP) network inside your physical local area network (LAN) for your tests. You need to prepare two servers for this test.
Completion time	5 minutes

- **PART A: Preparing the Server## Computer for Site-Configuration Testing**

1. On Server## Click Start > Administrative Tools > Server Manager to open the Server Manager if it is not already open.

2. Click View Network Connections. The Network Connections window is displayed.

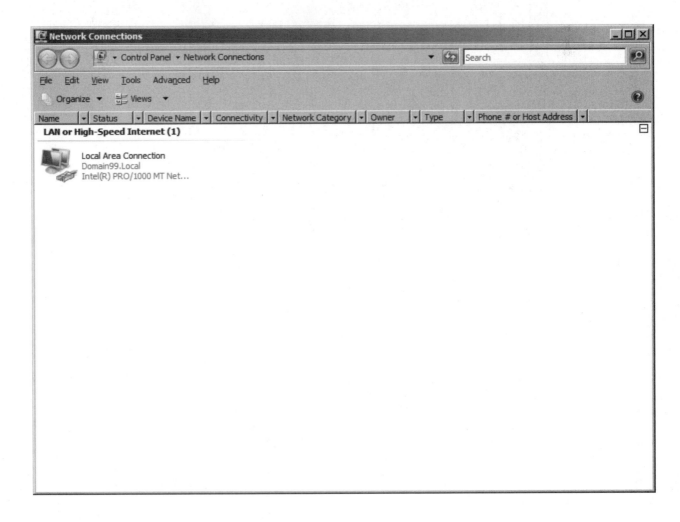

3. Right-click your network connection and select Properties. The network connection's Properties window is displayed.

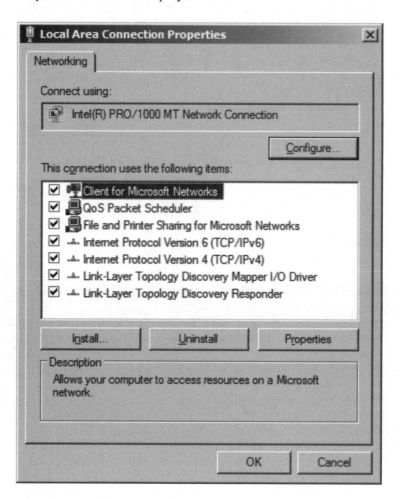

4. Click Internet Protocol Version 4 (TCP/IPv4) and select Properties. The Internet Protocol Version 4 (TCP/IPv4) Properties window is displayed.

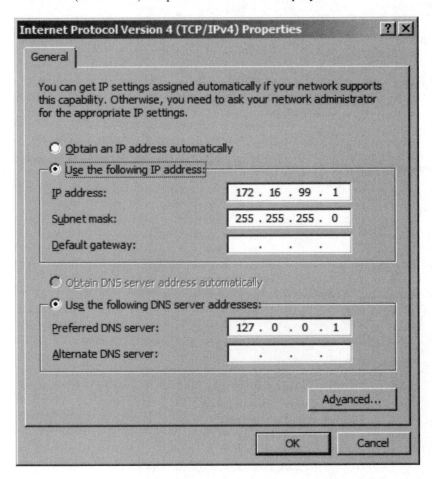

5. Click Advanced. The Advanced TCP/IP Settings window is displayed.

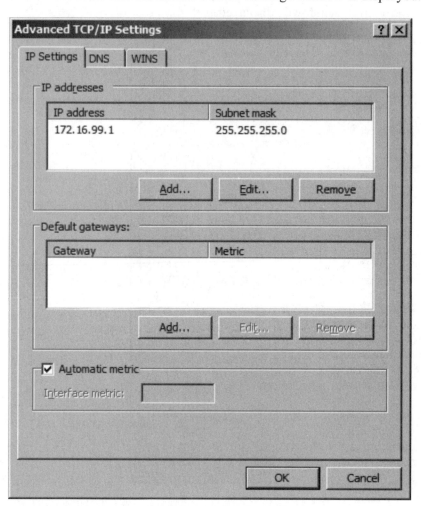

6. On the IP Settings tab, click Add. The TCP/IP Address dialog box is displayed.

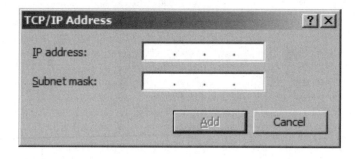

7. Enter the following additional IP address for this server:

   - Key the IP address **172.16.##.##**. For example, Server99 would be configured as 192.168.99.99.

   - Key the subnet mask **255.255.255.0**.

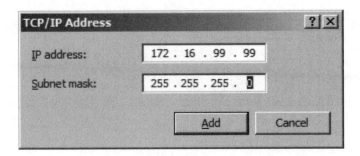

8. Click Add, and then click OK three times to save your settings.

- **PART B: Preparing the Server##A Computer for Site-Configuration Testing**

    1. On Server##A Click Start > Administrative Tools > Server Manager to open the Server Manager if it is not already open.

    2. Click View Network Connections. The Network Connections window is displayed.

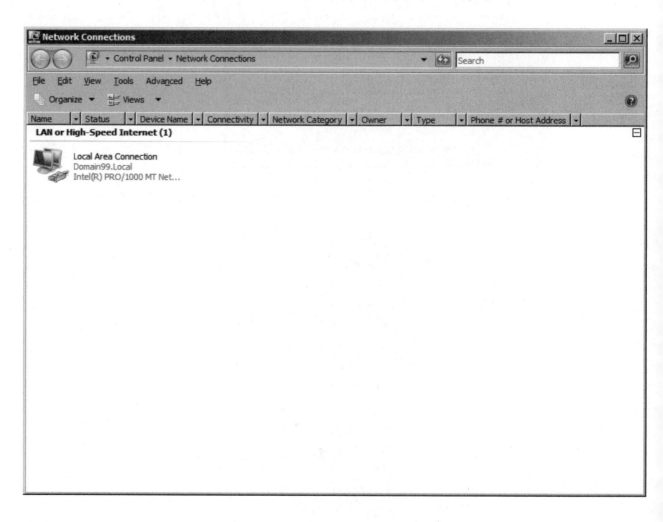

3. Right-click your network connection and select Properties. The network connection's Properties window is displayed.

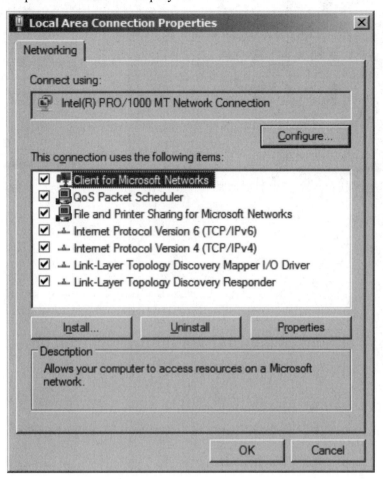

4. Click Internet Protocol Version 4 (TCP/IPv4) and select Properties. The Internet Protocol Version 4 (TCP/IPv4) Properties window is displayed.

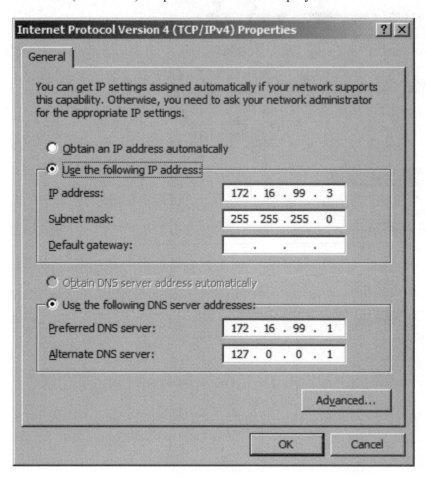

5. Click Advanced. The Advanced TCP/IP Settings window is displayed.

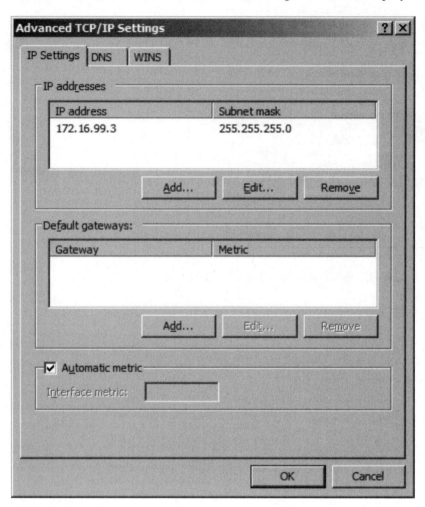

6. On the IP Settings tab, click Add. The TCP/IP Address dialog box is displayed.

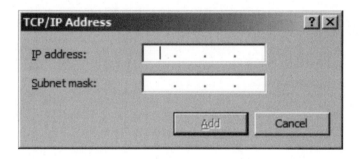

7. Enter the following additional IP address for this server:

    - Key the IP address **172.16.xx.xx**. Where xx is a number assigned by your instructor. For example, Server##A would be configured as 172.16.100.100.

    - Key the subnet mask **255.255.255.0**.

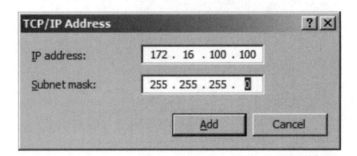

8. Click Add, and then click OK three times to save your settings.

Exercise 4.3	Configuring a Site
Overview	You decide to create the Main and Branch sites. Furthermore, you want to rename the Default-First-Site-Name to HQ.
Completion time	5 minutes

- **PART A: Creating a Site for the Server## Computer**

  1.   On the Server## computer, open the Active Directory Sites And Services console.

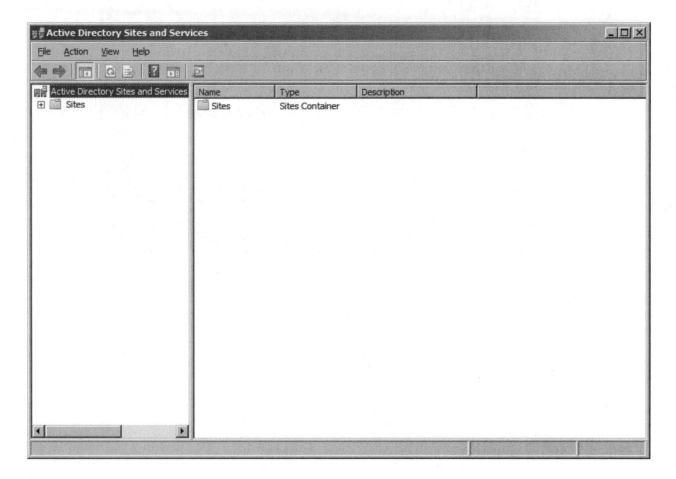

2.   In the left pane, right-click Sites and then click New Site. The New Object-Site dialog box is displayed.

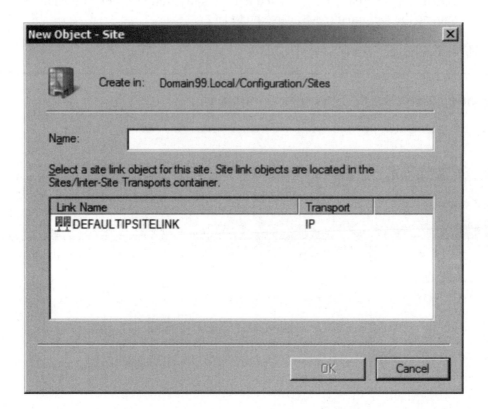

3. In the Name text box, key **MainSite**. Click DEFAULTIPSITELINK and then click OK. A message box is displayed, indicating that you must complete additional steps to configure the site.

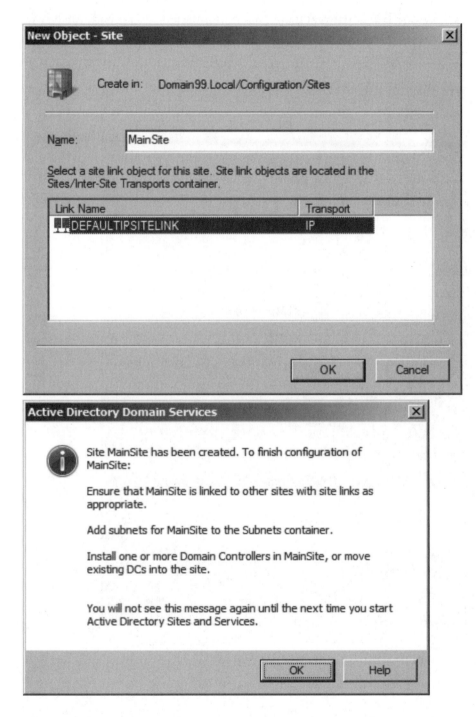

4. Click OK.

- **PART B: Creating a Site for the Server##A Computer and Renaming the Default-First-Site-Name Site**

    1. On the Server##A computer, open the Active Directory Sites And Services console. If you receive an error message indicating that the naming information cannot be located, wait a few minutes to ensure that the two domain controllers have had time to replicate and then try opening the console again.

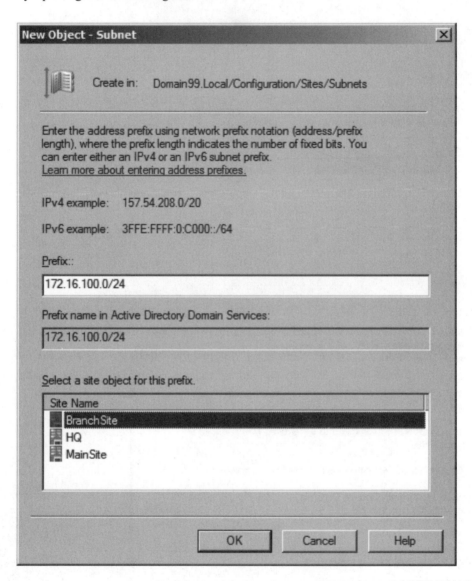

2. In the left pane, right-click Sites and then click New Site. The New Object-Site dialog box is displayed.

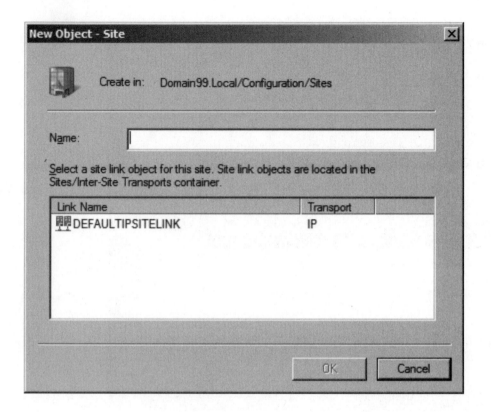

3. In the Name text box, key **BranchSite**. Click DEFAULTIPSITELINK and then click OK. A message box is displayed, indicating that you must complete additional steps to configure the site.

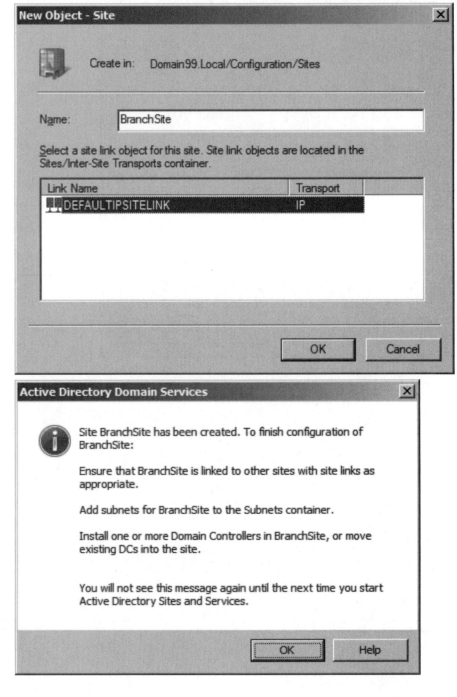

4. Click OK.

5. In the left pane, right-click Default-First-Site-Name and then click Rename. Key **HQ** as the new name for Default-First-Site-Name and then press Enter.

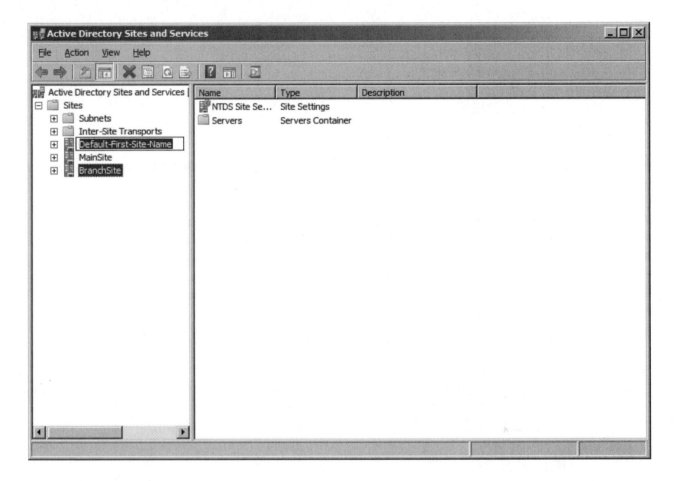

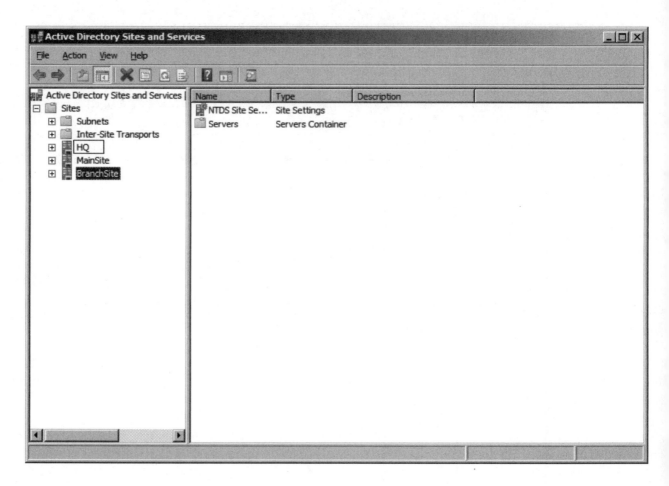

Exercise 4.4	Configuring a New Subnet
Overview	To simulate inter-site Active Directory replication, you decide to create two new subnets for use in the two sites that you created in Exercise 4.3.
Completion time	5 minutes

- **PART A: Create a Subnet Object for the Server## Computer**

    1. On the Server## computer, open the Active Directory Sites And Services console. In the left pane, expand the Sites folder.

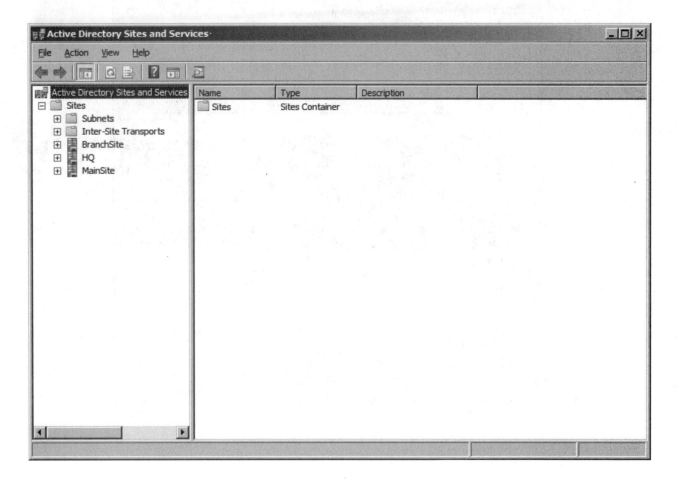

2. In the left pane, right-click Subnets and then click New Subnet. The New Object-Subnet dialog box is displayed.

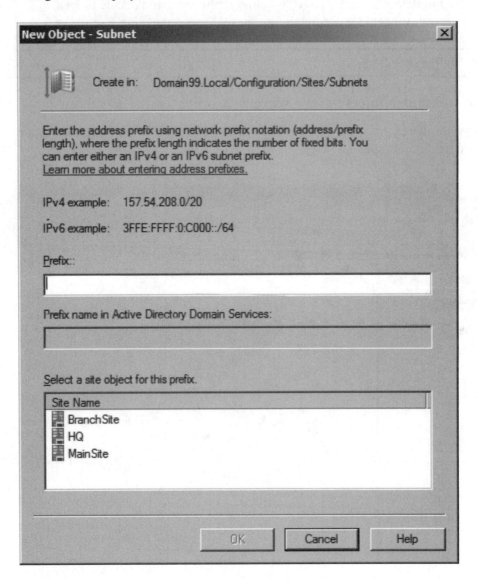

3. Key **172.16.##.0/24** in the Prefix text box; for example, on the Server99 computer, key 172.16.99.0/24. In the Site Name portion of the dialog box, click MainSite, and click OK.

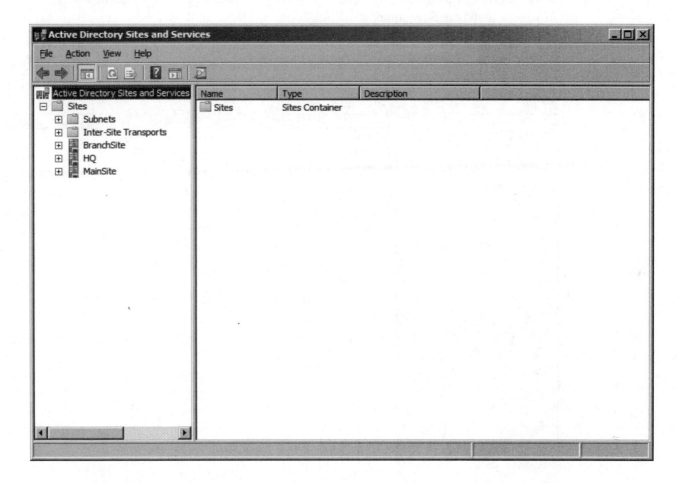

- **PART B: Create a Subnet Object for the Server##A Computer**

  1. On the Server##A computer, open the Active Directory Sites And Services console. In the left pane, expand the Sites folder.

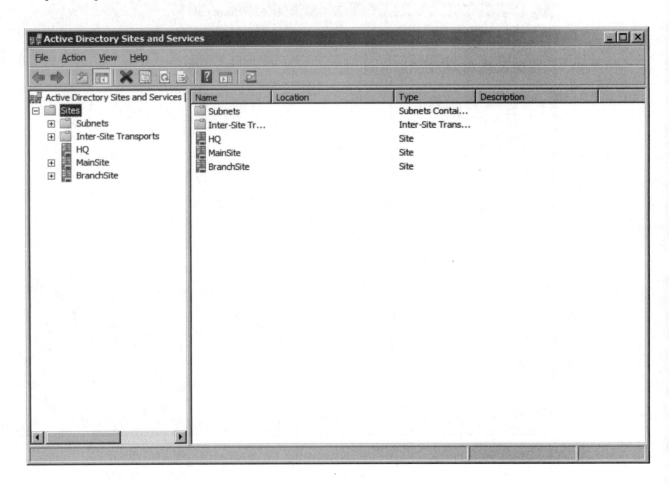

2. Right-click Subnets, and then click New Subnet. The New Object–Subnet dialog box is displayed.

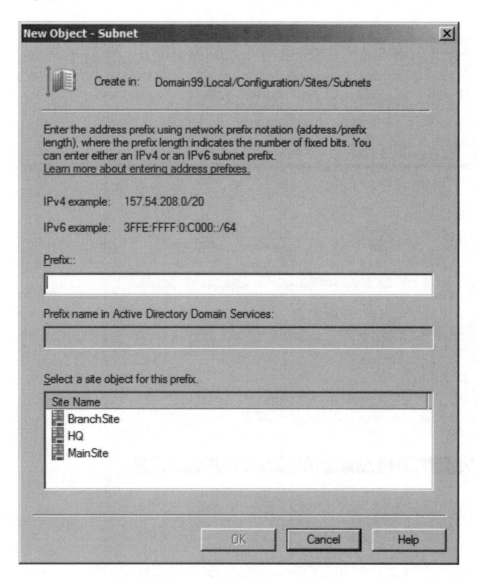

3. Key **172.16.xx.0/24** in the Prefix text box; for example, on the Server99A computer, key 172.16.100.0/24. In the Site Name portion of the dialog box, click BranchSite, and then click OK.

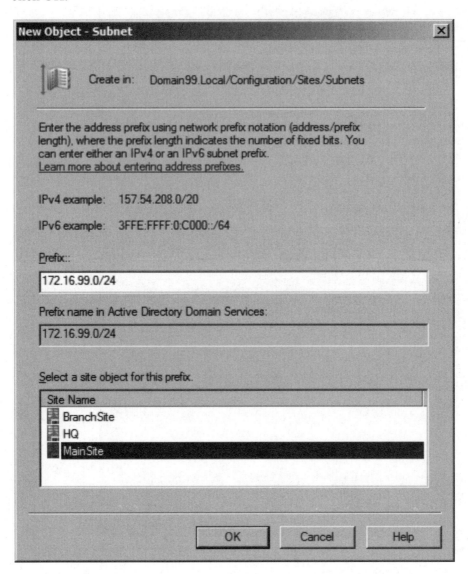

Exercise 4.5	Moving Computers and Creating Site Links
Overview	Now that you have created site and subnet objects, you want to move your computer accounts into their respective sites and configure site links between the sites.
Completion time	15 minutes

- **PART A: Moving the Server## and Server##A Computers to the Appropriate Site**

   1. On the Server## computer, open the Active Directory Sites And Services console. In the left pane, expand the Sites folder. Verify that the Default-First-Site-Name site was renamed to HQ. If you do not see this on the Server## computer, force replication with the Server##A computer and refresh the view. If a replication error is displayed, wait a few minutes and try again.

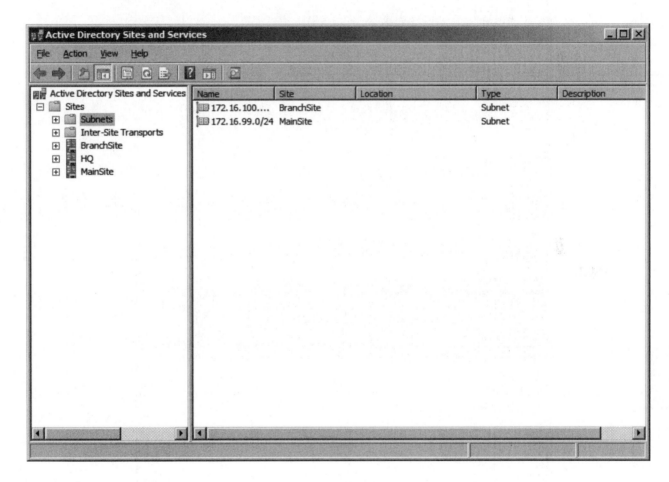

2. In the left pane, expand the HQ site and then expand the Servers folder.

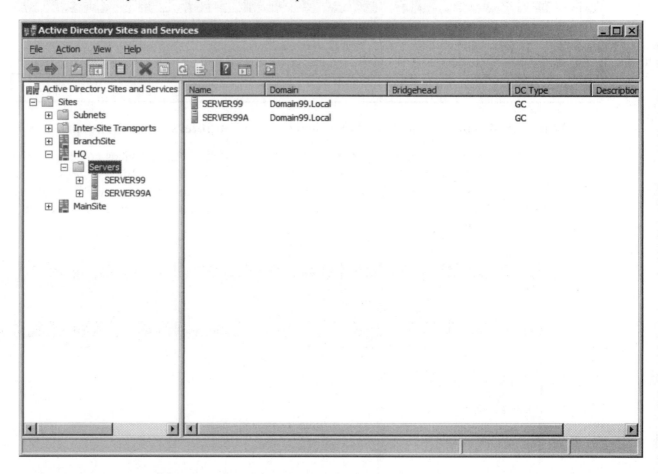

3. Right-click Server##, and then click Move. The Move Server dialog box is displayed.

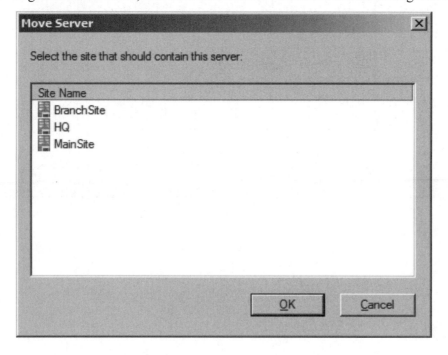

4. Click MainSite and then click OK.

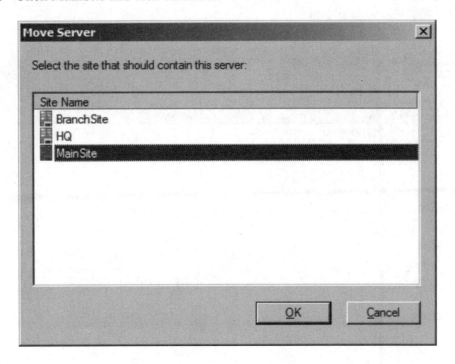

5. In the left pane, expand MainSite and then expand the Servers object below MainSite. You should see the Server## computer object.

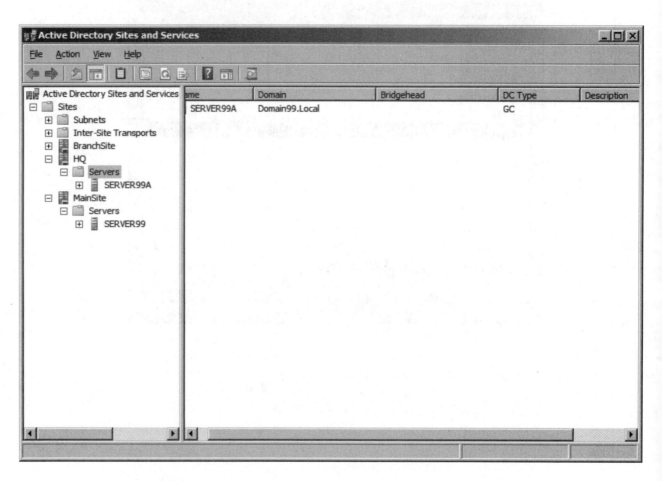

6. Try to force replicataion using the connection object of the Server## computer. You should see a message indicating that these servers are in different sites. Click OK.

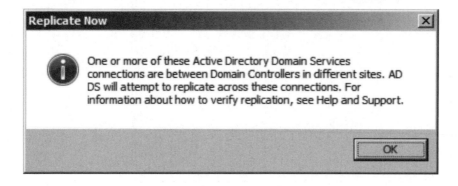

7. Right-click Server##A, and then click Move. The Move Server dialog box is displayed.

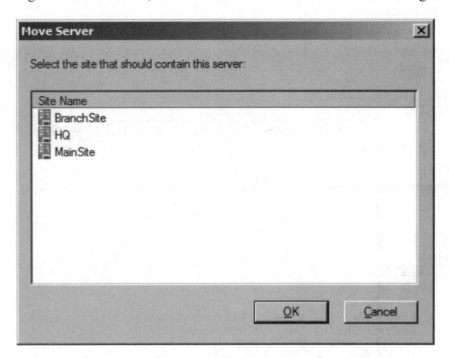

8. Click BranchSite and then click OK.

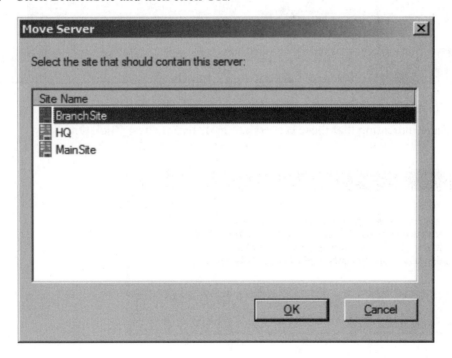

9. In the left pane, expand BranchSite and then expand the Servers folder. You should see the Server##A computer object.

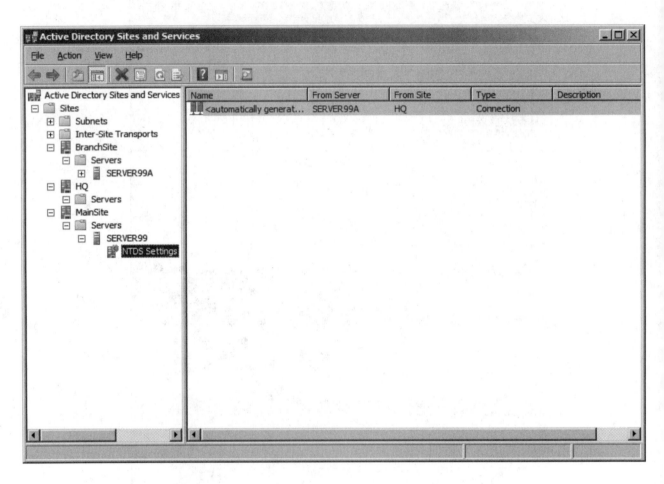

10. Try to force replication using the connection object of the Server##A computer. You should see a message indicating that these servers are in different sites. Click OK.

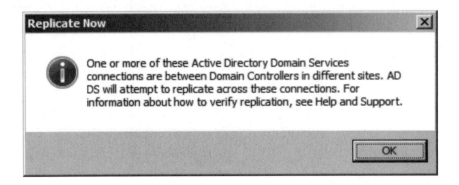

- **PART B: Creating a Site Link Object from the Server##A Computer**

For replication to take place between Server## and Server##A in separate sites, you must create a site link object between these sites.

1. On the Server##A computer, open the Active Directory Sites And Services console. In the left pane, expand the Sites folder.

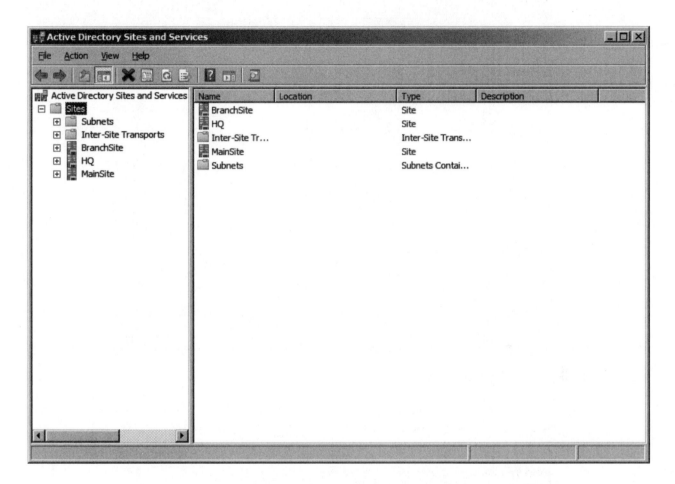

2. In the left pane, expand the Inter-Site Transports folder. Right-click IP and click New Site Link. The New Object-Site Link dialog box is displayed.

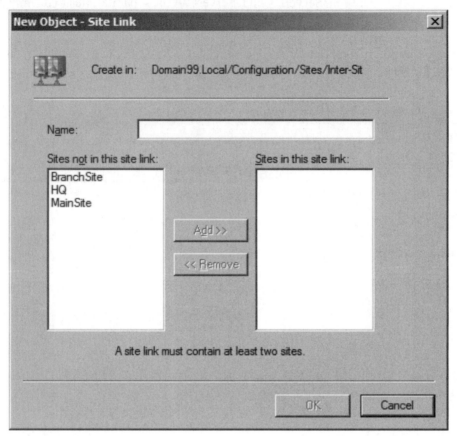

3. In the Name text box, key **EvenLink**. In the Sites Not In This Site Link box, click MainSite and then click Add.

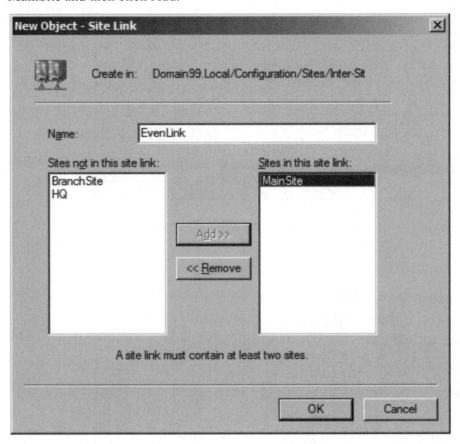

4. In the Sites Not In This Site Link box, click BranchSite and then click Add. Click OK to save your changes.

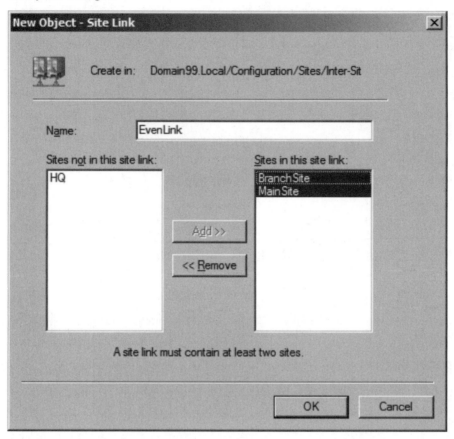

5. Click the IP object under Inter-Site Transports. The EvenLink site link should be visible in the right pane.

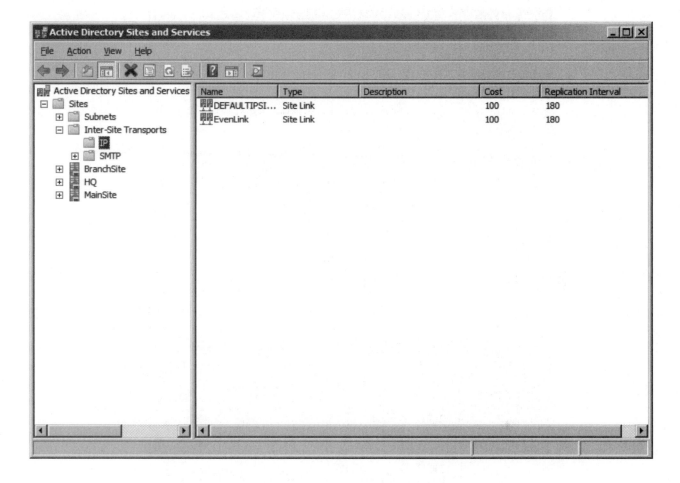

6. Right-click EvenLink and click Properties. The Evenlink Properties dialog box is displayed.

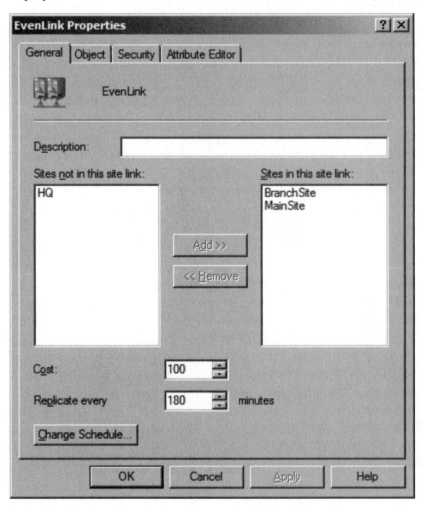

7. Change the value in the Replicate Every box to 15 minutes, and then click OK.

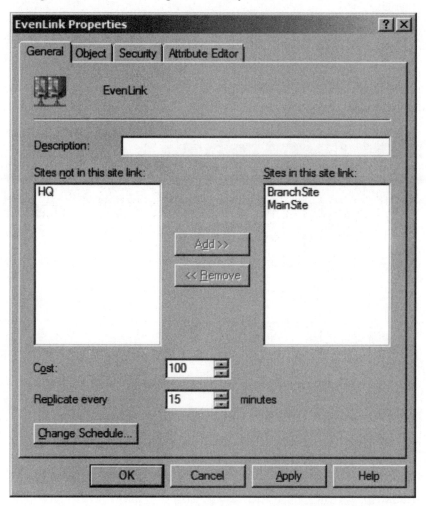

- **PART C: Creating a Site Link from the Server## Computer**

  In a production environment you would only create a single site link object between two sites. To allow both students to familiarize themselves with the process, however, in this project you will create two site link objects.

  1. On the Server## computer, open the Active Directory Sites And Services console. In the left pane, expand the Sites folder.

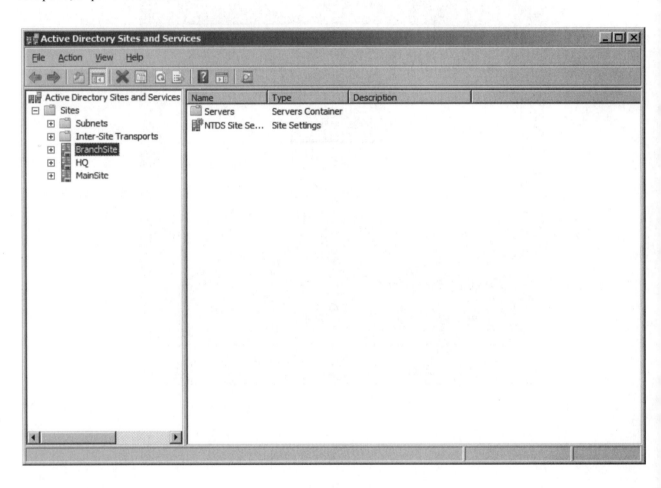

2. In the left pane, expand the Inter-Site Transports folder. Right-click IP and then click New Site Link. The New Object-Site Link dialog box is displayed.

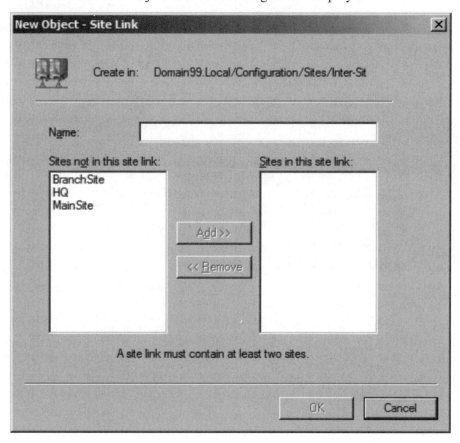

3. In the Name text box, key **OddLink**. In the Sites Not In This Site Link box, click MainSite and then click Add.

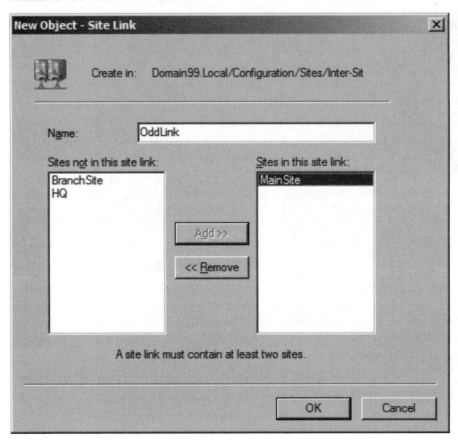

4. In the Sites Not In This Site Link box, click BranchSite and then click Add. Click OK to save your changes.

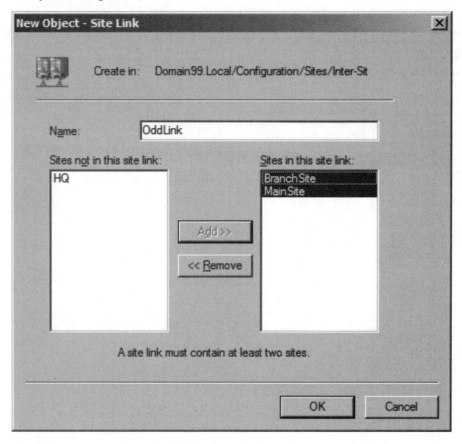

5. Click the IP object under Inter-Site Transports. The OddLink site link should be displayed in the right pane.

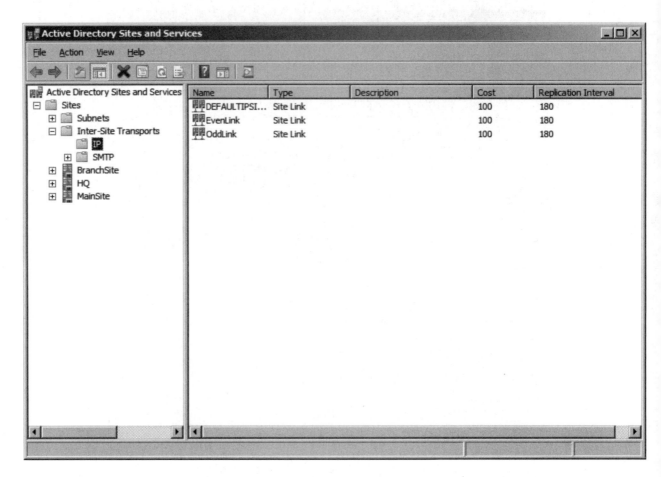

6. Right-click OddLink and click Properties. The Oddlink Properties dialog box is displayed.

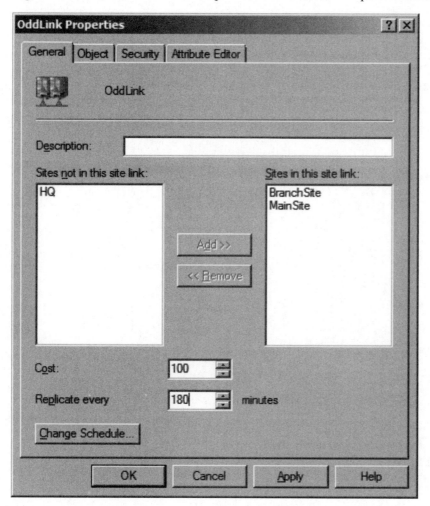

7. Change the value in the Replicate Every box to 15 minutes, and then click OK.

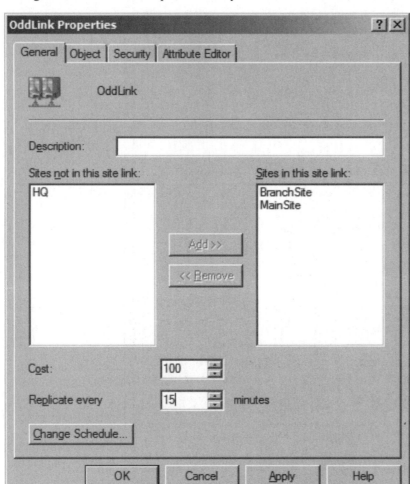

- **PART D: Verifying Replications**

1. Wait approximately 15 minutes for replication to complete. Return to either computer computer. Close and reopen Active Directory Sites And Services console by pressing the F5 key or clicking the Refresh button on the toolbar.

2. Click Inter-Site Transports and then click IP. You should see both site link objects added as a site link. This provides verification that your computers are replicating with each other.

POST-LAB CLEANUP

Overview	Use the techniques that you learned in this lab to complete the following steps from Server##. These cleanup steps are required to reset the lab configuration to perform exercises in the following Labs.
Completion time	10 minutes

1. Turn on the Server## computer and log on using your Student## account and the password P@ssw0rd (if it is not already on).

2. Turn on the Server##A computer and log on using your Student## account and the password P@ssw0rd (if it is not already on).

3. Move the Server## computer and the Server##A computer into the HQ site.

4. Rename the HQ site to Default-First-Site-Name.

5. Delete the two sites created in this lab. To delete a site in the Active Directory Sites And Services console, right-click the site object that you want to remove and then click Delete. Confirm this action by clicking Yes on each of the two warning message boxes that are displayed.

6. Delete the two subnets created in this lab. To delete a subnet in the Active Directory Sites And Services console, expand the Subnets object, right-click the subnet object that you wish to remove, and then click Delete. Confirm this action by clicking Yes on the warning message that is displayed.

7. Delete the two site links created in this lab. To delete a site link object in the Active Directory Sites And Services console, expand the Inter-Site Transports object and then select the IP object. In the right pane, right-click the site link object that you want to remove and then click Delete. Confirm this action by clicking Yes on the warning message that is displayed.

8. Remove the additional IP address configured for Server##.

9. After the Server## computer has finished rebooting, remove the additional IP address configured for Server##A computer and restart it.

LAB 5
GLOBAL CATALOG AND FLEXIBLE SINGLE MASTER OPERATIONS (FSMO) ROLES

This lab contains the following exercises:

Exercise 5.1   The Global Catalog and the Windows Server 2008 Domain Functional Level

Exercise 5.2   Enabling Universal Group Membership Caching

Exercise 5.3   Working with Flexible Single Master Operations Roles

Estimated lab time: 70 minutes

Exercise 5.1	The Global Catalog and the Windows Server 2008 Domain Functional Level
Overview	Now that your Domain Controllers are configured, your manager would like you to raise the domain and forest functional levels to Windows Server 2008 so that your organization can take full advantage of the features of Windows Server 2008. She would also like to know the implications of Global Catalog failure to your organization
Completion time	40 minutes

■ PART A: Raise the Domain Functional Level

1. Turn on the Server## computers and log on using your Administrator account and the password P@ssw0rd.1234

2. Turn on the Server##A computer, but do not logon yet.

NOTE	*Remember to use your domain adminstrator account and not the local administrator account.*

3. On Server## open the Active Directory Domains And Trusts console.

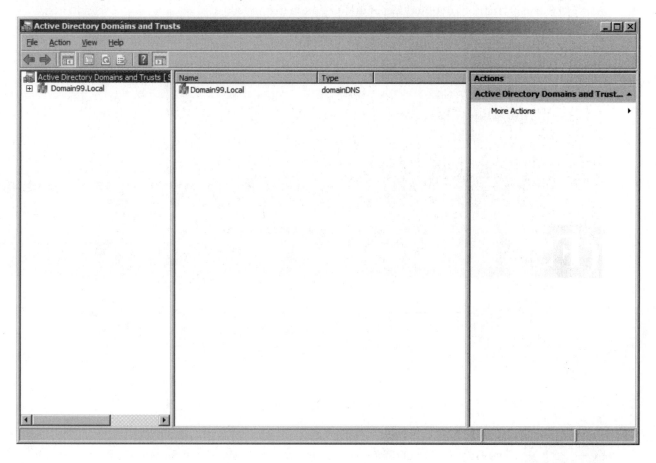

4. Right-click the Domain##.Local node and then click Raise Domain Functional Level. The Raise Domain Functional Level dialog box is displayed.

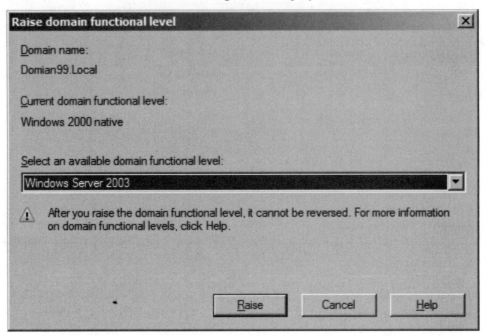

NOTE	*If the Domain Functional Level is already set to Windows Server 2008 skip steps 4 and 5.*

5. In the dropdown selection box, click Windows Server 2008 and then click Raise. A message box is displayed.

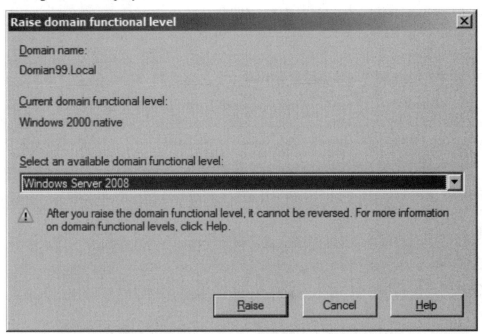

6. Read the message and then confirm it by clicking OK. A second message box is displayed, indicating that the domain functional level has been raised.

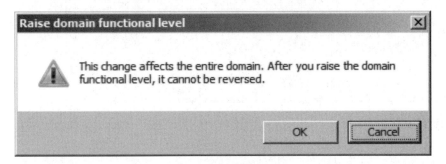

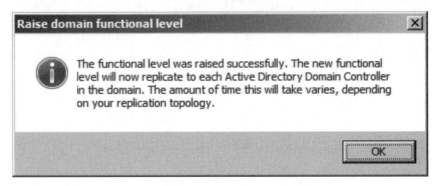

7. Press Ctrl+Prt Scr to take a screen shot of the message indicating that the domain functional level is Windows Server 2008, and then press Ctrl+V to paste the resulting image into the lab05_worksheet file in the page provided.

8. Click OK.

■ PART B: Raise the Forest Functional Level

1. On Server## in the Active Directory Domains And Trusts console, Right-click the top-level node Active Directory Domains And Trusts [Server##.Domain##.Local] and then click Raise Forest Functional Level. The Raise Forest Functional Level dialog box is displayed.

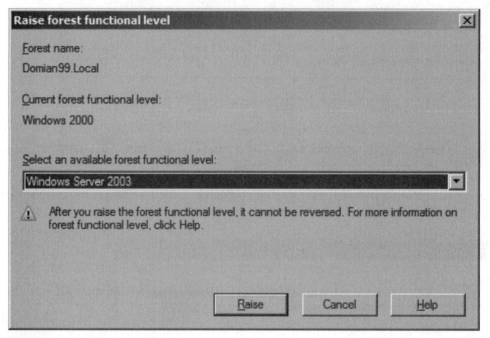

| | If the Forest Functional Level is already set to Windows Server 2008 skip steps 2 and 3. |
| NOTE | |

2.   In the dropdown selection box, click Windows Server 2008 and then click Raise. A message box is displayed.

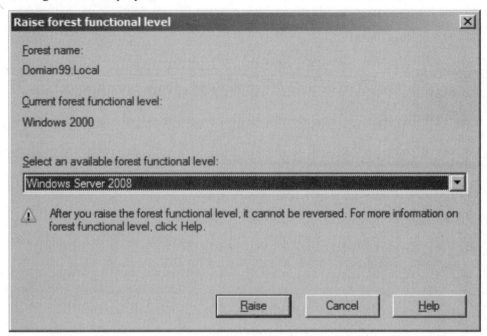

3.   Read the message and then confirm it by clicking OK. A second message box is displayed, indicating that the forest functional level has been raised.

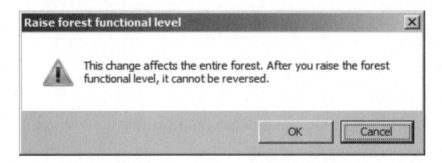

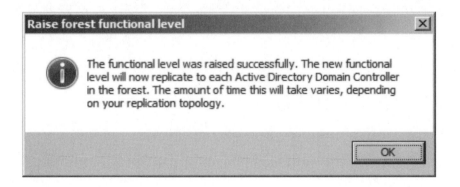

4. Press Ctrl+Prt Scr to take a screen shot of the message indicating that the forest functional level is Windows Server 2008, and then press Ctrl+V to paste the resulting image into the lab05_worksheet file in the page provided.

5. Click OK.

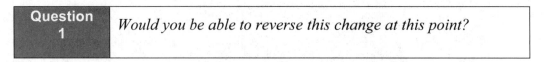

Question 1	*Would you be able to reverse this change at this point?*

6. Close Active Directory Domains And Trusts.

■ PART C: Simulate a Global Catalog Failure

1. On the Server## computer open the Active Directory Sites And Services console.

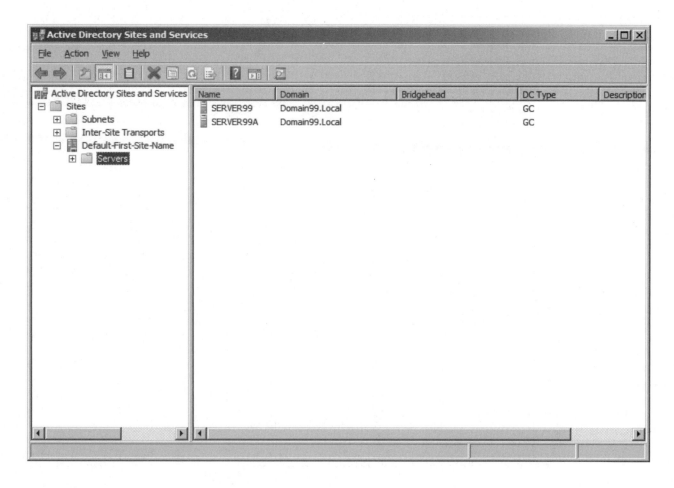

2.   Click Sites, click Default-First-Site-Name, click Servers, and then click Server##. Right-click NTDS Settings and select Properties. The NTDS Settings Properties dialog box is displayed.

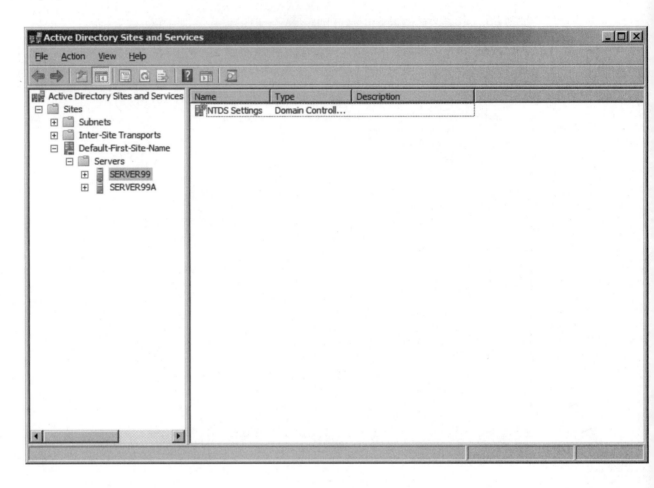

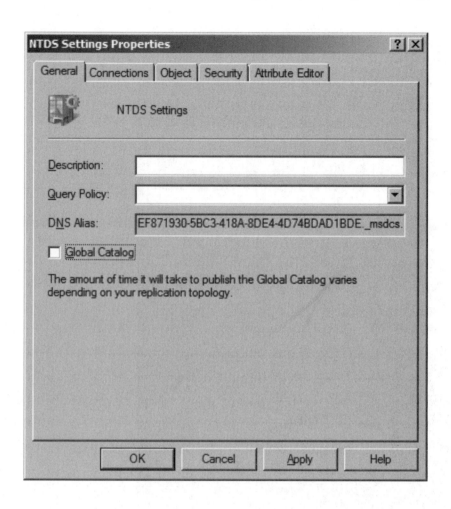

3. Remove the checkbox next to Global Catalog and click OK.

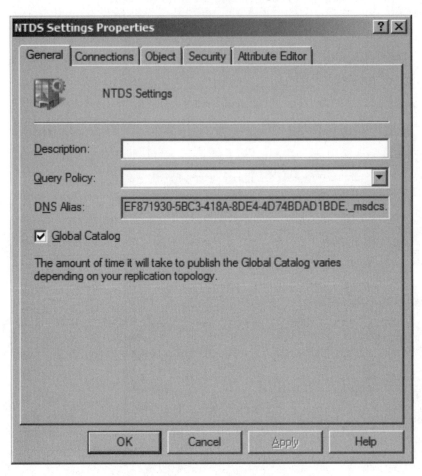

4. Repeat steps 3 and 4 for Server##A. A warning message will be displayed indicating that clients will be unable to log on if they cannot locate a global catalog. Click OK to acknowledge the error and then click OK again to save your changes.

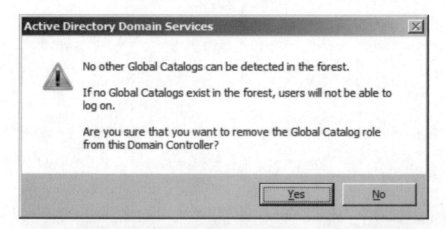

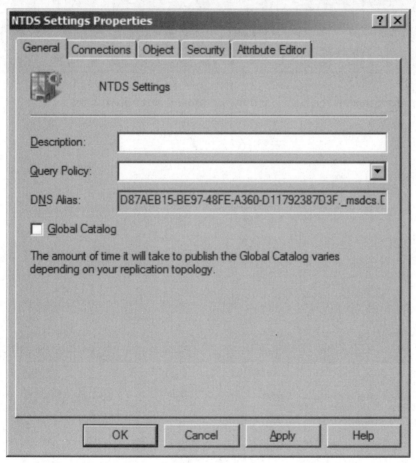

5.   Open a Command prompt window and key Repadmin /syncall in order to force replication so that the changes propoagate to Server##A.

```
Administrator: Command Prompt

Microsoft Windows [Version 6.0.6001]
Copyright (c) 2006 Microsoft Corporation.  All rights reserved.

C:\Users\Administrator>Repadmin /syncall
CALLBACK MESSAGE: The following replication is in progress:
    From: d87aeb15-be97-48fe-a360-d11792387d3f._msdcs.Domain99.Local
    To  : ef871930-5bc3-418a-8de4-4d74bdad1bde._msdcs.Domain99.Local
CALLBACK MESSAGE: The following replication completed successfully:
    From: d87aeb15-be97-48fe-a360-d11792387d3f._msdcs.Domain99.Local
    To  : ef871930-5bc3-418a-8de4-4d74bdad1bde._msdcs.Domain99.Local
CALLBACK MESSAGE: SyncAll Finished.
SyncAll terminated with no errors.


C:\Users\Administrator>
```

6.   Close Active Directory Sites and Services and the command prompt window.

■ PART D: Creating An Account in Order to Test the Global Catalog Failure

1. On Server## open the Active Directory Users And Computers MMC snap-in. Expand the domain object Domain##.Local in the left window pane, if necessary.

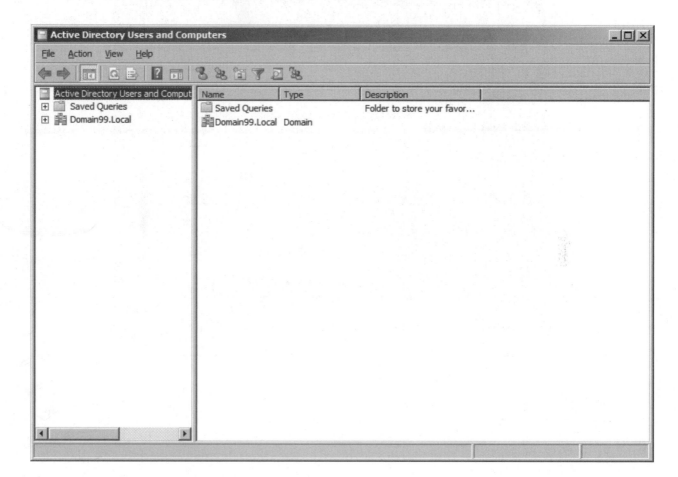

2. In the left window pane, right-click the Users container. Click New, and then click User. The New Object–User dialog box is displayed.

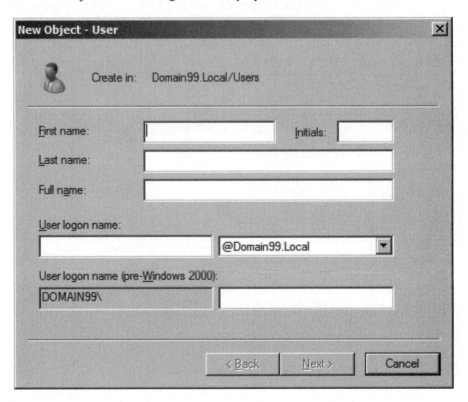

3. Create a new user account named Tst in the default Users container. In the Full Name text box, key **TestUser**.

4. Click the User Logon Name text box, key **TestUser** the same name used in Step 3, and then click Next. An Active Directory Domain Services message will appear. Click OK to continue.

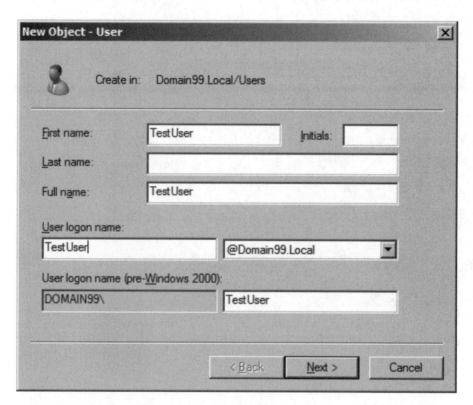

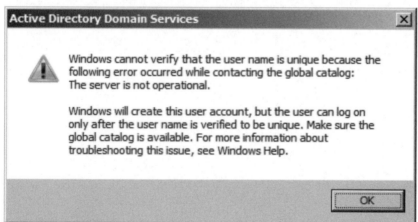

Question 2	*What does this message indicate?*

5. Key **P@ssw0rd** in the Password text box and in the Confirm Password text box.

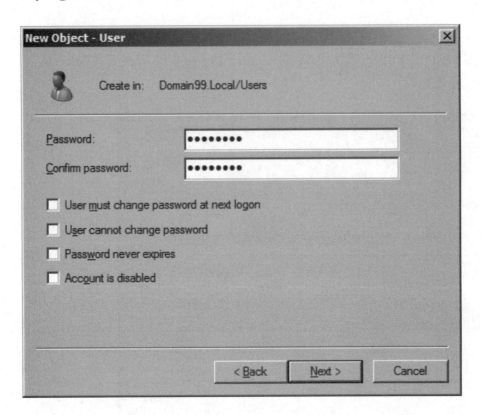

6. Clear the User Must Change Password At Next Logon checkbox. Click Next, and then click Finish.

7. Close Active Directory Users and Computers.

■ PART E: Resolve the Global Catalog Failure

1. On the Server## computer open the Active Directory Sites And Services console.

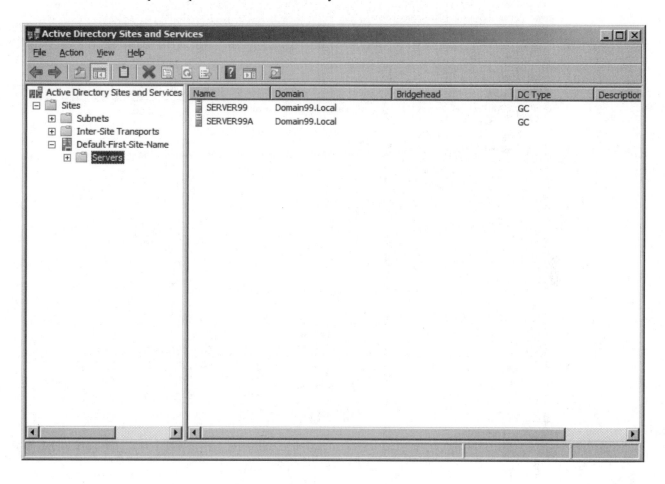

2. Click Sites, click Default-First-Site-Name, click Servers, and then click Server##. Right-click NTDS Settings and select Properties. The NTDS Settings Properties dialog box is displayed.

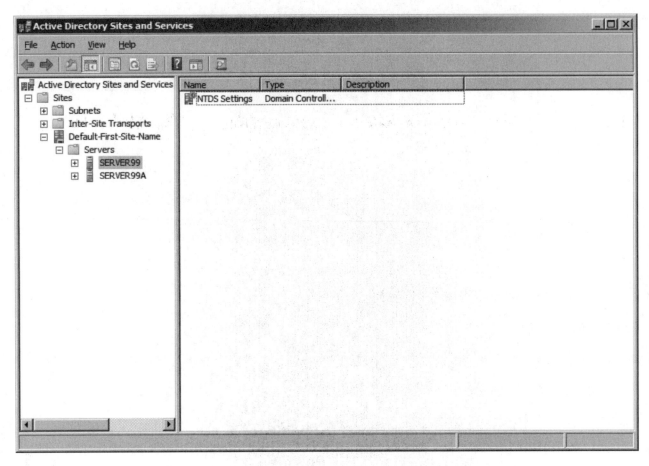

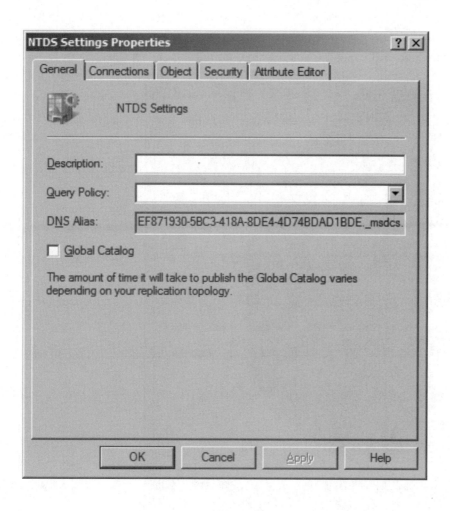

3. Place a check in the checkbox next to Global Catalog and click OK. An Active Directory Domain Services message will appear. Click Yes to continue.

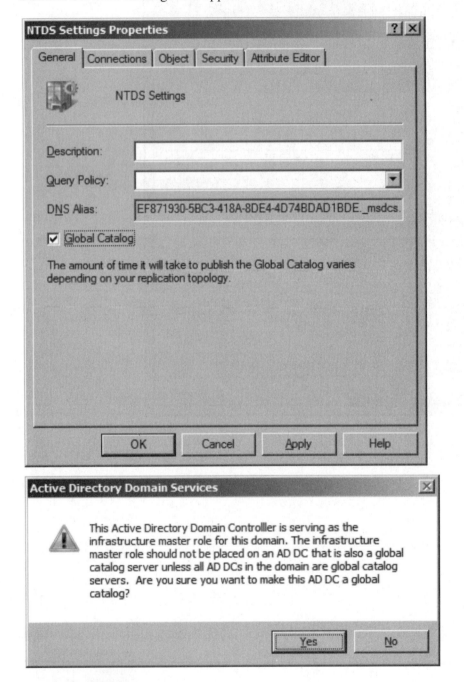

Question 3	*What does this message indicate?*

4. Repeat steps 3 and 4 for Server##A.

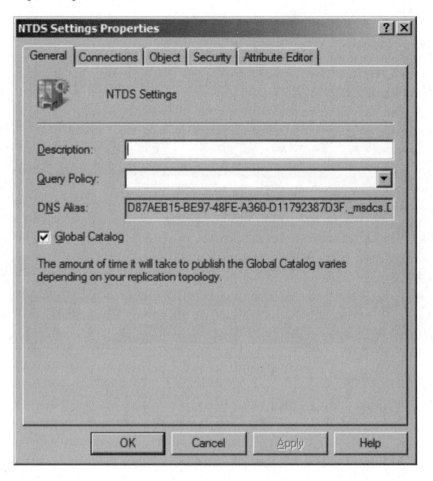

5. Open a Command prompt window and key Repadmin /syncall in order to force replication so that the changes propoagate to Server##A.

6. Close Active Directory Sites and Services and the command prompt window.

■ PART F: Test the Availability of the Global Catalog

> **NOTE** *Wait at least 5 minutes after performing Part E before you attempt this portion of the lab.*

1. On Server## open the Active Directory Users And Computers MMC snap-in. Expand the domain object Domain##.Local in the left window pane, if necessary.

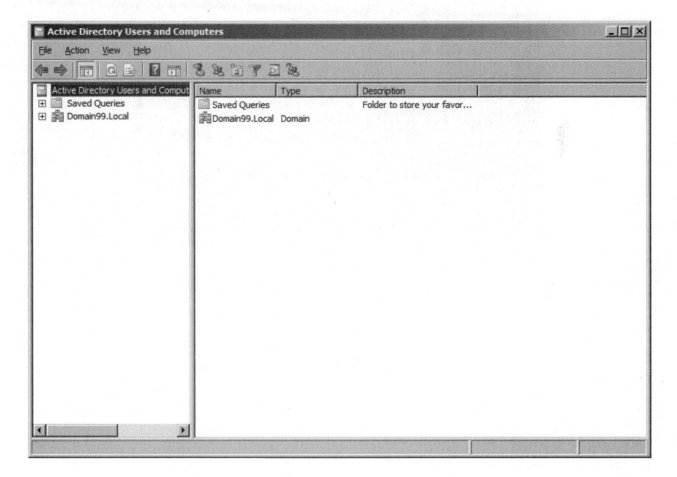

2. In the left window pane, right-click the Users container. Click New, and then click User. The New Object–User dialog box is displayed.

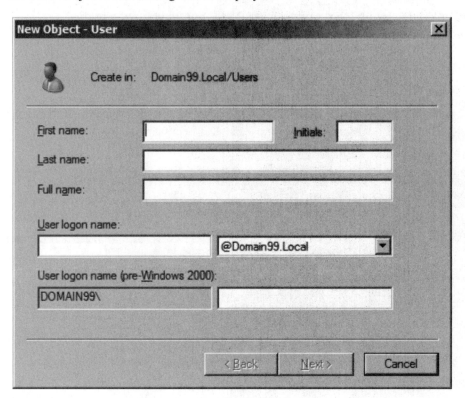

3. Create a new user account named Tst in the default Users container. In the Full Name text box, key **TestUser2**.

4. Click the User Logon Name text box, key **TestUser2** the same name used in Step 3, and then click Next. An Active Directory Domain Services message will appear. Click OK to continue.

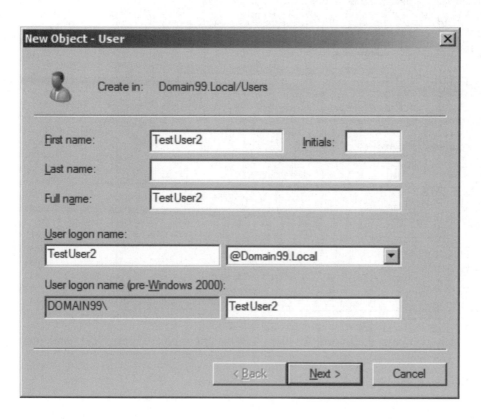

5. Key **P@ssw0rd** in the Password text box and in the Confirm Password text box.

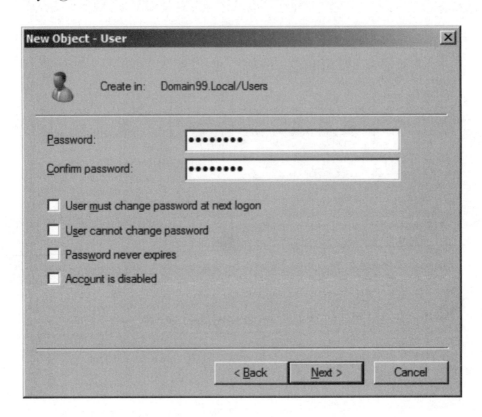

6. Clear the User Must Change Password At Next Logon checkbox. Click Next, and then click Finish.

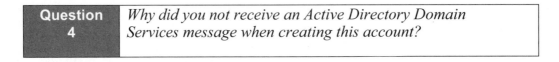

Question 4	*Why did you not receive an Active Directory Domain Services message when creating this account?*

7. Close Active Directory Users and Computers.

Exercise 5.2	Enabling Universal Group Membership Caching
Overview	Your manager wants to know if the universal group membership caching feature will alleviate her concerns about user logon dependency on the global catalog. You decide to run an experiment in your test lab to see how universal group membership caching works in the event of a global catalog failure.
Completion time	10 minutes

■ PART A: Enabling Universal Group Membership Caching

1. On the Server ## computer open the Active Directory Sites And Services console.

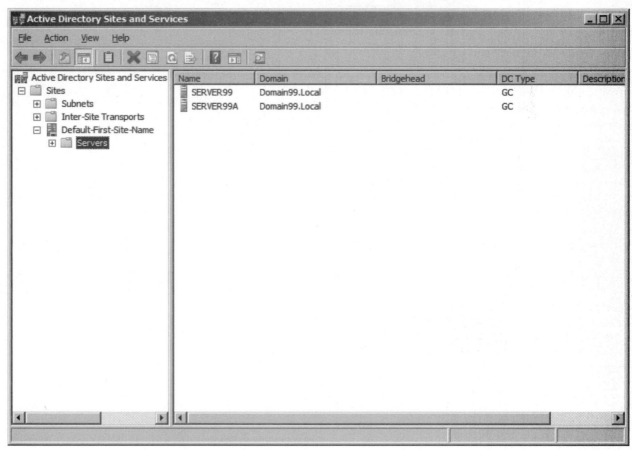

2.   In the left pane, click Sites, and then click Default-First-Site-Name. Right-click NTDS Site Settings and click Properties. The NTDS Site Settings Properties dialog box is displayed.

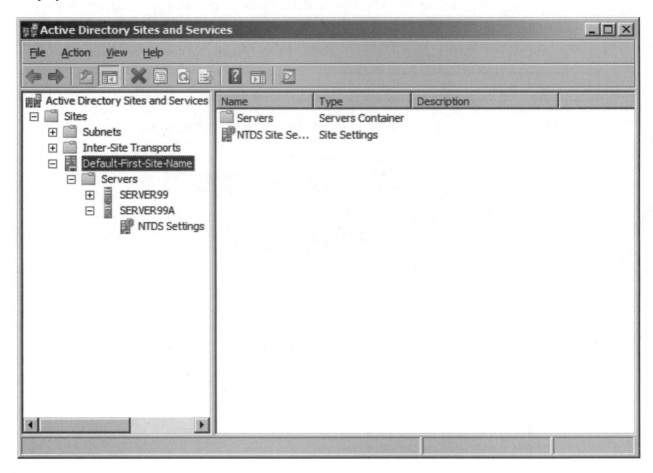

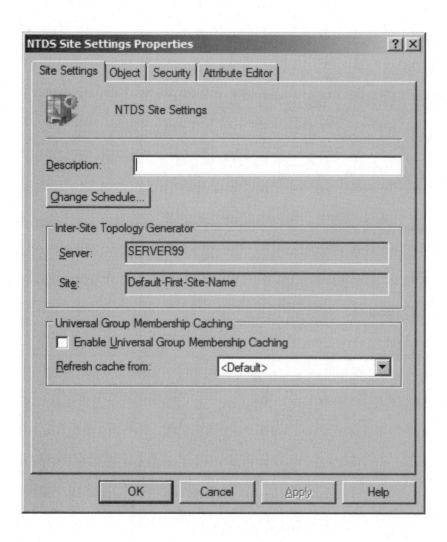

3. Place a checkmark next to Enable Universal Membership Group Caching and click OK.

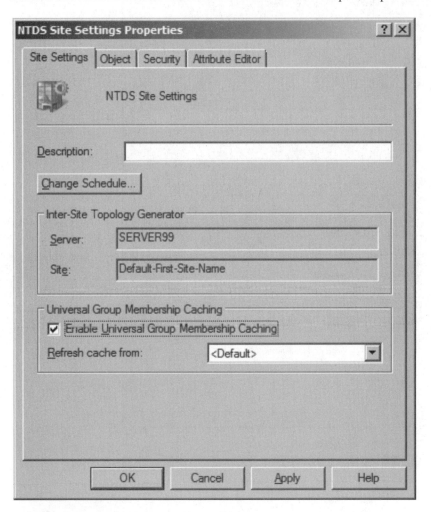

| Question | What are the benefits of enabling Universal Group |
| 5 | Membership Caching? |

4. Open a Command prompt window and key Repadmin /syncall in order to force replication so that the changes propoagate to Server##A.

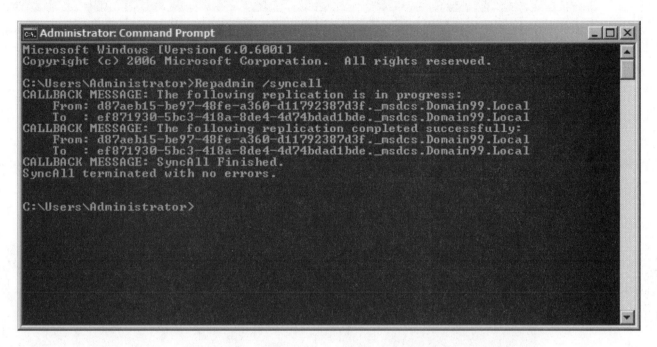

5. Close Active Directory Sites and Services and the command prompt window.

Exercise 5.3	Working with Flexible Single Master Operations Roles
Overview	Your manager tells you that the computer holding the schema operations master role must be replaced soon. She asks you to transfer that role to another server for a short period until a new domain controller can be put in place.
Completion time	20 minutes

■ PART A: Viewing Operations Masters

First, you must determine which server holds the schema operations master role.

1. On the Server## computer click the Start button, key **ntdsutil**, and then press Enter.

2. Key **roles** and then press Enter.

3. Key **connections** and then press Enter.

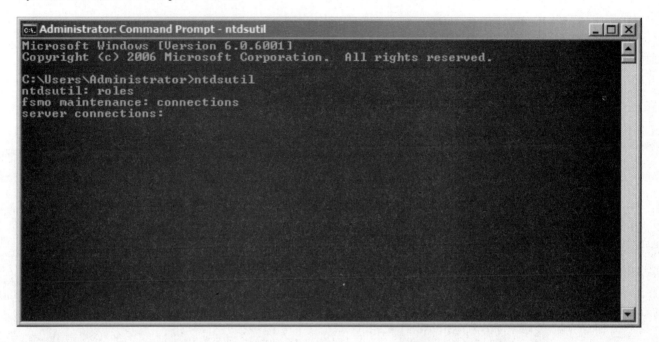

4. Key **connect to server Server##.domain##.local** and then press Enter.

5. Key **quit** and then press Enter.

6. Key **select operation target** and then press Enter.

7. Key **list roles for connected server** and then press Enter. Review the output information.

Question 6	*What FSMO roles are assigned to the Server## computer?*

8. Key **quit**.

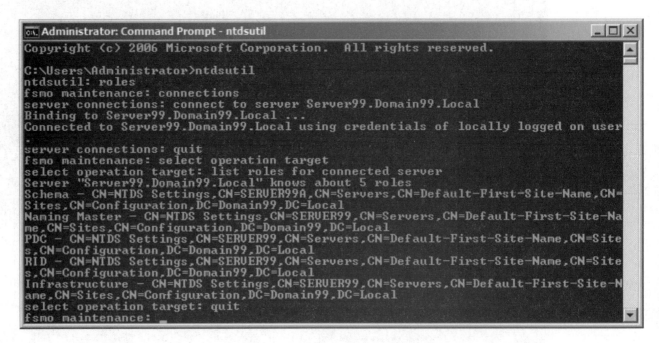

9. Key **connections** and then press Enter.

10. Key **connect to server Server##A.Domain##.Local** and then press Enter.

11. Key **quit** and then press Enter.

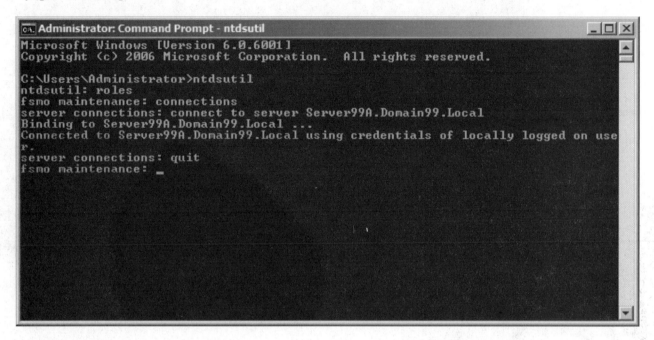

```
Administrator: Command Prompt - ntdsutil                              _ □ ×
Microsoft Windows [Version 6.0.6001]
Copyright (c) 2006 Microsoft Corporation.  All rights reserved.

C:\Users\Administrator>ntdsutil
ntdsutil: roles
fsmo maintenance: connections
server connections: connect to server Server99A.Domain99.Local
Binding to Server99A.Domain99.Local ...
Connected to Server99A.Domain99.Local using credentials of locally logged on use
r.
server connections: quit
fsmo maintenance: _
```

12. Key **select operation target** and then press Enter.

13. Key **list roles for connected server** and then press Enter.

Question 7	*What FSMO roles are assigned to the Server##A computer?*

14. Key **quit** to return to the command-prompt window.

```
Administrator: Command Prompt - ntdsutil                                _ □ ×
Copyright (c) 2006 Microsoft Corporation.  All rights reserved.

C:\Users\Administrator>ntdsutil
ntdsutil: roles
fsmo maintenance: connections
server connections: connect to server Server99A.Domain99.Local
Binding to Server99A.Domain99.Local ...
Connected to Server99A.Domain99.Local using credentials of locally logged on use
r.
server connections: quit
fsmo maintenance: select operation target
select operation target: list roles for connected server
Server "Server99A.Domain99.Local" knows about 5 roles
Schema - CN=NTDS Settings,CN=SERVER99A,CN=Servers,CN=Default-First-Site-Name,CN=
Sites,CN=Configuration,DC=Domain99,DC=Local
Naming Master - CN=NTDS Settings,CN=SERVER99,CN=Servers,CN=Default-First-Site-Na
me,CN=Sites,CN=Configuration,DC=Domain99,DC=Local
PDC - CN=NTDS Settings,CN=SERVER99,CN=Servers,CN=Default-First-Site-Name,CN=Site
s,CN=Configuration,DC=Domain99,DC=Local
RID - CN=NTDS Settings,CN=SERVER99,CN=Servers,CN=Default-First-Site-Name,CN=Site
s,CN=Configuration,DC=Domain99,DC=Local
Infrastructure - CN=NTDS Settings,CN=SERVER99,CN=Servers,CN=Default-First-Site-N
ame,CN=Sites,CN=Configuration,DC=Domain99,DC=Local
select operation target: quit
fsmo maintenance:
```

15. Close the command-prompt window and leave the Server## computer logged in for the next exercise.

■ PART B: Transferring the Schema Master to a Different Domain Controller

Next, you must move the schema operations master to another domain controller. In a production environment, you should always leave the schema master FSMO role on a domain controller in the forest root domain. You are performing this activity to get the experience of transferring an operations master role with ntdsutil. To complete this exercise, the user account that you use must be a member of Schema Admins or have user rights that allow schema management. The default domain administrator of the parent domain has the appropriate rights.

1. On the Server## computer Click the Start button, key **ntdsutil**, and then press Enter.

2. Key **roles** and then press Enter.

3. Key **connections** and then press Enter.

4. Key **connect to server Server##A.Domain##.Local** and then press Enter.

5. Key **quit** and then press Enter.

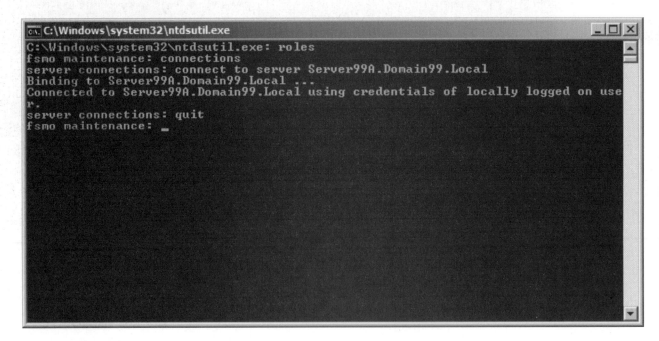

6. Key **transfer schema master** and then press Enter. A Role Transfer Confirmation dialog message is displayed.

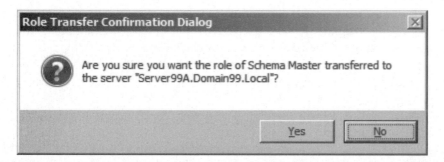

7. Press Ctrl+Prt Scr to take a screen shot of the Role Transfer Confirmation dialog message, and then press Ctrl+V to paste the resulting image into the lab05_worksheet file in the page provided.

8. Read the message and then click Yes.

9. Review the output of the ntdsutil window to confirm that the Server##A computer is now listed as the schema operations master.

10. Key **quit** to return to the command-prompt window.

11. Close the command-prompt window and log off of the Server## computer.

■ PART C: Transferring the Schema Master to the New Domain Controller

Assume that the new server has replaced the old server. Now, you must transfer the schema operations master role back to the "new" server. To complete this exercise, the user account that you use must be a member of Schema Admins or have user rights that allow schema management. The default domain administrator of the parent domain has the appropriate rights.

1. On the Server##A computer, log on using your Administrator account and the password P@ssw0rd.

2. Click the Start button, key **ntdsutil**, and then press Enter.

3. Key **roles** and then press Enter.

4. Key **connections** and then press Enter.

5. Key **connect to server Server##.Domain##.Local** and then press Enter.

6. Key **quit** and then press Enter.

```
Administrator: Command Prompt - ntdsutil

Microsoft Windows [Version 6.0.6001]
Copyright (c) 2006 Microsoft Corporation.  All rights reserved.

C:\Users\Administrator>ntdsutil
ntdsutil: roles
fsmo maintenance: connections
server connections: connect to server Server99.Domain99.Local
Binding to Server99.Domain99.Local ...
Connected to Server99.Domain99.Local using credentials of locally logged on user
.
server connections: quit
fsmo maintenance:
```

7. Key **transfer schema master** and then press Enter. A Role Transfer Confirmation dialog message is displayed.

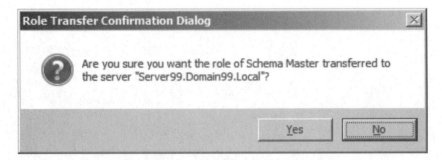

8. Press Ctrl+Prt Scr to take a screen shot of the Role Transfer Confirmation dialog message, and then press Ctrl+V to paste the resulting image into the lab05_worksheet file in the page provided.

9. Read the message and then click Yes.

10. Review the output of the ntdsutil window to confirm that the Server## computer is now listed as the schema operations master.

11. Key **quit** to return to the command-prompt window.

12. Close the command-prompt window and log off of the Server##A computer.

LAB 6
CREATING AND MANAGING USERS AND GROUPS

This lab contains the following exercises:

Exercise 6.1   Creating Administrative Accounts

Exercise 6.2   Testing Administrative Access

Exercise 6.3   Configuring Groups and Permissions

Exercise 6.4   Using dsadd to Add a User Account

Estimated lab time: 75 minutes

Exercise 6.1	Creating Administrative Accounts
Overview	Your manager wants to know what would happen if the global catalog server in your environment fails. She has asked you to run some tests on your test network to determine the effect of an unavailable global catalog server on the success or failure of network logons. In addition, she would like you to test the implications of raising the domain and forest functional levels to Windows Server 2008.
Completion time	20 minutes

■ PART A: Creating Administrative Accounts on the Domain

1. Turn on the Server## and Server##A computers and log on using your Administrator account and the password P@ssw0rd.

> **NOTE** *You can perform the following tasks from eitherWindows Server 2008 machine.*

NOTE	*Remember to use your domain adminstrator account and not the local administrator account.*

2. To open the Active Directory Users And Computers MMC snap-in, click Start, click Administrative Tools, and then click Active Directory Users And Computers. Expand the domain object Domain##.Local in the left window pane, if necessary.

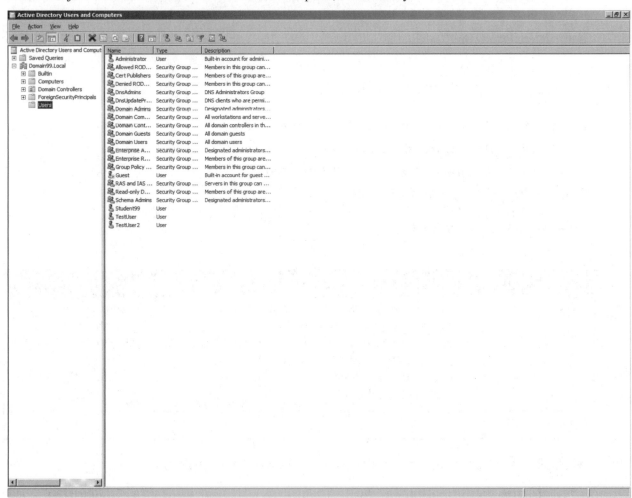

3. In the left window pane, right-click the Users container. Click New, and then click User. The New Object–User dialog box is displayed.

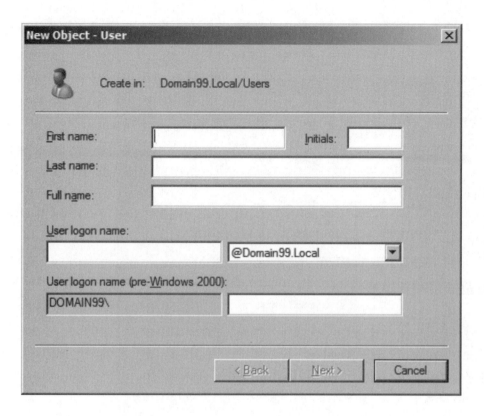

4. Create a new user account named DomAdmin in the default Users container. In the Full Name text box, key **DomAdmin**.

5. Click the User Logon Name text box, key **DomAdmin**, the same name used in Step 4, and then click Next.

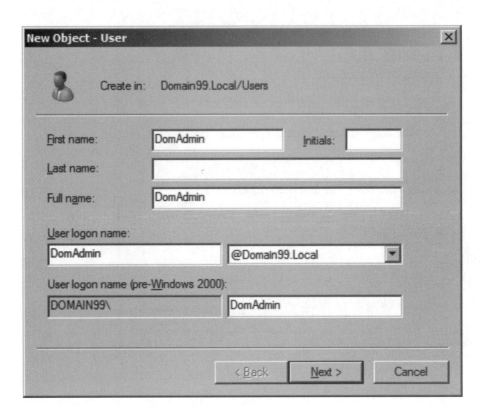

6. Key **P@ssw0rd** in the Password text box and in the Confirm Password text box.

7. Clear the User Must Change Password At Next Logon checkbox. Click Next, and then click Finish.

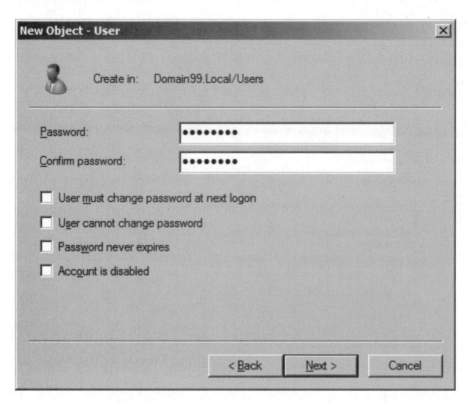

8. Ensure that the Users container is selected. In the right window pane of Active Directory Users And Computers, right-click DomAdmin and click Properties. The DomAdmin Properties dialog box is displayed.

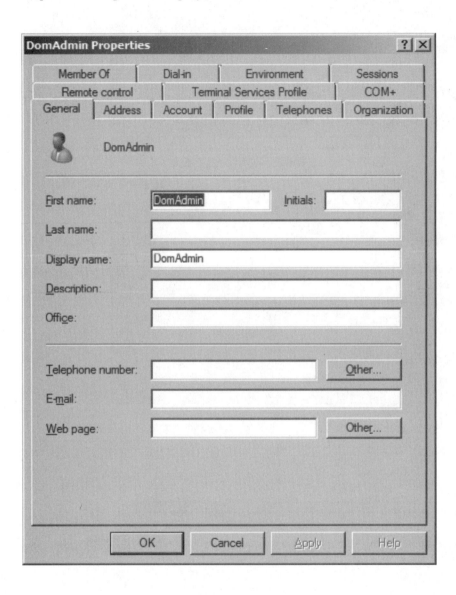

9. Click the MemberOf tab. Click Add. The Select Groups dialog box is displayed.

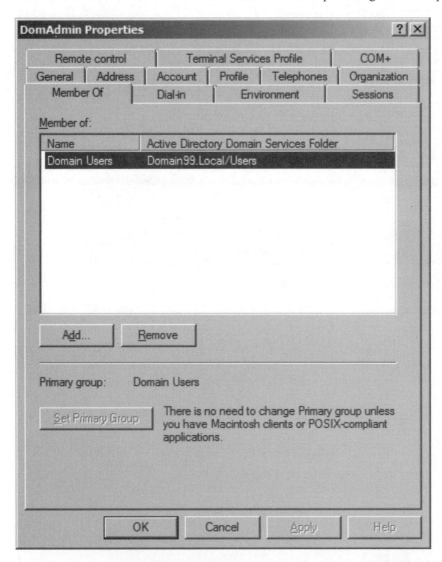

10. Key **Domain Admins** in the Enter The Object Name To Select text box. Click OK.

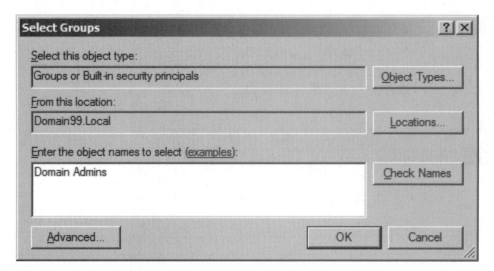

11. In the DomAdmin Properties dialog box, click Domain Admins in the MemberOf selection box. Click Set Primary Group to make the primary group Domain Admins.

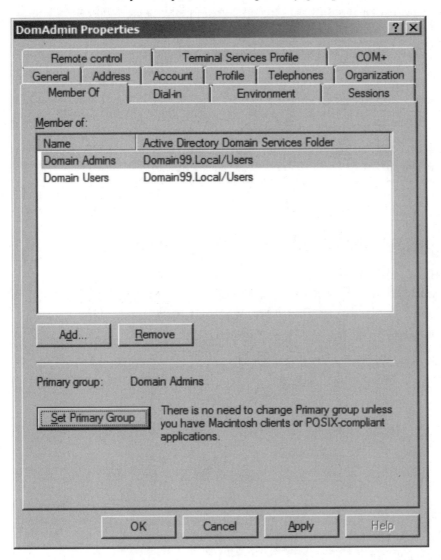

12. Click Domain Users in the MemberOf selection box. Click Remove to make Domain Admins the only group membership for this user account. A message about removing a user from the group text is displayed. Read the message and click Yes.

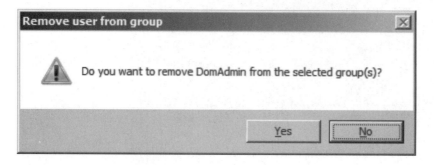

13. Click OK in the DomAdmin Properties dialog box.

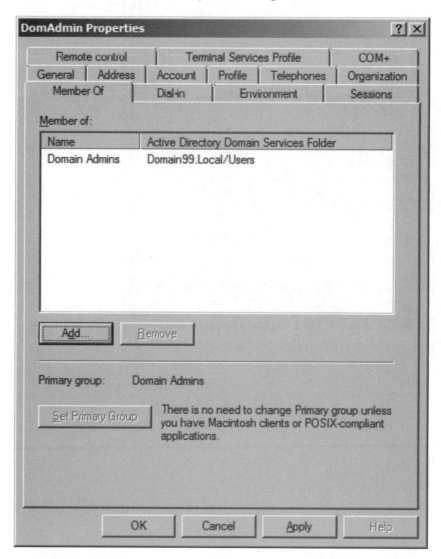

14. Repeat the previous steps to create two additional accounts named SchAdmin and EntAdmin. Ensure that the SchAdmin account is a member of only the Schema Admins group and that the EntAdmin account is a member of only the Enterprise Admins group.

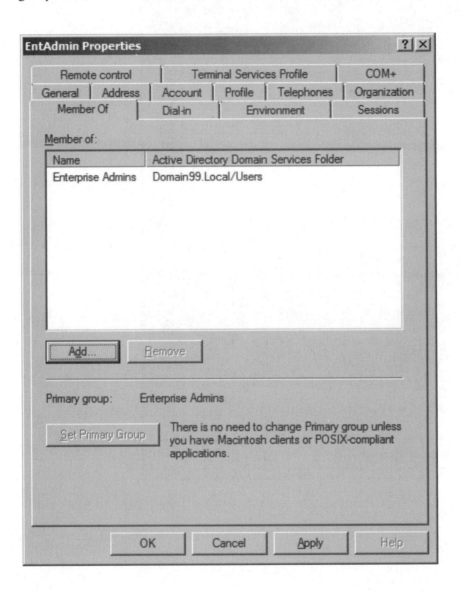

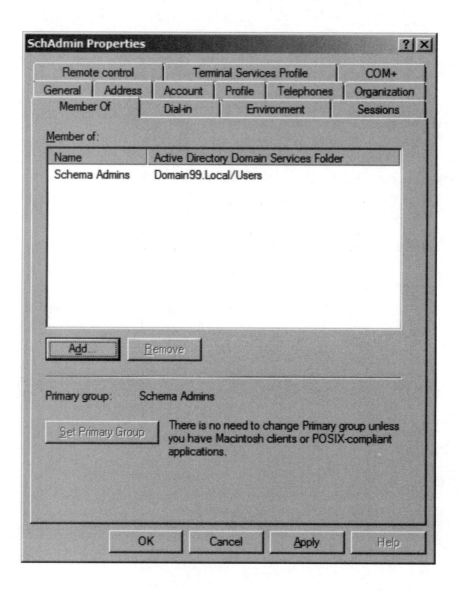

■ PART B: Allowing Users to Log On to Domain Controllers

> **NOTE**
>
> *You are about to allow nonadministrative users to log on to a domain controller. You are doing this only for testing purposes; you typically would not want domain users to be able to interactively (locally) log on to a domain controller.*

1. On the Server## computer open the Group Policy Management Console. Expand the Forest: Domain##.Local node, expand the Domains node, expand the Domain99.Local node and expand the Domain Controllers node. Right-click the Default Domain Controllers Policy and click Edit. The Group Policy Management Editor window is displayed.

> **NOTE**
>
> *Ensure you choose Default Domain Controllers Policy and not Deafult Domain Policy.*

> **NOTE**
>
> *You can perform the following tasks from eitherWindows Server 2008 machine.*

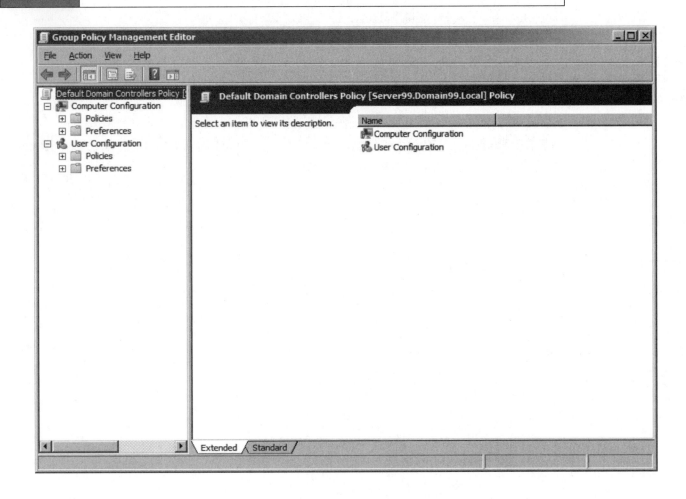

2. In the left console pane, expand Computer Configuration, expand Policies, expand Windows Settings, expand Security Settings, expand Local Policies, and then click User Rights Assignment.

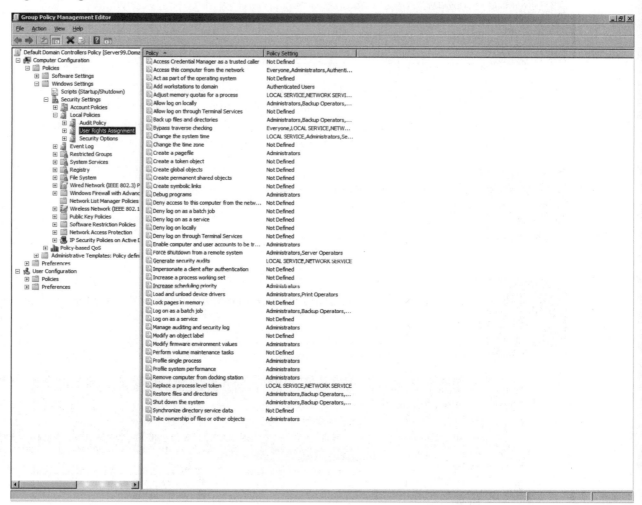

3. In the right pane, double-click the Allow Logon Locally policy object. The Allow Logon Locally Properties dialog box is displayed.

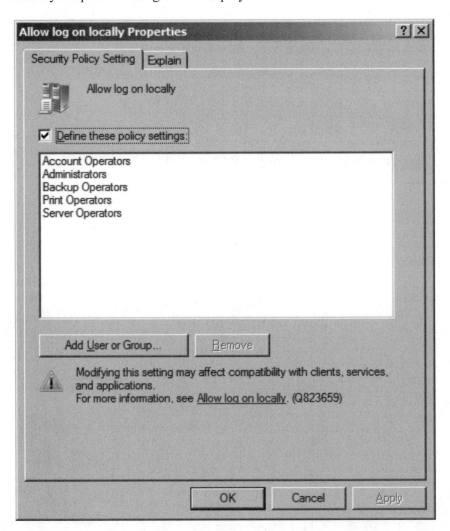

4. Make sure the check the box for Define these Policy settings is checked. Click Add User Or Group. An Add User Or Group dialog box is displayed.

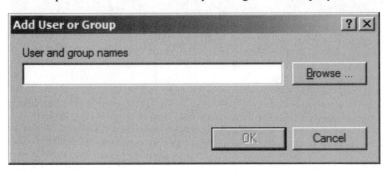

5. Check to make sure Administrators is already listed. Key **Users** in the User And Group Names text box. Click OK, and then click OK again in the Allow Logon Locally Properties dialog box.

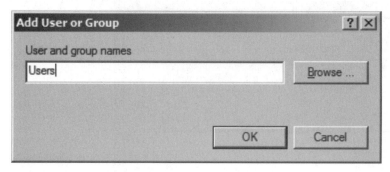

6. Close the Group Policy Management Editor and the Group Policy Management Console.

7. Open a Command prompt window and key gpupdate in order to force replication so that the changes to group policy take effect.

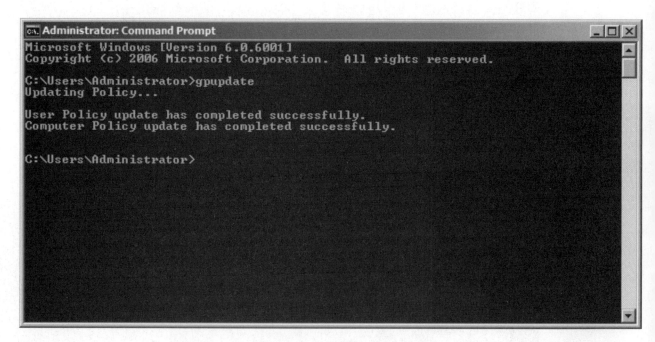

8. Log off of Server##A and leave Server## logged in for the next exercise.

Exercise 6.2   Testing Administrative Access

Overview	You must now test the capabilities of each of the user accounts you created in the previous project.
Completion time	30 minutes

■ PART A: Determine Which Accounts Can Create Sites

1. On the Server##A computer log on with one of the accounts to be tested (such as DomAdmin) and the password P@ssw0rd.

NOTE	In order to log using another account click switch user, then other user and enter the username of the account.

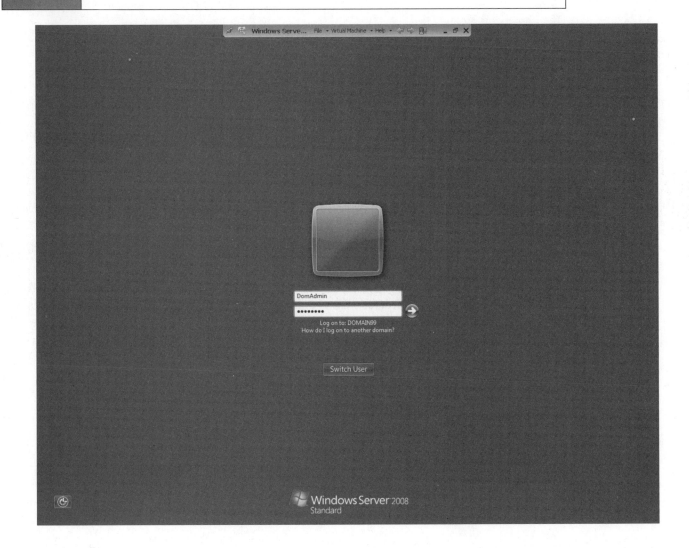

2. Using the Active Directory Sites And Services MMC snap-in, attempt to create a site. Try to create a unique site name with each administrative account. Record the names of the accounts that can be used to create a new site. Refer to Lab 4.3 if you need directions for creating a site.

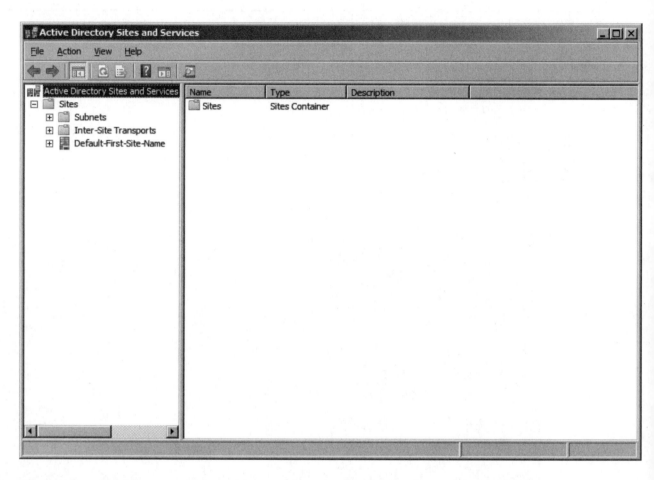

3. If a site is created successfully, right-click the site name and click Delete in the left window pane of Active Directory Sites And Services. An Active Directory message is displayed. Read the message and click Yes to confirm that you want to delete the site. Another Active Directory message box is displayed. Read the message and click Yes to confirm.

4. Repeat steps 1 through 3 for the SchAdmin and EntAdmin administrative accounts.

Question 1	Which administrative user accounts can create a site?

5. Close the Active Directory Sites and Services console and log off.

■ PART B: Determine Which Accounts Can Create Users

1. On the Server##A computer log on with one of the accounts to be tested (such as DomAdmin) and the password P@ssw0rd.

2. Using the Active Directory Users And Computers MMC snap-in, attempt to create a unique user account on the local domain.

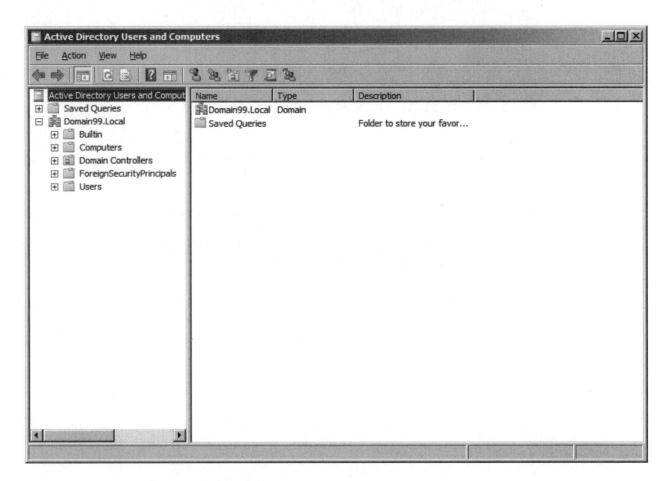

3. Repeat steps 1 and 2 for the SchAdmin and EntAdmin administrative accounts.

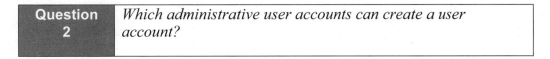

Question 2	*Which administrative user accounts can create a user account?*

4. Close the Active Directory Users And Computers console and log off.

■ PART C: Determine Which Accounts Can Manage the Schema

1. On the Server##A computer log on using your Administrator account and the password P@ssw0rd.

2. Click the Start button, key **regsvr32 schmmgmt.dll**, and press Enter.

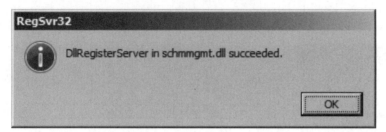

3. Press Ctrl+Prt Scr to take a screen shot of the registration succeeded message box, and then press Ctrl+V to paste the resulting image into the lab06_worksheet file in the page provided.

4. Click OK in the message box indicating that the registration succeeded.

5. Log off of the Administrator account and log on with one of the accounts to be tested (such as DomAdmin) and the password P@ssw0rd.

6. Click the Start button, key **mmc**, and press Enter. The MMC console is displayed.

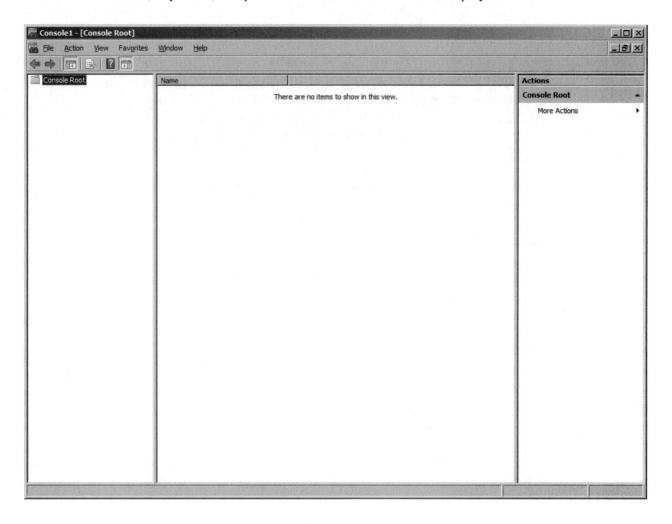

7. Click File, and then click Add/Remove Snap-in. The Add/Remove Snap-in window is displayed.

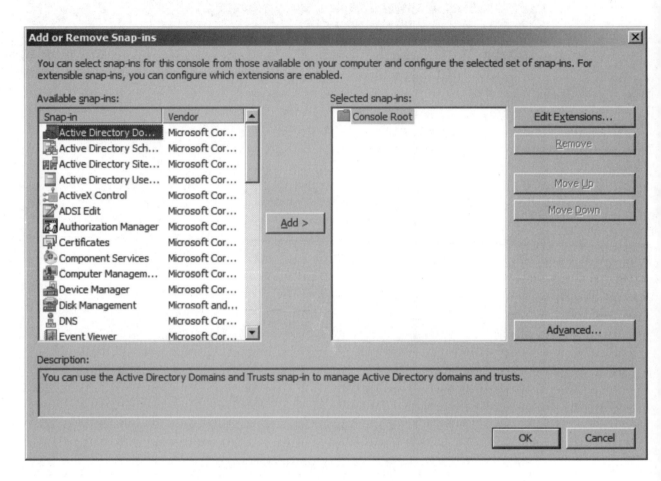

8. Locate and click the Active Directory Schema snap-in.

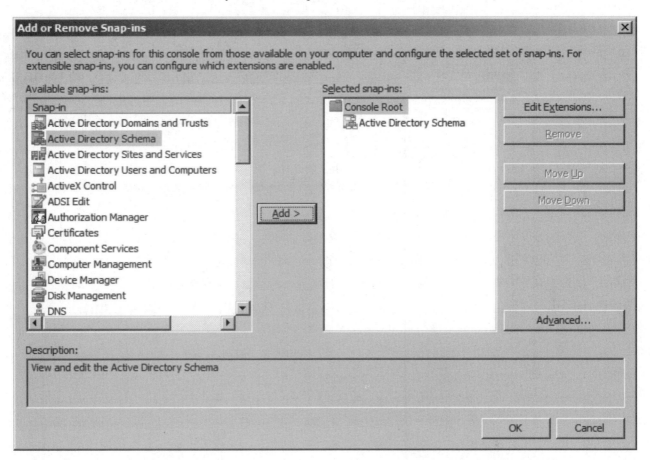

9. Click Add, and then click OK.

10. Expand the Active Directory Schema node to reveal the Classes and Attribute nodes.

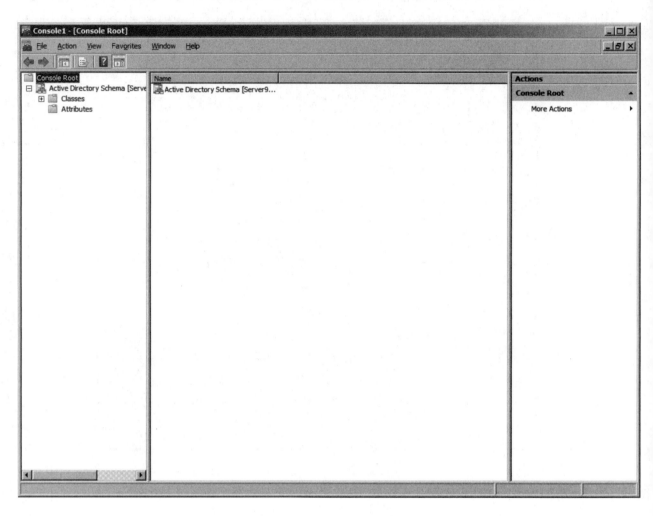

11. Click Attributes. A list of schema attributes will be displayed in the right window pane.

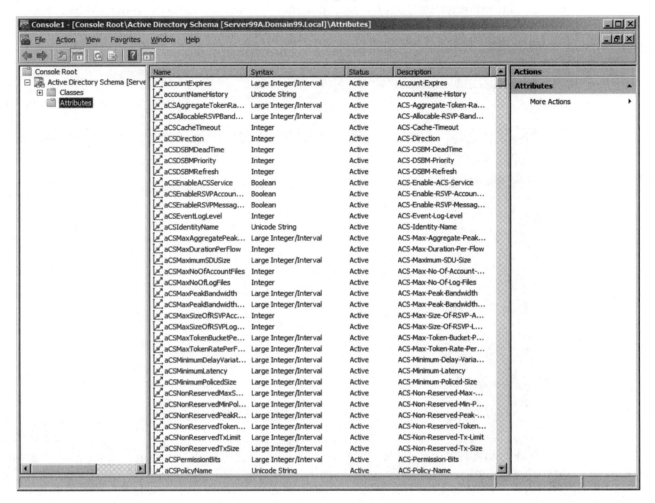

12. Right-click the Attributes object. If you see that the option to Create Attribute is gray in the context menu, then this user account does not have the ability to modify the schema.

13. Click the File menu, and then click Save As.

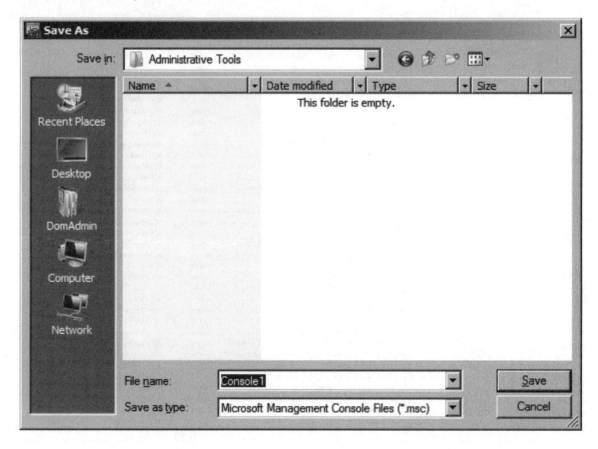

14. Key **c:\schema.msc** in the File Name text box. Click Save and close the Schema console.

15. Log off of the Server##A computer.

16. Log on as the SchAdmin user you created and the password P@ssw0rd.

17. Click Start, key **c:\schema.msc**, and press Enter. The Schema console should be displayed. If you can view the list of Active Directory Schema attributes, the user account has the ability to view the schema.

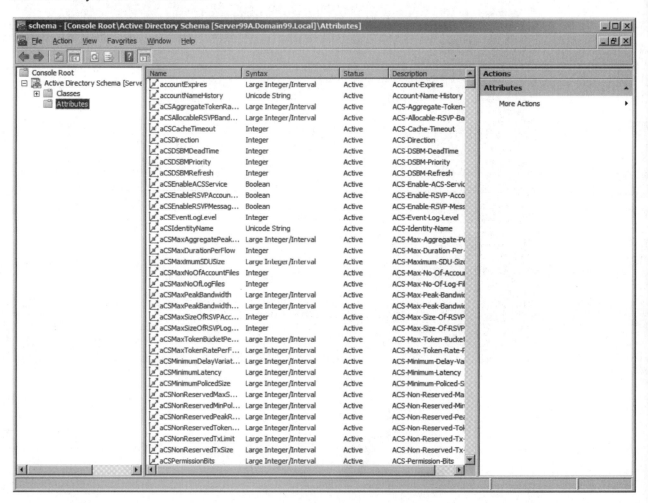

18. Right-click the Attributes object. If you see that the Create Attribute option is available in the context menu, the user account has the ability to modify the schema.

19. Log off and log on as the EntAdmin user. Repeat steps 16 through 18 to determine whether the EntAdmin user has the ability to view and/or modify the schema.

Question 3	*Which administrative user accounts can view or modify the schema?*

Exercise 6.3	Configuring Groups and Permissions
Overview	You must now create an administrative structure that you can use for new administrators. Group administrators into separate global groups. Then, create a universal group that can be used to give new administrators permissions equivalent to the local administrators of each domain.
Completion time	15 minutes

■ PART A: Creating Global Groups

1. On the Server## computer log on using your Administrator account and the password P@ssw0rd.

2. Open the Active Directory Users And Computers console.

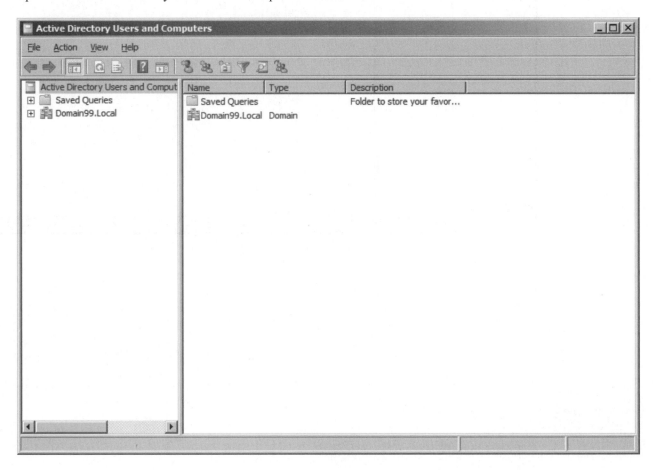

3. Expand the Domain##.Local domain, and then right-click the Users container.

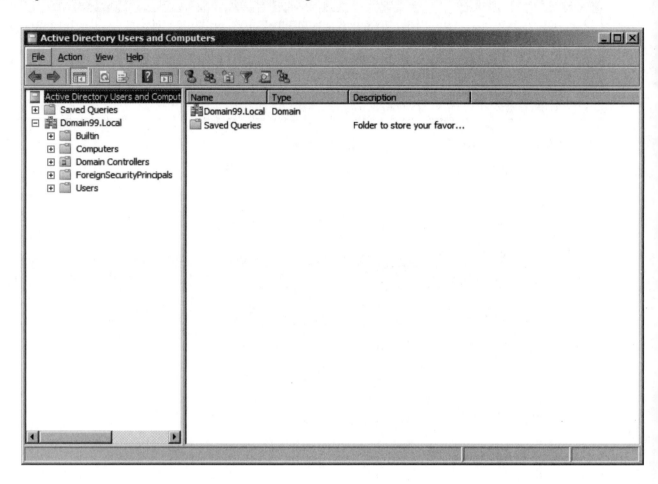

4. Click New, and then click Group. The New Object–Group dialog box is displayed. Notice that the Group Scope default is Global and the Group Type default is Security. Keep these default settings.

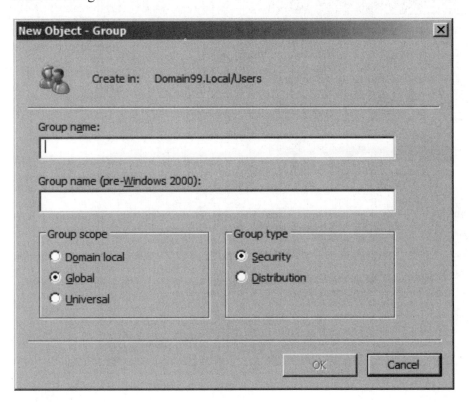

5. Key **LAdmins##** in the Group Name text box and click OK.

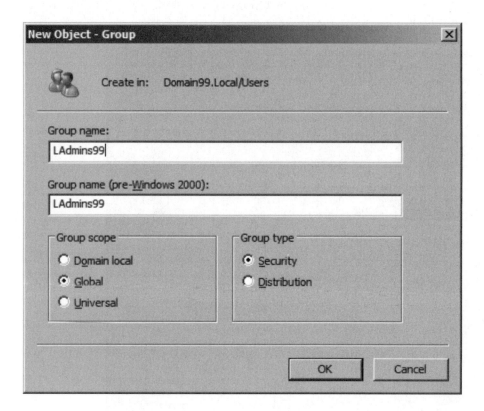

■ PART B: Creating Universal Groups

1. On the Server## computer, right-click the Users container.

2. Click New, and then click Group. The New Object–Group dialog box is displayed.

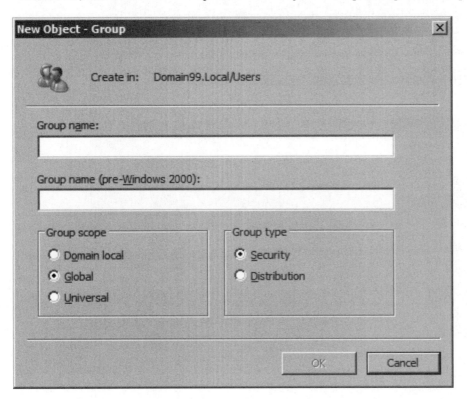

3. Key **LAdmins** in the Group Name text box.

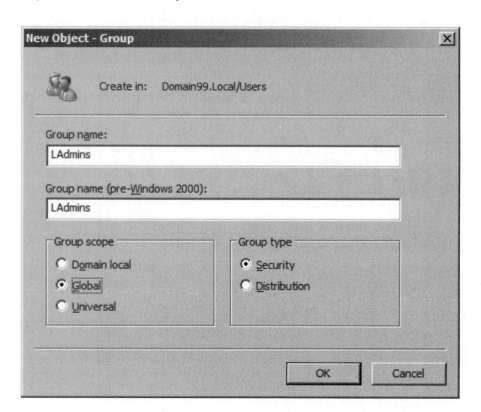

4. In the Group Scope area, select the Universal radio button. Verify that the Group Type is set to Security and click OK.

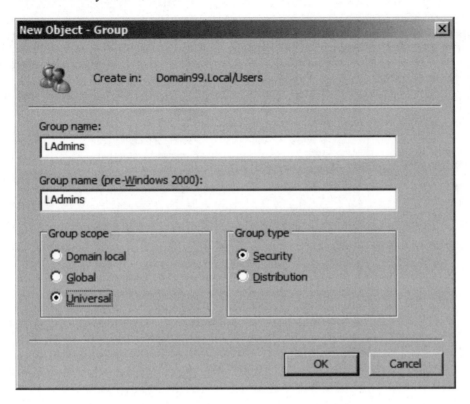

5.   Verify that the Users container is selected. In the right pane of Active Directory Users And Computers, right-click LAdmins, and then click Properties.

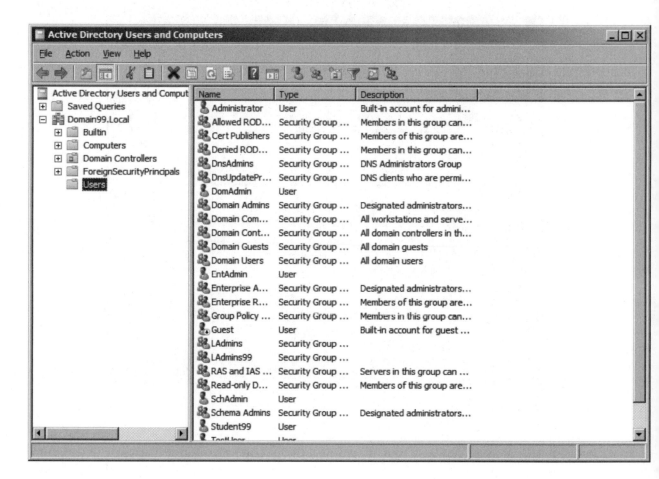

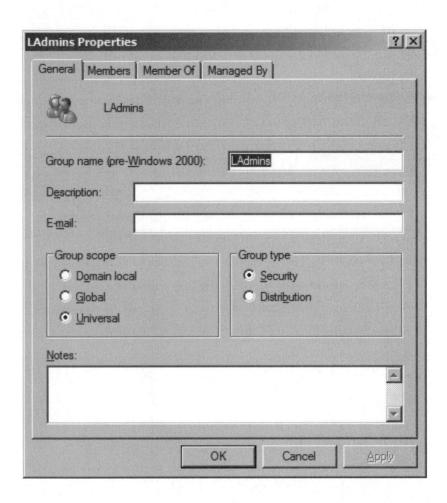

6.   Click the Members tab. Click Add. The Select Users, Contacts, Computers, Or Groups dialog box is displayed.

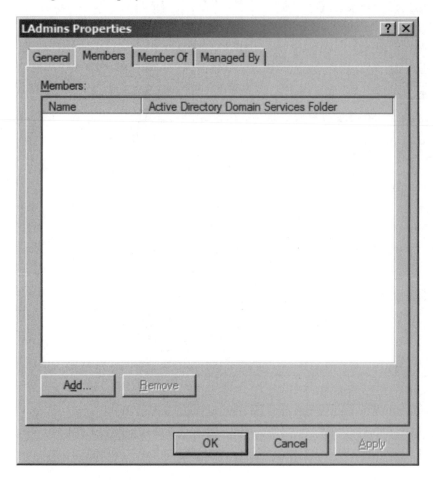

7. Key **LAdmins##** in the Enter The Object Names To Select text box, and then click OK. Remember that LAdmins## is a global group.

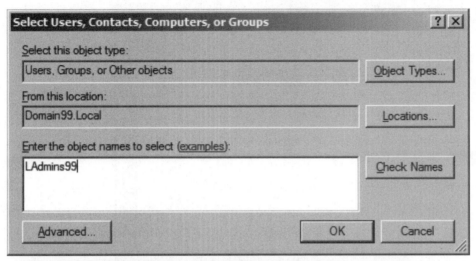

8. Click the Member Of tab and click Add. The Select Groups dialog box is displayed.

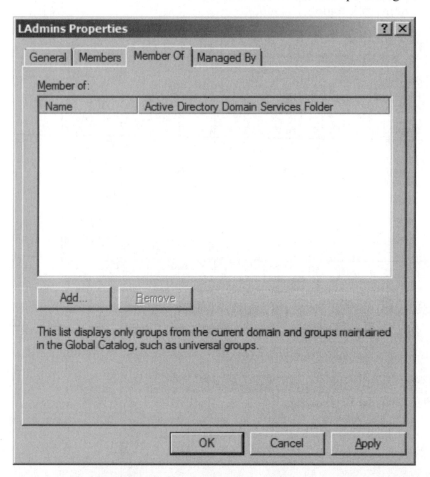

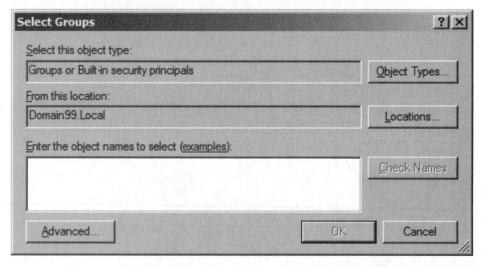

9. Key **Administrators** in the Enter The Object Names To Select text box. Click OK.

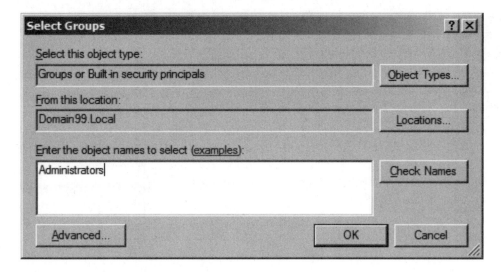

10. Click OK in the LAdmins Properties dialog box.

■ PART C: Assigning Permissions Through Group Membership

1. On the Server## computer, create a user acount named LocalAdmin## in the Domain##.Local domain. Refer to Project 5.1, Creating Administrative Accounts on the Parent Domain.

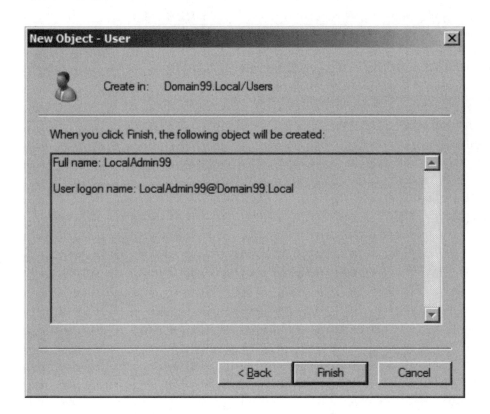

2. Make the LocalAdmin## user a member of the LAdmins## group.

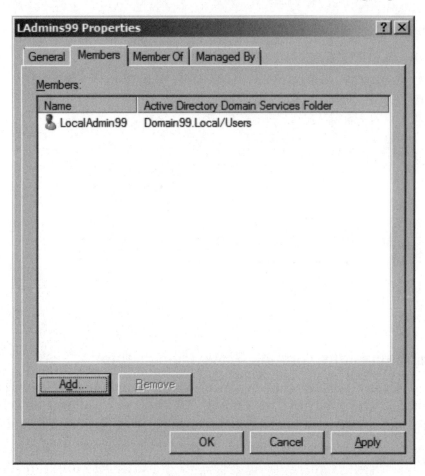

3. Close the Active Directory Users And Computers console.

4. Log on to the Server##A computer using the LocalAdmin## account.

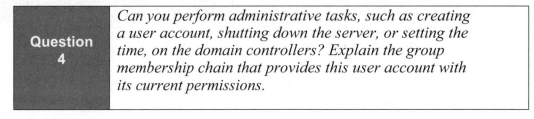

Question 4	*Can you perform administrative tasks, such as creating a user account, shutting down the server, or setting the time, on the domain controllers? Explain the group membership chain that provides this user account with its current permissions.*

5. Log off of the Server##A computer and leave the Server## computer logged on for the next exercise.

Exercise 6.4	Using dsadd to Add a User Account
Overview	Your organization is growing and you need to add new OUs and users.
Completion time	10 minutes

■ PART A: Using dsadd to Create an OU and User in the Parent Domain

A Sales department was added to your organizational structure, and you decide to create a new OU to help you manage the resources of this new department. Additionally, a new manager, Kim Ralls, was just hired for the Sales department. You must create a user account for Kim in the new OU. Use dsadd to add these new objects.

1. On the Server## computer open a command-prompt window.

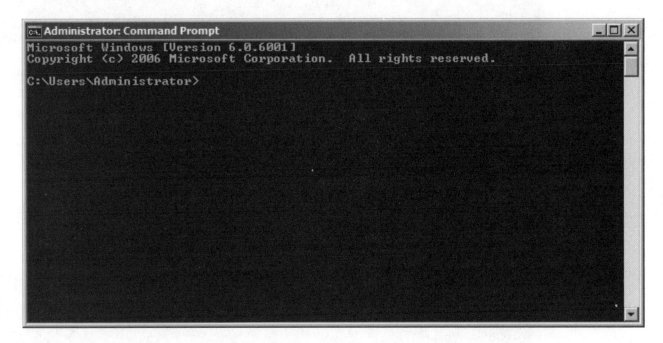

2. Key **dsadd ou ou=Sales,dc=Domain##,dc=Local –desc Lab5** in the command-prompt window, and then press Enter.

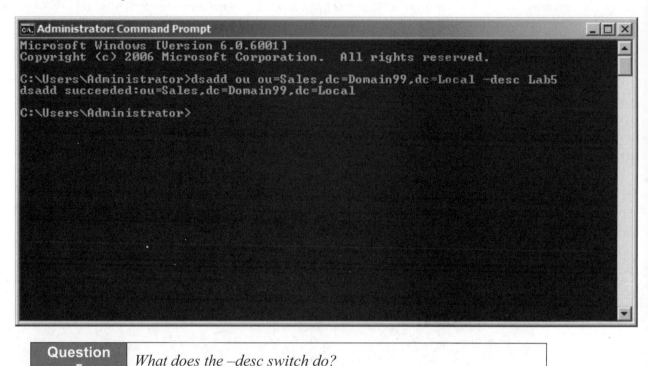

Question 5	*What does the –desc switch do?*

3. Key **dsadd user cn=Kim,ou=Sales,dc=Domain##,dc=local –pwd P@ssw0rd –samid KimR –upn Kim@domain##.Local** in the command-prompt window. Press Enter.

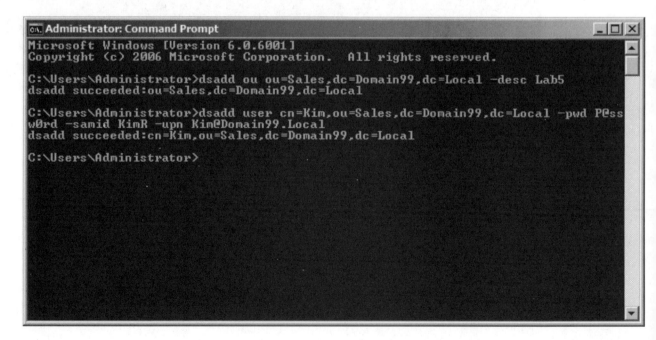

4. Open the Active Directory Users And Computers console and verify that the Sales OU exists and that the Kim user account exists inside the OU.

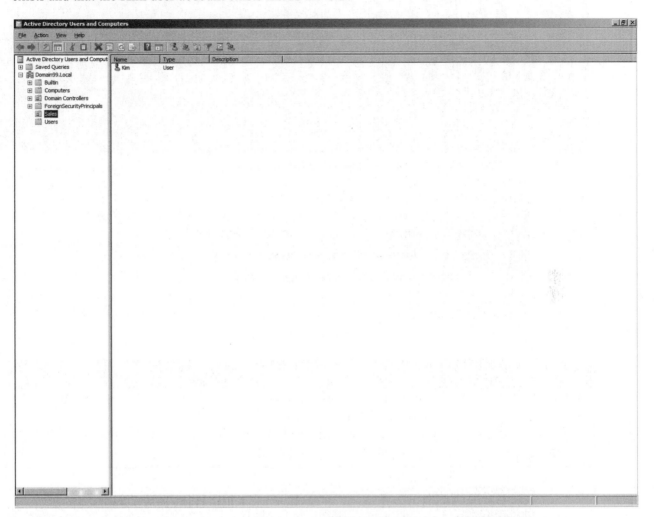

5. Press Ctrl+Prt Scr to take a screen shot of the users and Computers console showing that the sales OU exists and that the Kim user account exists inside the OU, and then press Ctrl+V to paste the resulting image into the lab06_worksheet file in the page provided.

6. Close the Active Directory Users And Computers console and log off of the Server## computer.

LAB 7
EMPLOYING SECURITY CONCEPTS

This lab contains the following exercises:

Exercise 7.1   Using Naming Standards and Secure Passwords

Exercise 7.2   Employing Administrator Account Security

Exercise 7.3   DelegatIng Administrative Responsibility

Estimated lab time: 55 minutes

Exercise 7.1	Using Naming Standards and Secure Passwords
Overview	Company policy states that each employee's user account name must be created from the first letter of the employee's first name, the employee's entire last name, and the employee's unique identification number. All employee passwords will be complex.
Completion time	5 minutes

1. Turn on the Server## computer and log on using your Administrator account and the password P@ssw0rd.

NOTE	*Remember to use your domain adminstrator account and not the local administrator account.*

2. Turn on the Server##A computer, but do not logon yet.

3. On Server## use the Active Directory Users And Computers console to create a user account based on your name in the Users container. Use the naming standard described in the scenario for this project. Substitute ## for the employee identification number. For example, a user named Reed Koch who is using Computer99 would have the following values:

    *   **First Name: Reed**
    *   **Last Name: Koch**
    *   **Full Name: Reed Koch**
    *   **Logon Name: RKoch99**
    *   **Password: P@ssw0rd**
    *   **User Must Change Password at Next Logon: Not selected**

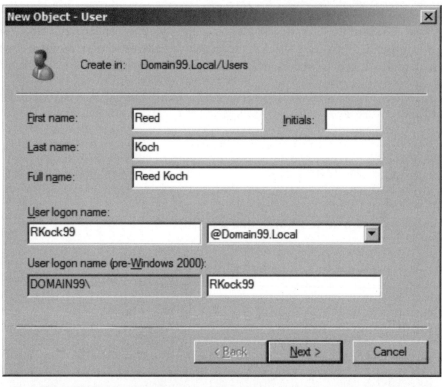

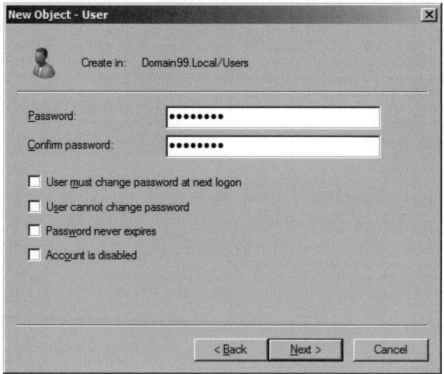

4. Log off of both computers.

Exercise 7.2	Employing Administrator Account Security
Overview	You must demonstrate the various methods for using the runas utility to allow administrators to reduce the exposure of administrative accounts.
Completion time	20 minutes

■ PART A: Using Runas from the Command Prompt

1. Turn on the Server##A computer and log on to Server##A using the account that you created in Project 6.1.

> **NOTE**
>
> *In order to log using another account click switch user, then other user and enter the username of the account.*

2. Open the Active Directory Users And Computers console.

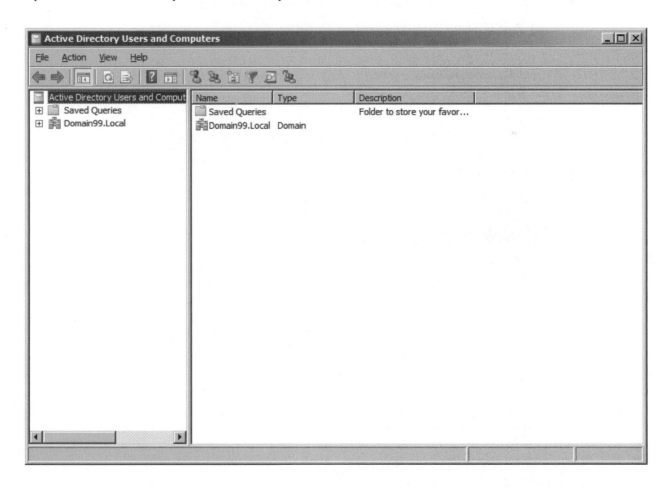

3. Try to reset your password. Click the Users container in the left window pane. In the right window pane, right-click your user account and click Reset Password. A Reset Password dialog box is displayed. Key **Password#1** in both of the password boxes. Click OK. A message box is displayed. Read the message and click OK.

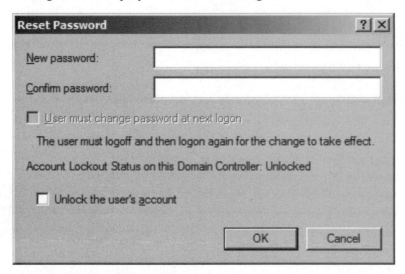

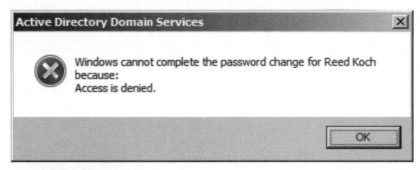

Question 1	*Were you able to reset your password?*

4.   Close the Active Directory Users And Computers console.

5.   Open a command prompt window. Key **runas /user:administrator@Domain##.Local "mmc dsa.msc"** Press Enter.

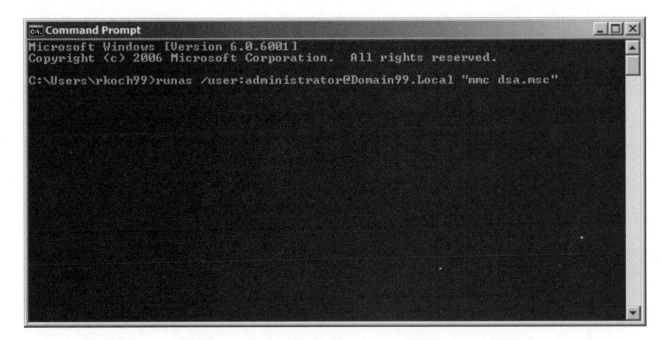

6.   When you are prompted for the password, key **P@ssw0rd**. Press Enter. Wait a few seconds and the Active Directory Users And Computers console will be displayed.

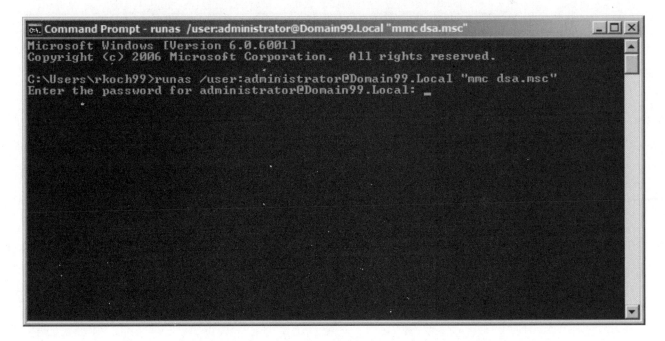

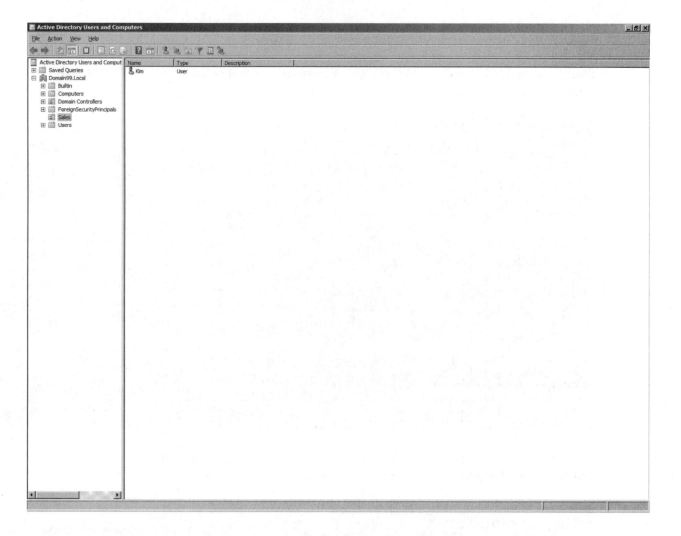

7. Try to reset your password. Click the Users container in the left window pane. In the right window pane, right-click your user account and click Reset Password. The Reset Password dialog box is displayed. Key **Password#1** in both of the password boxes. A message box is displayed.

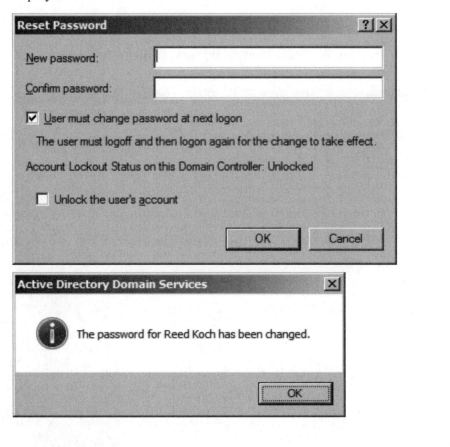

| Question 2 | *Why were you successful this time?* |

8. Click OK.

9. Close the Active Directory Users And Computers console and the command-prompt window.

■ PART B: Creating and Using a Runas Shortcut

You want to create a shortcut on your desktop that will allow you to easily manage your domains and forest without requiring you to log off when using your domain user account.

1. Find an area of the desktop where there are no icons and right-click that area.

2. Click New, and then click Shortcut. A Create Shortcut Wizard is displayed.

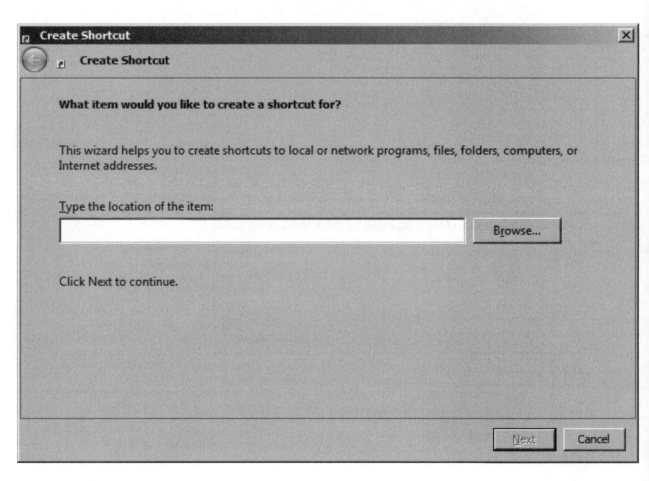

3. Key **runas /user:administrator@Domain##.Local "mmc domain.msc"** in the Type
    The Location Of The Item text box. Click Next.

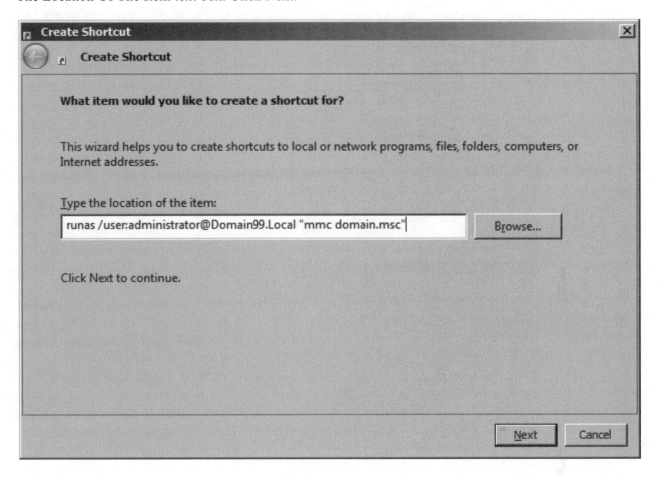

4. Key **Domains and Trusts** in the Type A Name For This Shortcut text box. Click Finish.

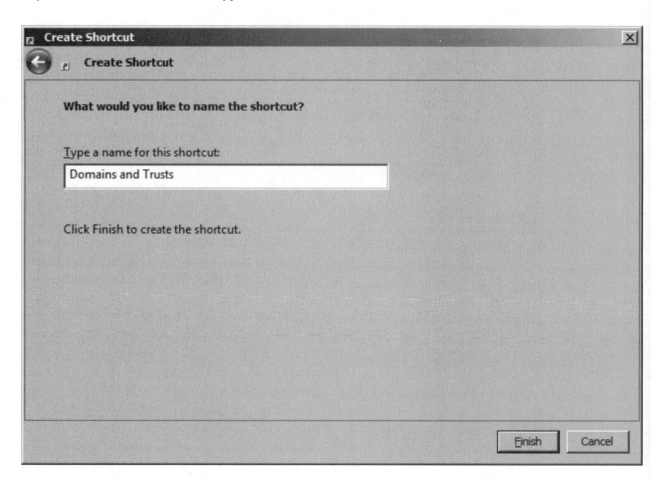

5. Double-click the icon on the desktop that you just created. A command-prompt window is displayed.

6. Key **P@ssw0rd** and Press Enter. The Active Directory Domains And Trusts console is displayed.

7. Close the Active Directory Domains and Trusts console.

■ PART C: Attempting to Run Multiple Runas Consoles Simultaneously

You want to see if you can run multiple consoles simultaneously with the runas utility.

1. Click the Start button. Key **runas /user:administrator@Domain##.Local "mmc dsa.msc"**. Press Enter. A command-prompt window is displayed.

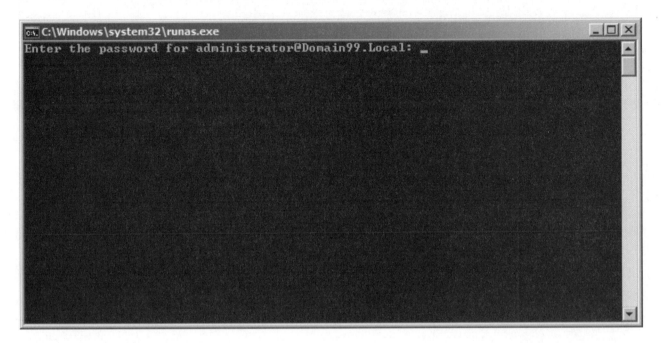

2. Key **P@ssw0rd** in the command-prompt window. Press Enter. The Active Directory Users And Computers console is displayed.

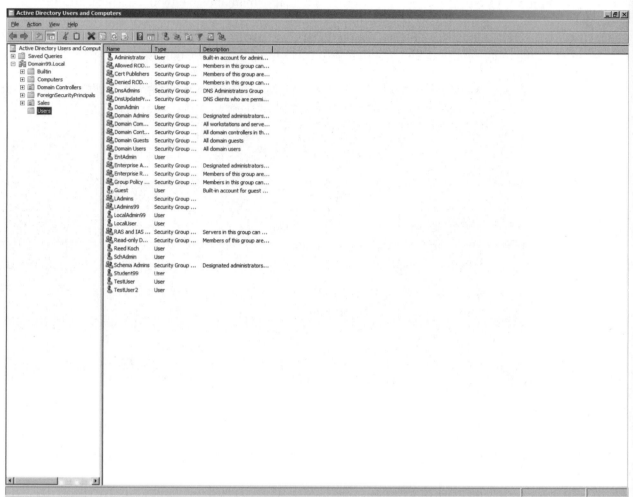

3. Click the Start button again. Key **runas /user:administrator@Domain##.Local "mmc dssite.msc"**. Press Enter. A command-prompt window is displayed.

4. Key **P@ssw0rd** in the command-prompt window. Press Enter. The Active Directory Sites And Services console is displayed.

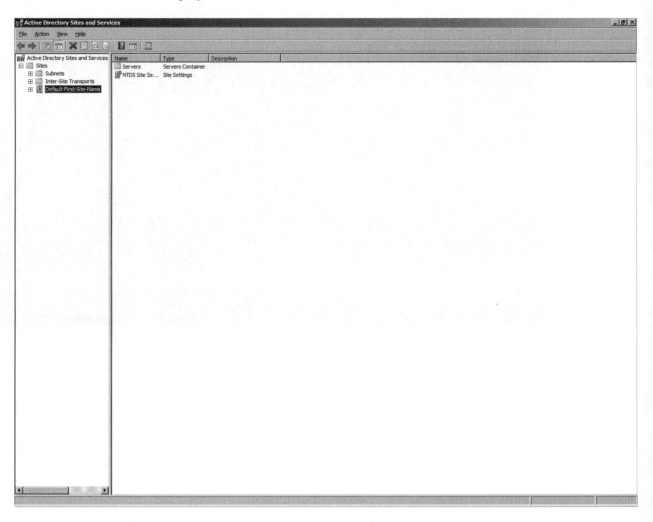

5. Click the Start button again. Key **runas /user:administrator@Domain##.Local "mmc domain.msc"**. Press Enter. A command-prompt window is displayed.

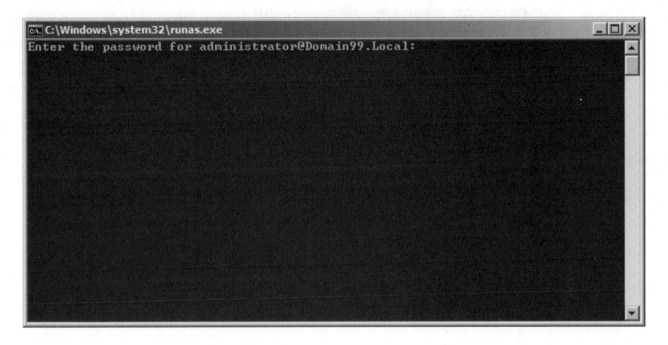

6. Key **P@ssw0rd** in the command-prompt window. Press Enter. The Active Directory Domains And Trusts console is displayed.

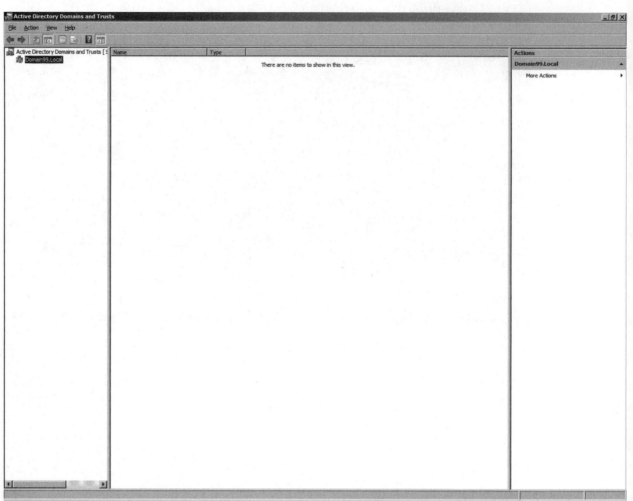

7. Close all open consoles and log off Server##A.

Exercise 7.3	Delegating Administrative Responsibility
Overview	You must now create an administrative structure that you can use for new administrators. Group administrators into separate global groups. Then, create a universal group that can be used to give new administrators permissions equivalent to the local administrators of each domain.
Completion time	30 minutes

■ PART A: Delegating Control on the Domain

1. On Server## open a command-prompt window and key the following three commands to create user accounts that you will delegate limited permissions to:

    -   **dsadd user cn=User1,cn=Users,dc=Domain##,dc=Local –samid User1 –upn user1@Domain##.Local –pwd P@ssw0rd**

    -   **dsadd user cn=User2,cn=Users,dc=Domain##,dc=Local –samid User2 –upn user2@Domain##.Local –pwd P@ssw0rd**

    -   **dsadd user cn=Manager,cn=Users,dc=Domain##,dc=Local –samid Manager –upn manager@Domain##.Local –pwd P@ssw0rd**

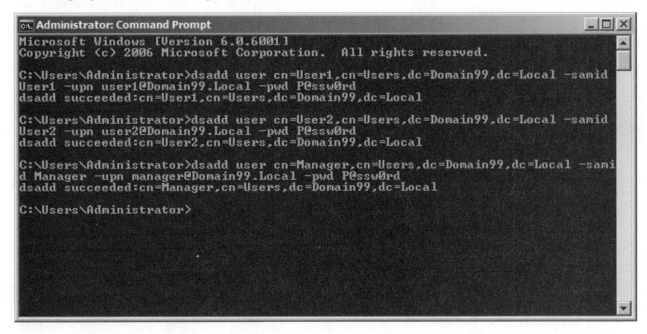

2. Press Ctrl+Prt Scr to take a screen shot of the copmmand prompt windows showing the three user accounts were succesffully added, and then press Ctrl+V to paste the resulting image into the lab07_worksheet file in the page provided.

3. Open the Active Directory Users And Computers console. Right-click the Domain##.Local object in the left pane. Click New, and then click Organizational Unit. A New Object–Organizational Unit dialog box is displayed.

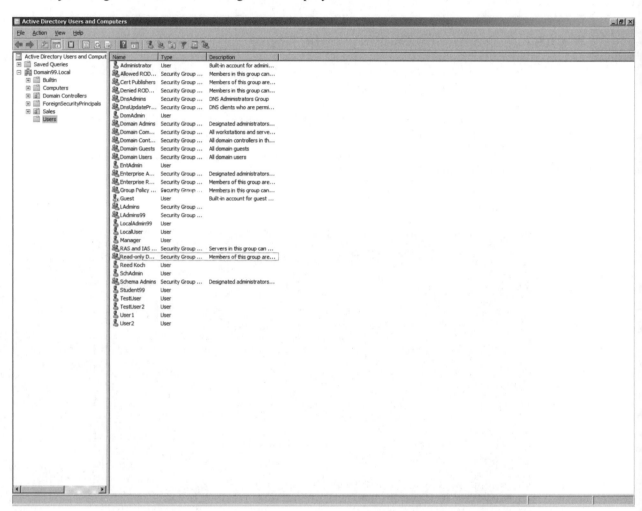

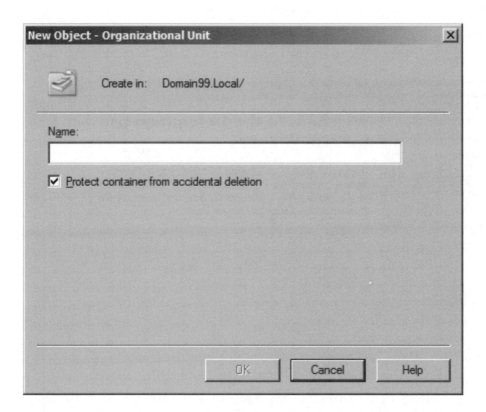

4. Key **Mgmt1** in the Name text box, and then click OK.

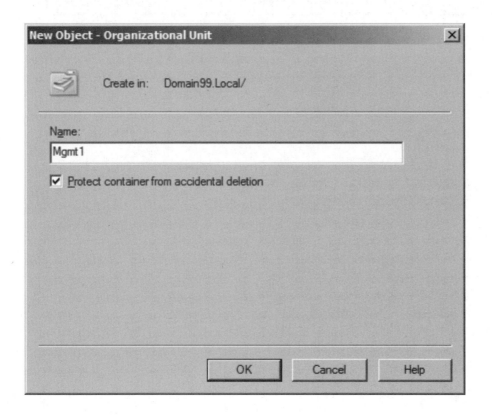

5. In the left pane of the Active Directory Users And Computers console, right-click the Mgmt1 OU and click Delegate Control. The Delegation Of Control Wizard is displayed.

6. Click Next. The *Users Or Groups* page is displayed.

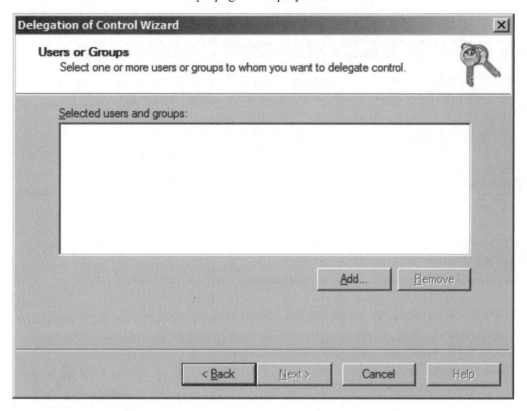

7. Click Add. The Select Users, Computers, Or Groups dialog box is displayed.

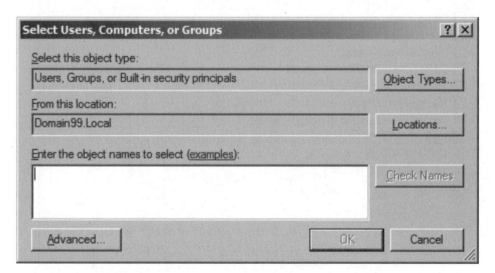

8. Key **Manager** in the Enter The Object Names To Select text box, and then click Check Names. The Manager username should now appear underlined. Click OK.

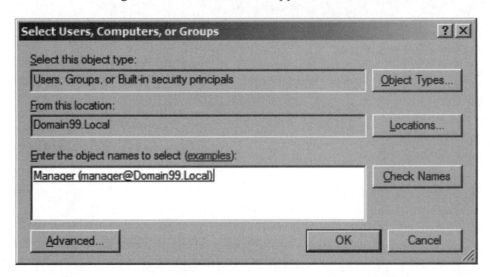

9. In the *Users Or Groups* page, click Next. The *Tasks To Delegate* page is displayed.

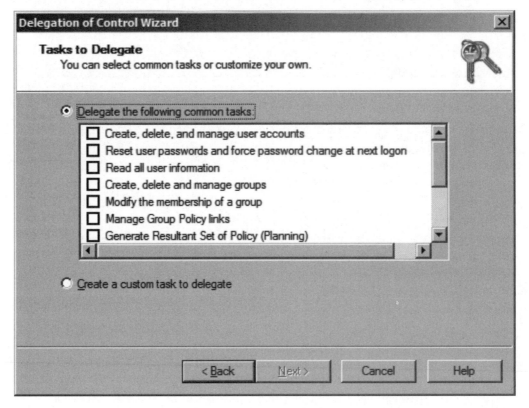

10. Place a checkmark next to Reset User Passwords and Force Password Change At Next Logon. Click Next, and then click Finish.

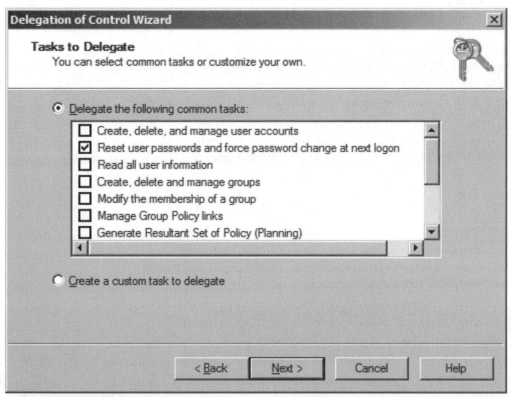

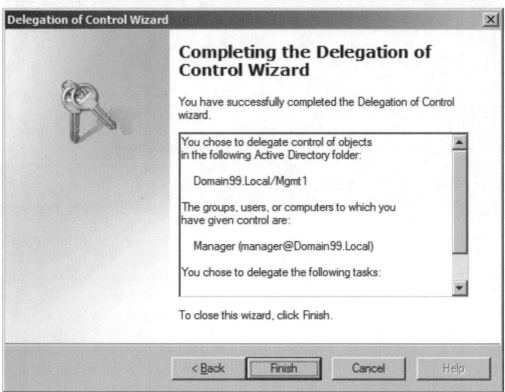

11. Move the User1 account from the Users container to the Mgmt1 OU. You can use the drag-and-drop method to move the user account. You can also right-click the user account and then click Move. A Move dialog box is displayed. Select the Mgmt1 OU, and then click OK. An Active Directory Domain Services message about moving accounts appears, click Yes.

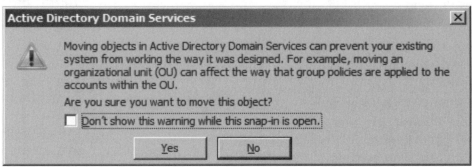

12. Open a command-prompt window. Key the following command and then press Enter:

- **dsmove cn=user2,cn=users,dc=Domain##,dc–Local –newparent ou=Mgmt1,dc=Domain##,dc=Local**

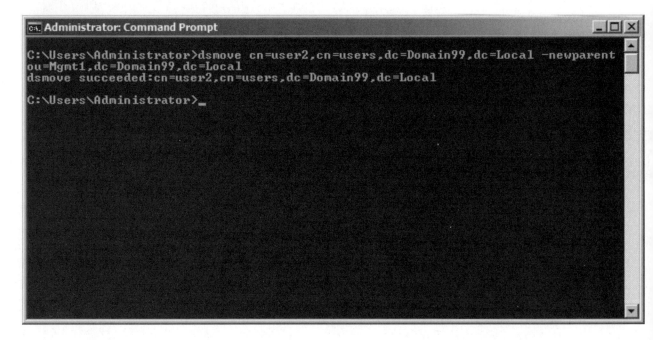

13. In the left pane of the Active Directory Users And Computers console, select the Mgmt1 OU. Refresh the display by clicking Refresh on the Action menu or by pressing F5. User1 and User2 should be displayed in the right pane.

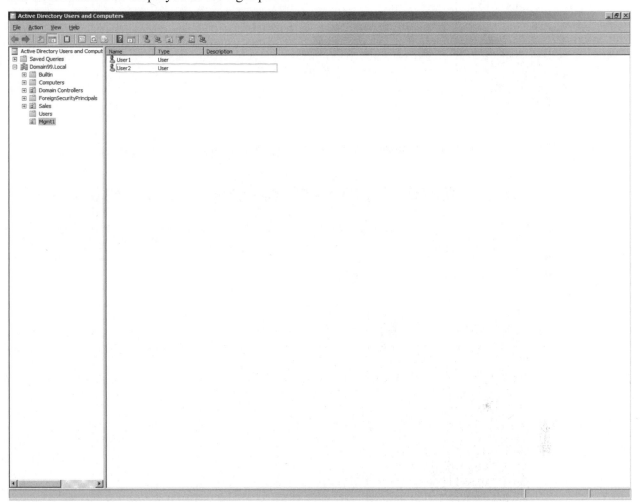

14. Press Ctrl+Prt Scr to take a screen shot of the Active Directory Users and Computers console showing that the User1 and User2 accounts have been moved to the Mgmt1 OU, and then press Ctrl+V to paste the resulting image into the lab07_worksheet file in the page provided.

15. Close the command-prompt window, close the Active Directory Users And Computers console, and log off of the computer.

■ PART B: Testing Delegated Permissions on the Parent Domain

1. On the Server##A computer, log on using the Manager user account and the password P@ssw0rd.

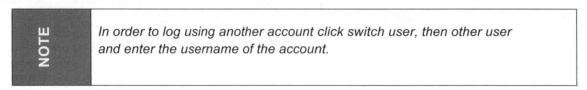

> **NOTE**
>
> *In order to log using another account click switch user, then other user and enter the username of the account.*

2. Open the Active Directory Users And Computers console.

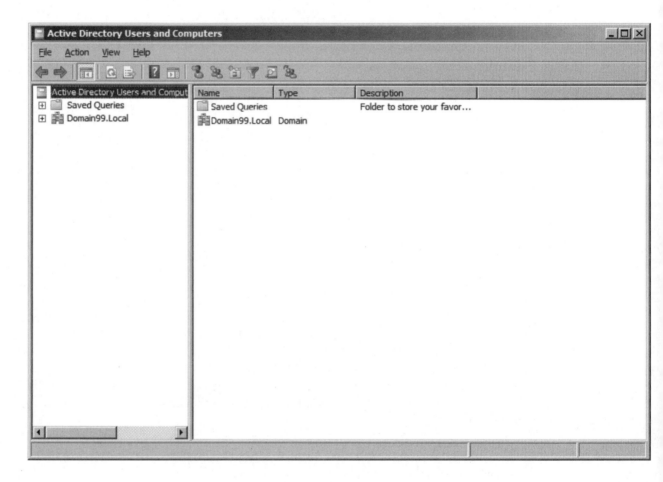

3. In the left window pane, expand the Domain##.Local object and click the Mgmt1 OU.

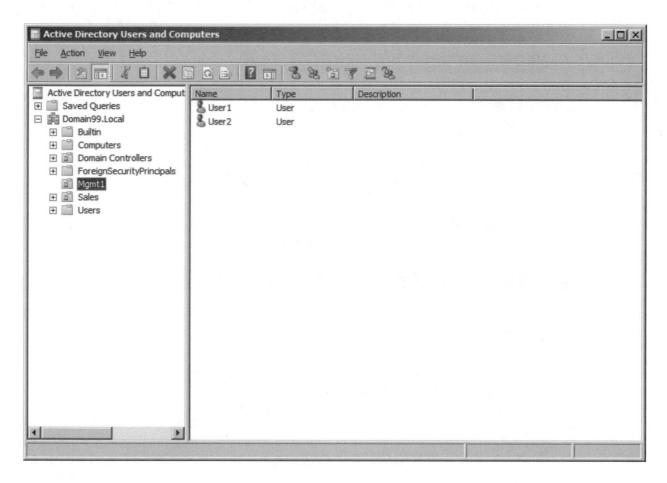

4. In the right pane, right-click User2 and click Reset Password. The Reset Password dialog box is displayed.

5. Key **Password#1** in the New Password text box and in the Confirm Password text box. Click OK. The Active Directory message box is displayed, verifying that the user's password has changed. Click OK.

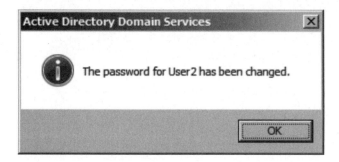

6. In the right window pane, right-click User1 and click Delete. An Active Directory warning message is displayed asking you to confirm the deletion of the account. Click Yes.

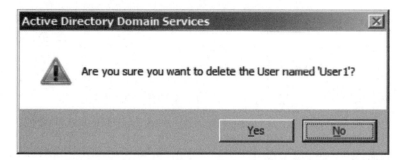

7. The Active Dirctory message box is displayed, telling you that you do not have sufficient privileges to delete the user account. Click OK.

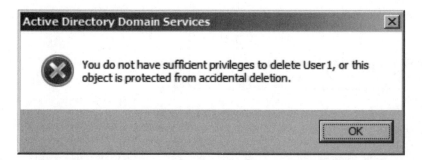

Question 3	*Why can the manager change a user's password in the Mgmt1 OU but cannot delete a user's account?*

8. Try changing the password for another user that is not a member of the Mgmt1 OU; for example, the Administrator in the Users container.

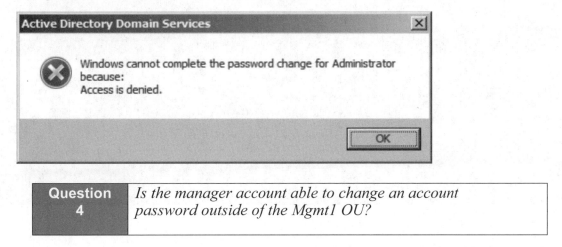

Question 4	*Is the manager account able to change an account password outside of the Mgmt1 OU?*

9. Close the Active Directory Users And Computers console and log off of both computers.

LAB 8
EXPLORING GROUP POLICY ADMINISTRATION

This lab contains the following exercises:

Exercise 8.1   Configuring the Local Computer Policy

Exercise 8.2   Configuring Processing Order

Exercise 8.3   Configuring Priority Order

Exercise 8.4   Using Block Policy Inheritance and Enforce

Exercise 8.5   Cleanup for Exercise 8.6

Exercise 8.6   Configuring Account Policies

Post-Lab Cleanup

Estimated lab time: 130 minutes

Exercise 8.1	Configuring the Local Computer Policy
Overview	In this exercise you will be configuring Group Policy to see its effects on a Winodws 7 machine (Workstation##) that is a member of the domain. You will also test the implementation of a Local GPO before you move on to testing Group Policy Objects (GPOs.)
Completion time	20 minutes

■ **PART A: Configure the Workstation## Computer to Remove the Properties Option When Right-Clicking My Computer**

1. Turn on the Server## computer and log on using your Administrator account and the password P@ssw0rd.

NOTE	*You are opening your server machine in preperation for later exercises.*

> **NOTE**
>
> *Remember to use your domain adminstrator account and not the local administrator account.*

2. Turn on the Workstation## (your Windows 7 machine) computer and log on using your Student## account for the local machine and the password P@ssw0rd.

> **NOTE**
>
> *In order to log using a local machine account click switch user, then other user and enter Workstation##\Student## as the username.*

3. Click the Start button. Key gpedit.msc and press Enter. The Group Policy Object Editor opens to the Local Computer Policy.

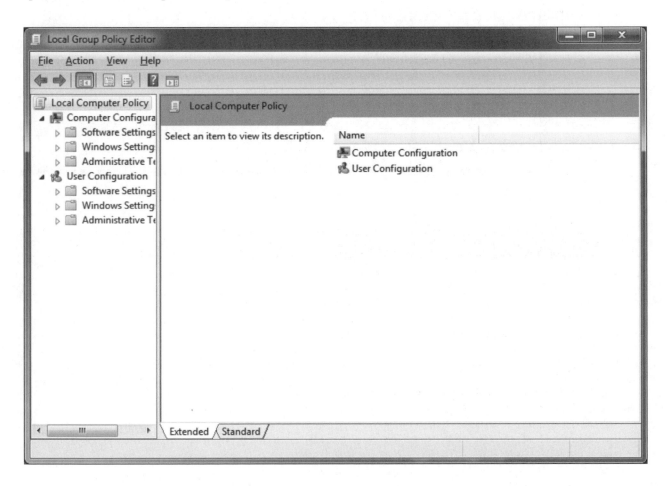

4. Under the User Configuration node, click Administrative Templates.

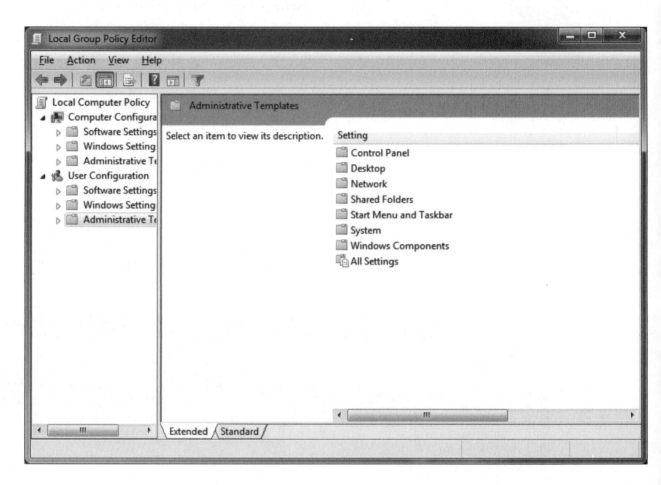

5. Click the Desktop node.

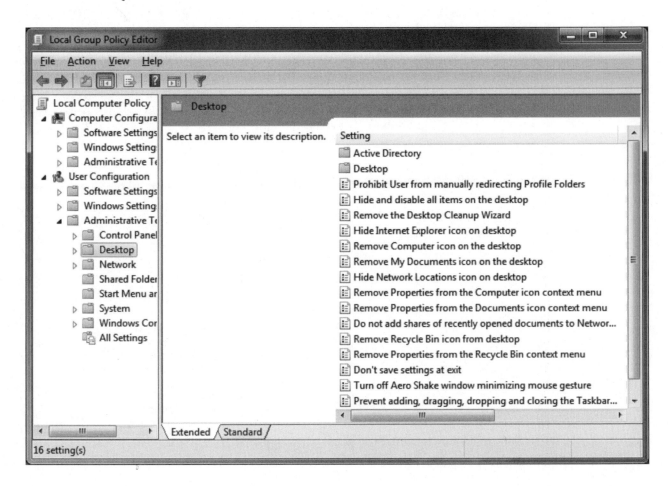

6. In the right window, double-click the Remove Properties From The Computer Icon
   Context Menu setting. The Remove Properties From The Computer Icon Context Menu
   dialog box is displayed.

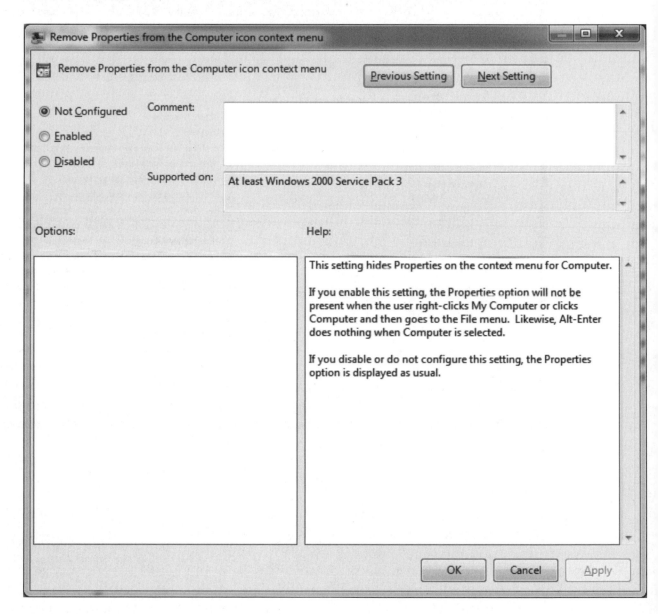

7. Click the Enabled radio button. Click OK.

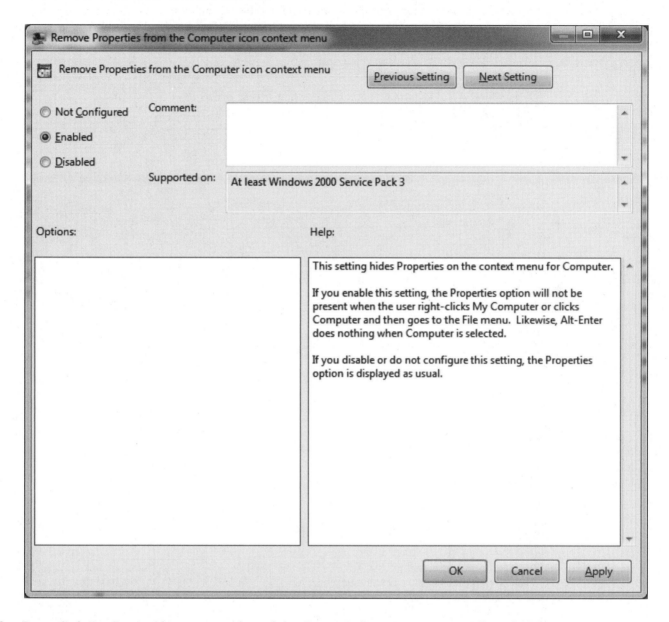

8. Press Ctrl+Prt Scr to take a screen shot of the Group Policy Management Editor showing that the Remove Properties from the Computer icon text menu is enabled, and then press Ctrl+V to paste the resulting image into the lab08_worksheet file in the page provided.

9. Close the Group Policy Management Editor.

> **NOTE**
>
> *Ensure your Windows 7 virtual machines IP address is set to an adress in the 172.16.##.0 subnet (for example 172.16.99.5) and its DNS Server address is set to 172.16.##.1.*

10. Log off of the computer and then log on again as the Student## account for the local computer. This will update the Group Policy for this user account.

11. Click the Start button, and then right-click the Computer icon.

Question 1	*Do you see the Properties menu option?*

Exercise 8.2	Configuring Processing Order
Overview	In this exercise you will test to see whether or not domain policies override configured computer settings. In the previous exercise you configured a local GPO and this exercise will test which GPO will take precedence if a conflict occurs between a local and domain based GPO.
Completion time	30 minutes

■ **PART A: Configure the Computer Properties Context Menu Setting on the Domain**

1. On Server## open the Group Policy Management Console from the Administrative Tools folder. Drill down to the Group Policy Objects node.

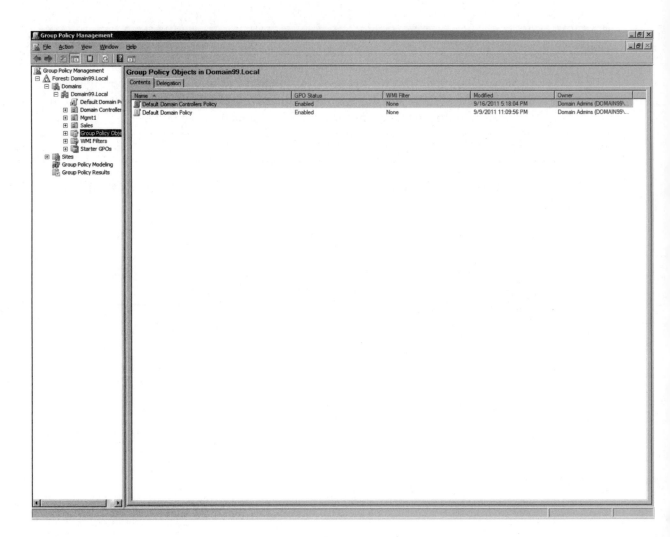

2. Right-click Default Domain Policy and click Edit. The Group Policy Management Editor
    window is displayed.

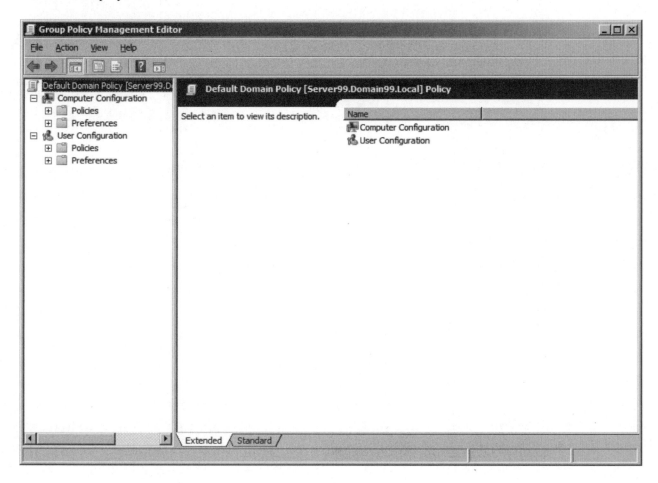

3. Under the User Configuration node, click Policies, and then click Administrative Templates.

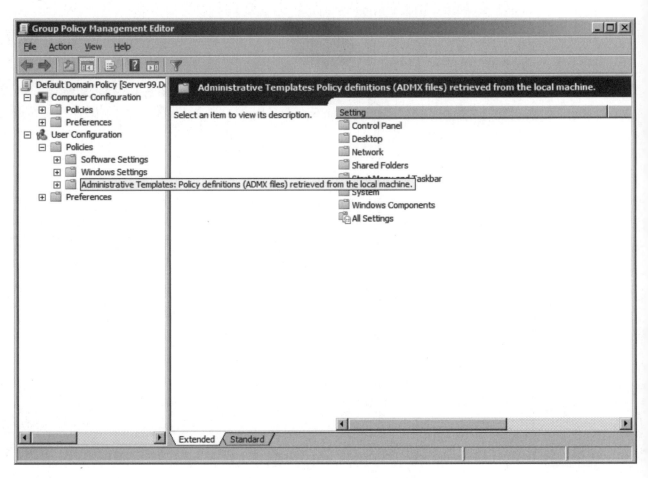

4. Click the Desktop node.

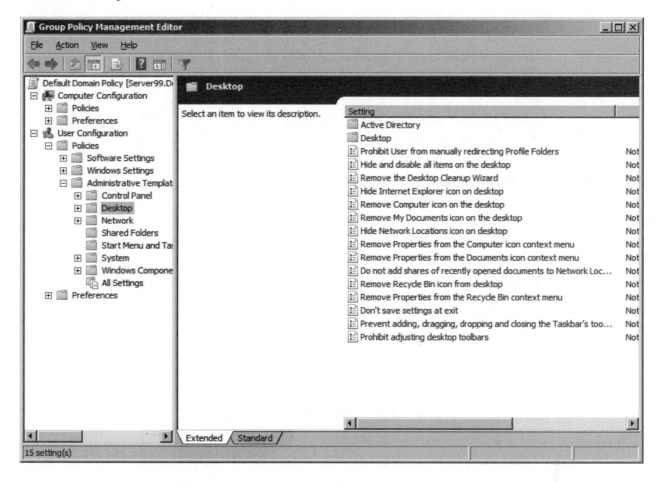

5. In the right window, double-click the Remove Properties From The Computer Icon Context Menu setting. The Remove Properties From The Computer Icon Context Menu dialog box is displayed.

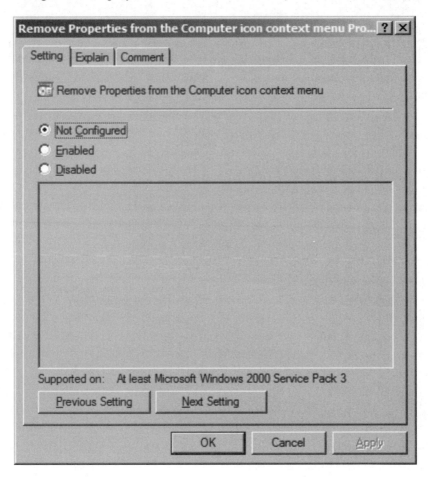

6. Click the Disabled radio button, and then click OK.

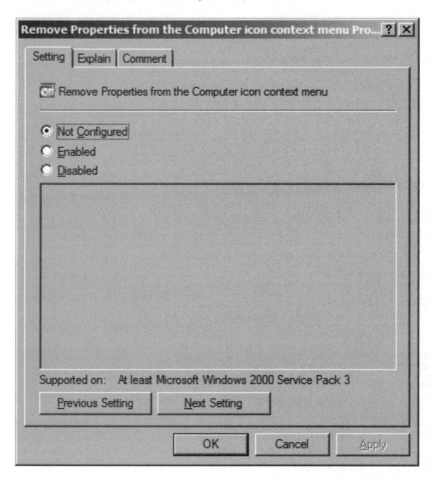

7. Close the Group Policy Management Editor and the Group Policy Management Console.

■ PART B: Verify that the Domain GPO Overrides the Local Computer Policy

1. On the Workstation## computer, log off and then log on using your Student##account and the password P@ssw0rd.

> **NOTE**
>
> *In order to log using a domain administrator click switch user, then other user and enter Domain##\Student## as the username.*

2. Click the Start button, and then right-click the Computer icon.

> **Question 2**
>
> *Do you see the Properties menu option? Based on the results, what does this tell you about how Group Policy Objects are processed?*

■ PART C: Create Domain Users for Testing

1. On the Server## computer, open the Active Directory Users And Computers console.

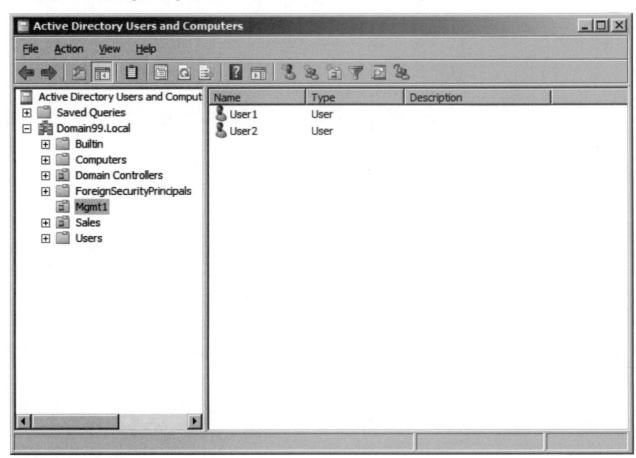

2. Create a user account named L7DomUser in the Users container of Domain##.Local.

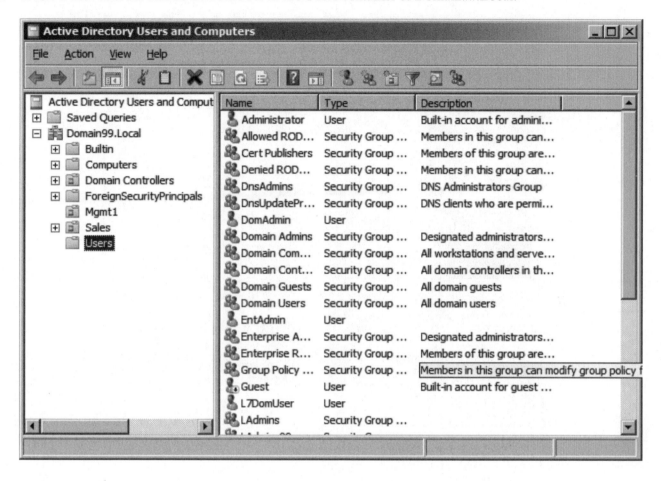

3. Create a new top-level OU named L7Test1.

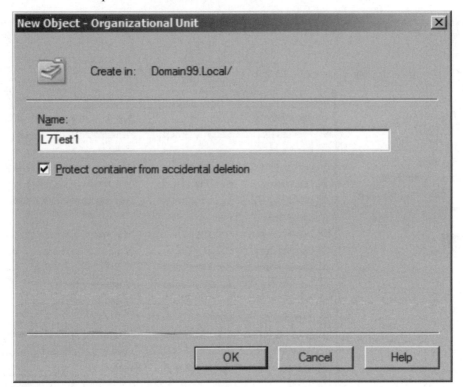

4. Create a user account in the L7Test1 OU named L7Test1User.

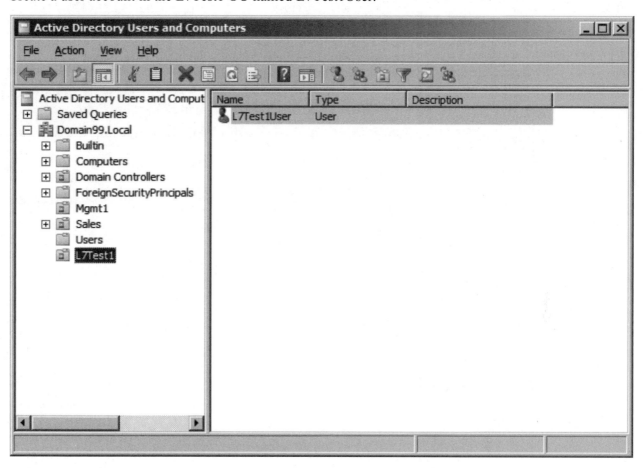

■ PART D: Create GPO Links for the Domain

1. On the Server## computer, open the Group Policy Management Console from the Administrative Tools folder. Drill down to the Domain## node.

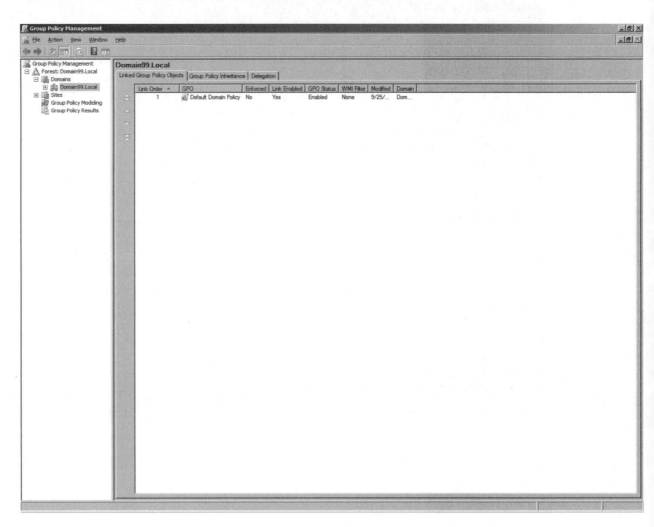

2. Right-click the Domain## node and select Create A GPO In This Domain, And Link It Here.

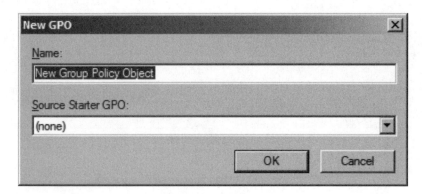

3. Name the new GPO RemoveHelp1 and press Enter.

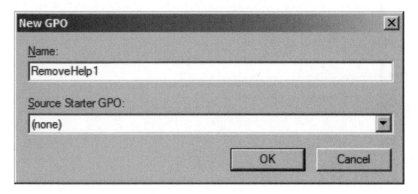

4. Navigate to the Group Policy Objects node. Right-click the RemoveHelp1 GPO and click Edit. The Group Policy Management Editor is displayed.

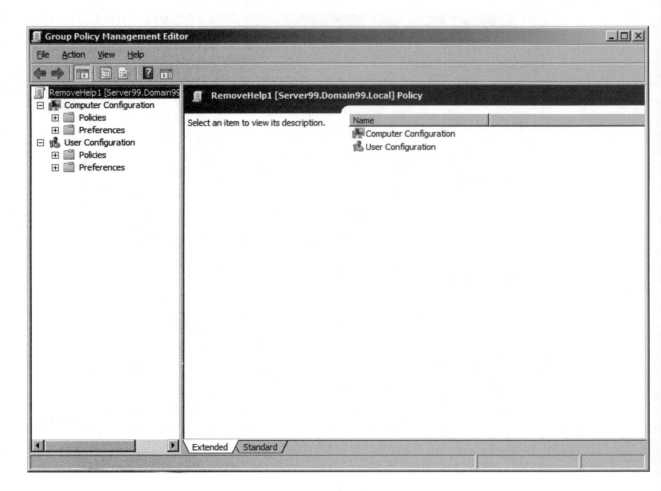

5. Browse to User Configuration, click Policies, and then click the Administrative Templates node.

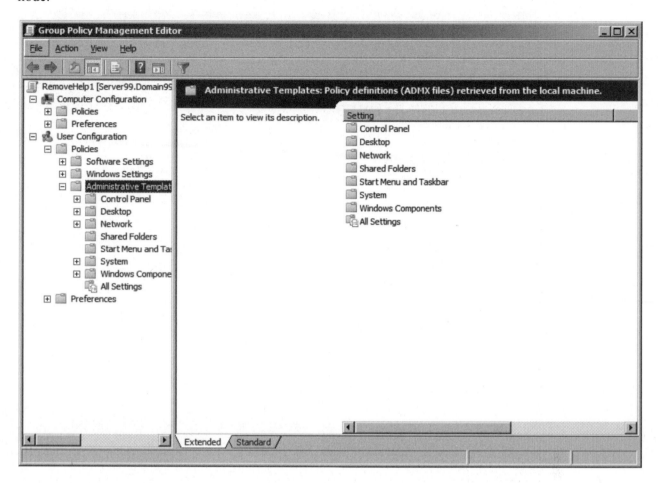

6. Select the Start Menu and Taskbar object.

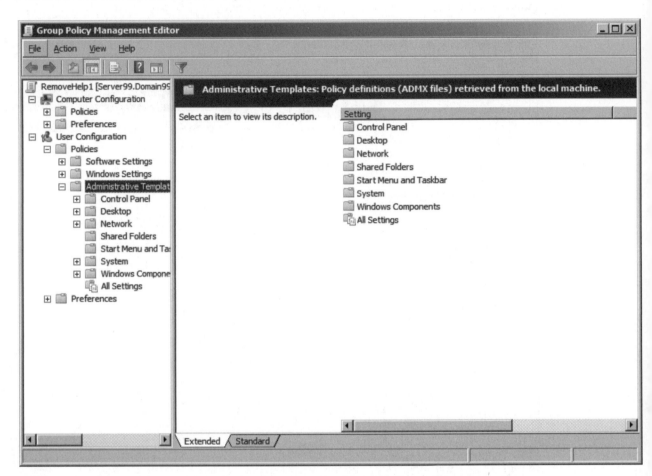

7. In the right pane, double-click the Remove Help Menu From Start Menu setting. The Remove Help Menu From Start Menu Properties dialog box is displayed.

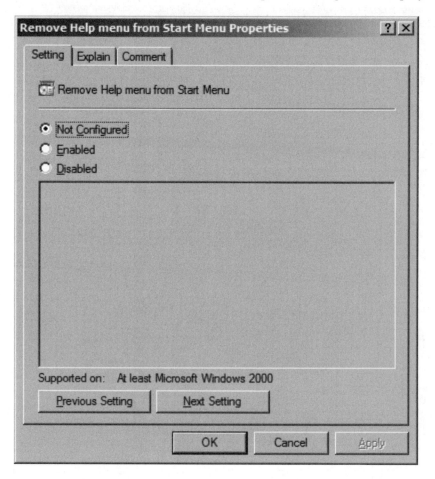

8. Select the Enabled radio button and click OK.

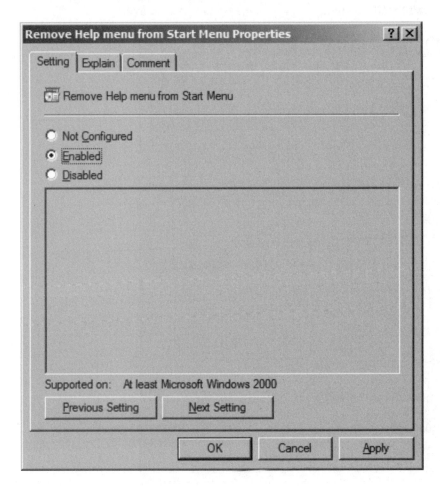

9. Close the Group Policy Management Editor.

10. Right-click the Domain## node and select Create A GPO In This Domain, And Link It Here.

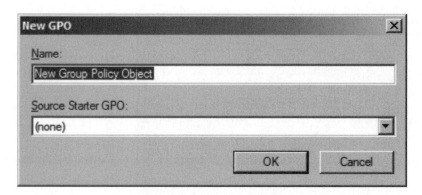

11. Name the new GPO RemoveMusic1 and press Enter.

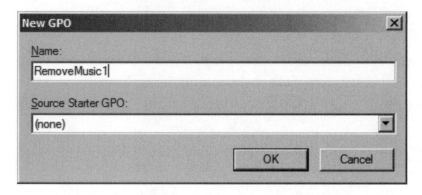

12. Repeat steps 5–10 to enable the Remove Music icon from Start Menu setting in the RemoveMusic1 GPO. Close the Group Policy Management Editor when you are finished.

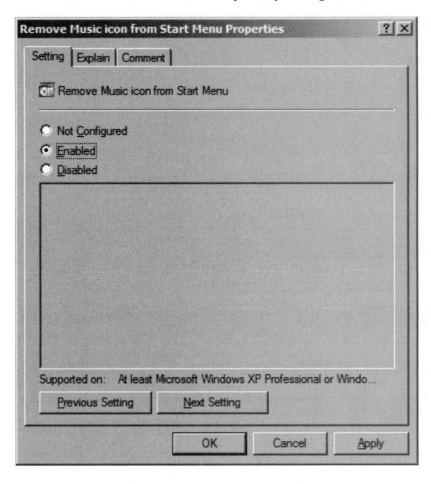

■ PART E: Create GPO Links for an OU

1. On the Server## computer, if it is not open, open the Group Policy Management Console. Drill down to the L7Test1 OU and select Create A GPO In This Domain, And Link It Here.

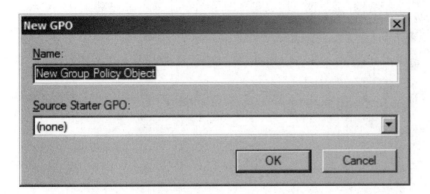

2. Name the new GPO AddHelp1 and press Enter.

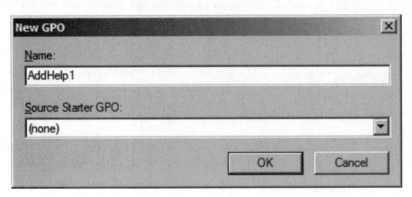

3. Use the technique that you used in Part D to disable the Remove Help Menu From Start Menu setting in the AddHelp1 GPO. Close the Group Policy Management Editor when you are finished.

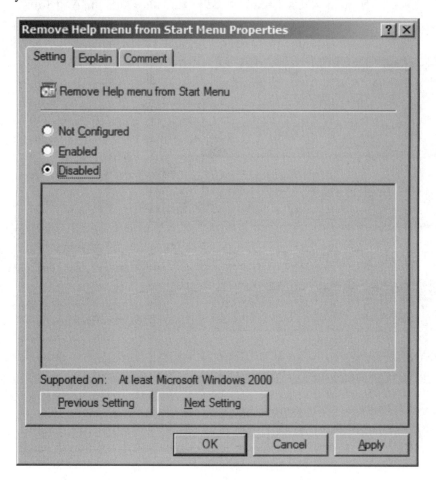

4. Create and link another GPO to the L7Test1 OU named RemoveComputerProperties2. Enable the Remove Properties From The Computer Icon Context Menu setting in the RemoveComputerProperties2 GPO.

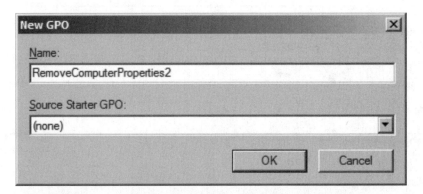

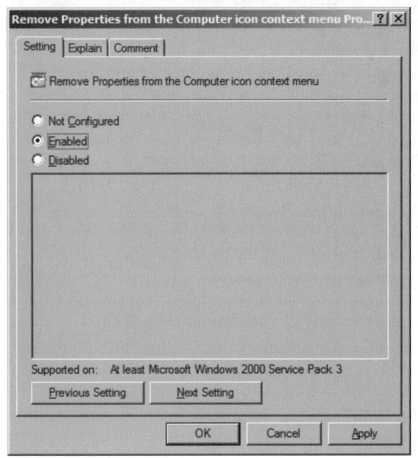

5. Close the Group Policy Management Editor and the Group Policy Management Console when you are finished.

■ PART F: Testing the Results

1. On the Workstation## computer, log on as L7DomUser in the Domain## domain.

NOTE	*In order to log using another account click switch user, then other user and enter the username of the account.*

2. Click the Start button.

Question 3	*Do you see a Music option? Do you see a Help and Support menu option?*

3. Click the Start button and right-click the Computer icon.

Question 4	*Do you see the Properties context menu option?*

4. Log off and then log on as L7Test1User in the Domain## domain.

5. Click the Start button.

Question 5	*Do you see a Music menu option? Do you see a Help and Support menu option?*

6. Click the Start button and right-click the Computer icon.

Question 6	*Do you see the Properties context menu option?*

Exercise 8.3   Configuring Priority Order

Overview	In this exercise you will create several new child OUs and test to see what will happen when you link two conflicting policies on the same OU.
Completion time	10 minutes

■ PART A: Create an Additional GPO for L7Test1

1. On the Server## computer, create a new GPO linked to the L7Test1 OU. Name it AddComputerProperties1.

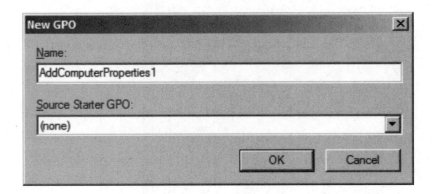

2. Edit the AddComputerProperties1 GPO and disable the Remove Properties From The Computer Icon Context Menu setting.

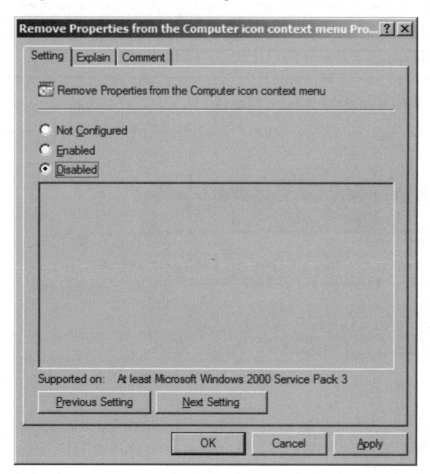

3. On the Workstation## computer, log off and log on as L7Test1User in the Domain## domain.

Question 7	*Can you see the Properties option when you right-click the Computer icon? Why did the AddComputerProperties1 GPO link not add this option to the Computer icon's right-click context menu?*

4. On the Server## computer, open the Group Policy Management Console and drill down to the L7Test1 OU.

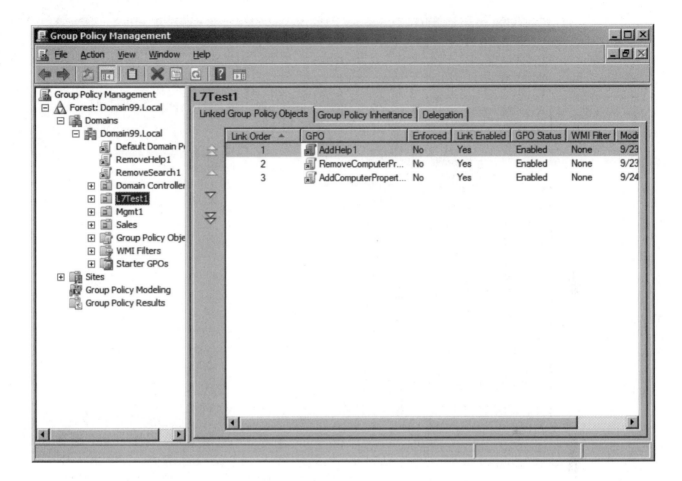

5. Click the AddComputerProperties1 GPO link and then click the up arrow twice. Verify that the AddComputerProperties1 GPO link is at the top of the Link Order.

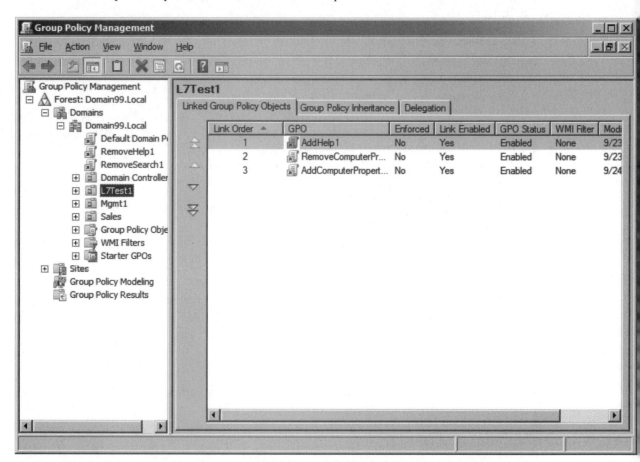

6. Press Ctrl+Prt Scr to take a screen shot of the Group Policy Management console showing that the priority of the AddHelp1 GPO has been changed and then press Ctrl+V to paste the resulting image into the lab08_worksheet file in the page provided.

7. Close the Group Policy Management Console.

8. On the Workstation## computer, log off of the computer and then log on again as the L7Test1User. This will update the Group Policy for this user account.

9. Click the Start button, and then right-click the Computer icon.

Question 8	*Can you see the Properties menu option? Why did the AddComputerProperties1 GPO add this option to the Computer icon's context menu?*

Exercise 8.4	Using Block Policy Inheritance and Enforce
Overview	It is not necessary that all GPO settings apply to all users or computers in the domain. Some users and computers do not need to receive some of the configuration options. In this exercise you will use Block Policy Inheritance and Enforce to control which settings are inherited from the domain by specific OUs.
Completion time	25 minutes

1. On the Server## computer, open the Group Policy Management Console. Drill down to the L7Test1 OU.

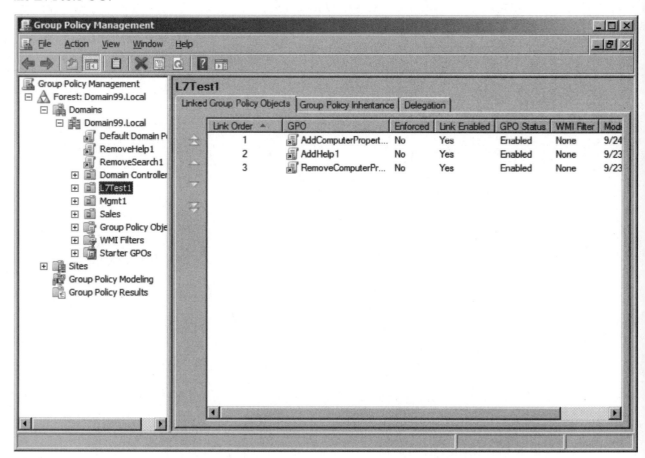

2. Right-click the AddComputerProperties1 GPO link and click Delete. A Group Policy Management dialog box is displayed. Read the message and click OK.

3. Right-click the AddHelp1 GPO link and click Delete. A Group Policy Management dialog box is displayed. Read the message and click OK. Right-click the RemoveComputerProperties2 GPO link and click Delete. A Group Policy Management dialog box is displayed. Read the message and click OK.

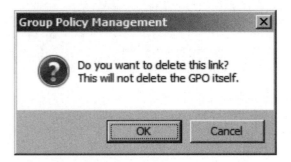

4. Close the Group Policy Management Console.

5. On the Workstation## computer, log off of the computer and then log on again as the L7Test1User. This will update the Group Policy for this user account.

6. Click the Start button.

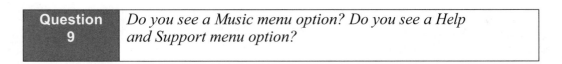

Question 9	*Do you see a Music menu option? Do you see a Help and Support menu option?*

7. Click the Start button and right-click the Computer icon.

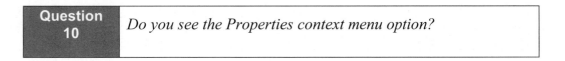

Question 10	*Do you see the Properties context menu option?*

8. On the Server## computer, open the Group Policy Management Console. Drill down to the L7Test1 OU.

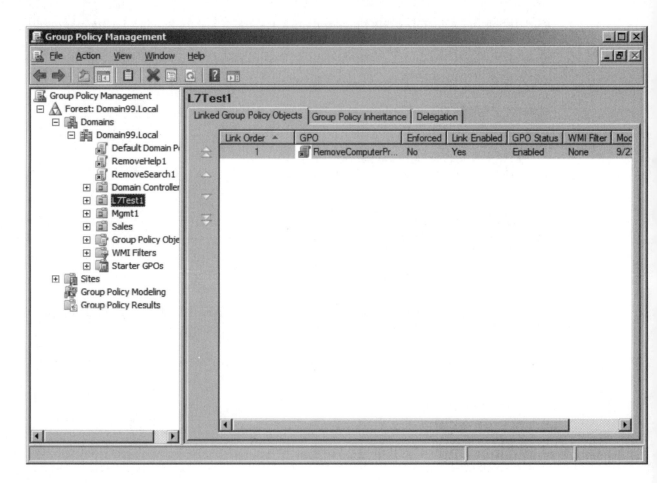

9. Right-click the L7Test1OU and click Block Inheritance.

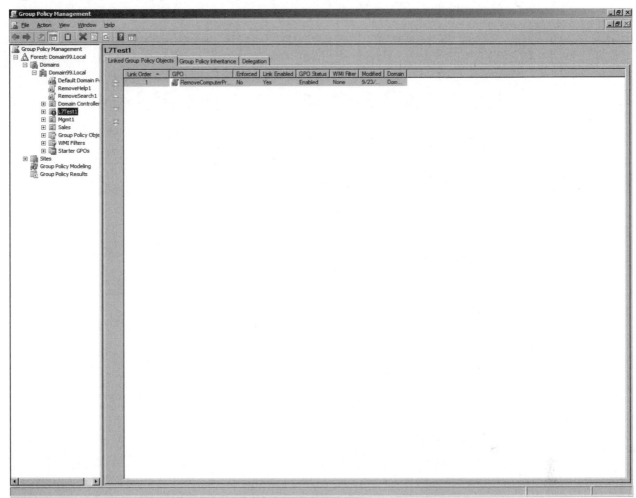

10. Close the Group Policy Management Console.

11. On the Workstation## computer, log off of the computer and then log on again as the L7Test1User. This will update the Group Policy for this user account.

12. Click the Start button.

Question 11	*Do you see a Music menu option? Do you see a Help and Support menu option?*

13. Click the Start button on the Workstation## computer and right-click the Computer icon.

Question 12	*Do you see the Properties context menu option?*

14. On the Server## computer open the Group Policy Management Console from the Administrative Tools folder. Drill down to the Domain## node.

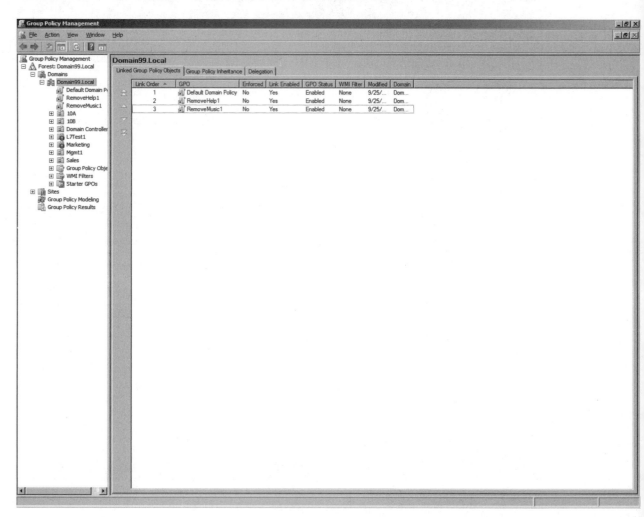

15. Right-click Default Domain Policy GPO link and click Enforced. A message will appear asking if you want to change the Enforced setting for this GPO link(s), click OK.

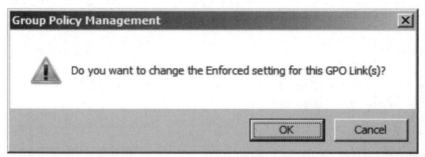

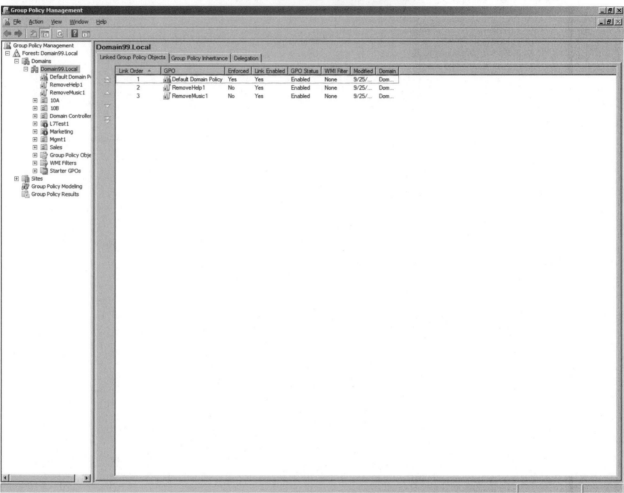

16. Close the Group Policy Management Console.

17. On the Workstation## computer, log off of the computer and then log on again as the L7Test1User. This will update the Group Policy for this user account.

18. Click the Start button.

Question 13	*Do you see a Music menu option? Do you see a Help and Support menu option?*

19. Click the Start button and right-click the Computer icon.

Question 14	*Do you see the Properties context menu option?*

Exercise 8.5   Cleanup For Exercise 8.6

Overview	In this exercise you will remove the configurations you made in the previous exercises in order to perform the tasks in exercise 8.6.
Completion time	20 minutes

1. Permanently delete all new GPO objects that you created in this Lab as follows:

    •   Open the Group Policy Management Console.

    •   Navigate to the Group Policy Objects node.

    •   Right-click the GPO and click Delete. A Group Policy Management dialog box will be displayed. Click Yes to delete the GPO.

    > **NOTE**
    >
    > *Do not delete the Default Domain Policy or the Default Domain Controllers Policy.*

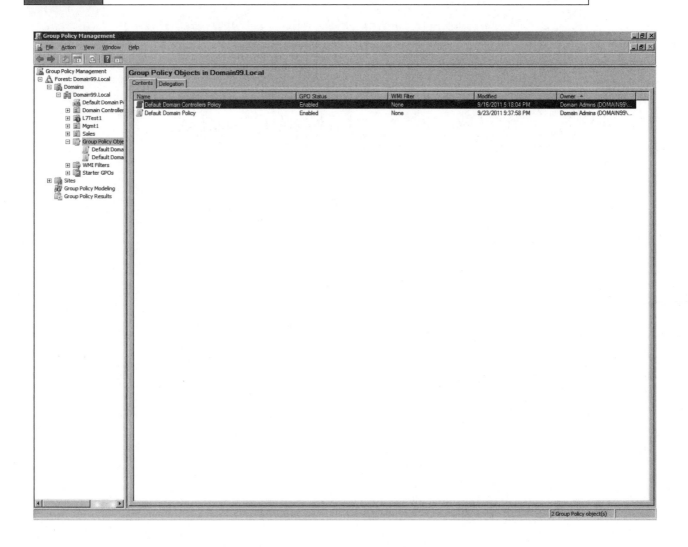

2. Edit the Default Domain Policy and set the Remove Properties from the Computer icon context menu setting to Not Configured.

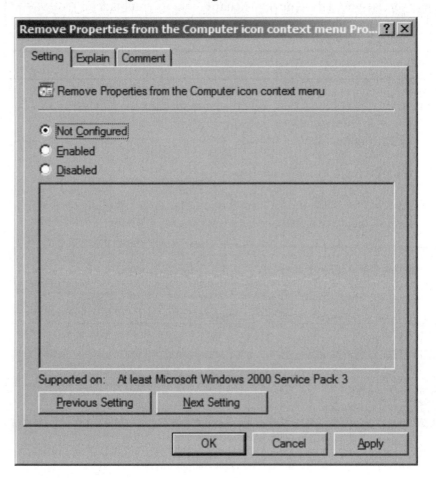

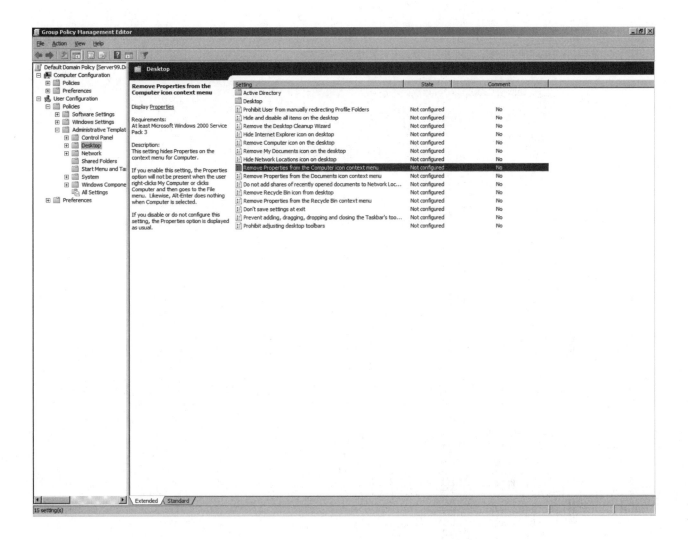

3. Navigate to the Domain##.Local node. Right-click the Default Domain Policy GPO link and remove the checkmark next to Enforced.

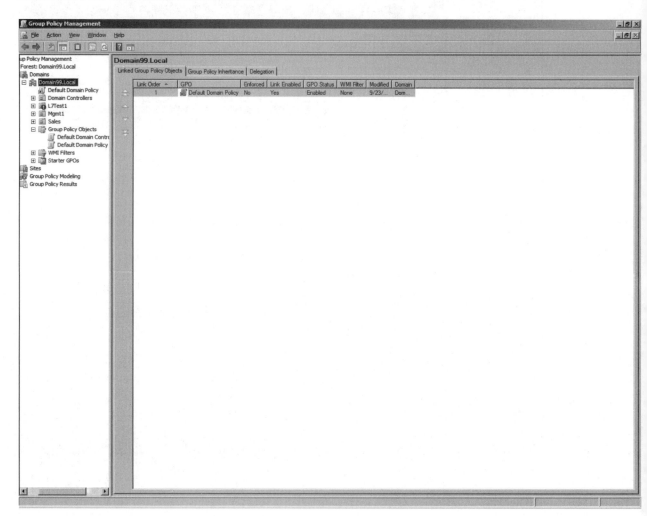

4. On the Workstation## computer, use gpedit.msc to edit the Local Computer Policy and change the Remove Properties From The Computer Icon Context Menu setting to Not Configured.

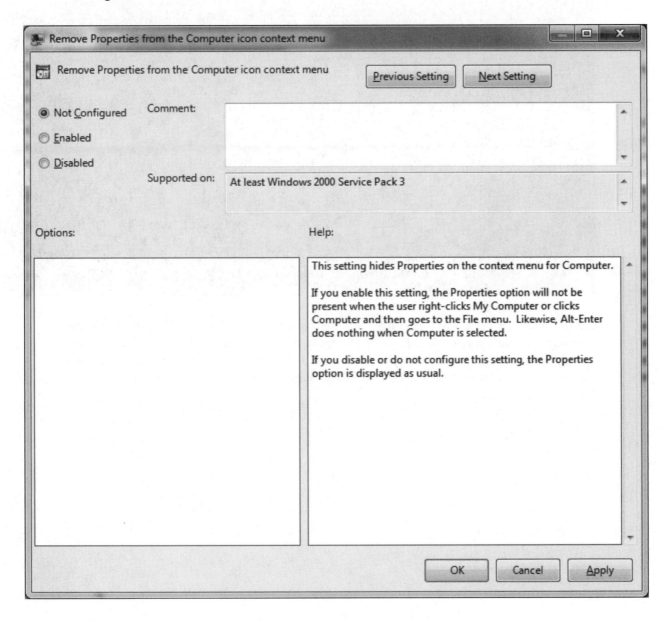

Remove Properties from the Computer icon context menu

Remove Properties from the Computer icon context menu   [Previous Setting]   [Next Setting]

○ Not Configured   Comment:

○ Enabled

○ Disabled

Supported on: At least Windows 2000 Service Pack 3

Options: Help:

This setting hides Properties on the context menu for Computer.

If you enable this setting, the Properties option will not be present when the user right-clicks My Computer or clicks Computer and then goes to the File menu. Likewise, Alt-Enter does nothing when Computer is selected.

If you disable or do not configure this setting, the Properties option is displayed as usual.

[OK]   [Cancel]   [Apply]

5. Execute **gpupdate /force** on both computers.

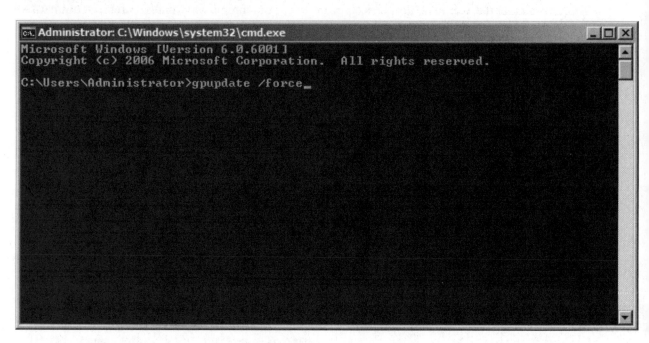

6. Log off of the Workstation## computer and log back on as the default administrator in the Domain## domain. Verify that the Help, Support, and Music options are available on the Start Menu. Verify that the Properties option is displayed when you right-click the Computer icon in the Start Menu. If not, try restarting the computers or verifying the Cleanup steps.

Exercise 8.6	Configuring Account Policies
Overview	Some departments in your company require a 14-character password for user accounts. You want to ensure that users are required to use 14-character passwords. Furthermore, you need to address the issue that the security consultants identified concerning account lockout. The security consultants were able to run a password cracker on your network without locking out a single user account. You want to ensure that anyone attempting to gain access to a user account by trying different passwords is locked out.
Completion time	20 minutes

■ PART A: Adjusting a Local Password Policy

1. On the Server## computer, use the Active Directory Users and Computers console to create an OU named Marketing.

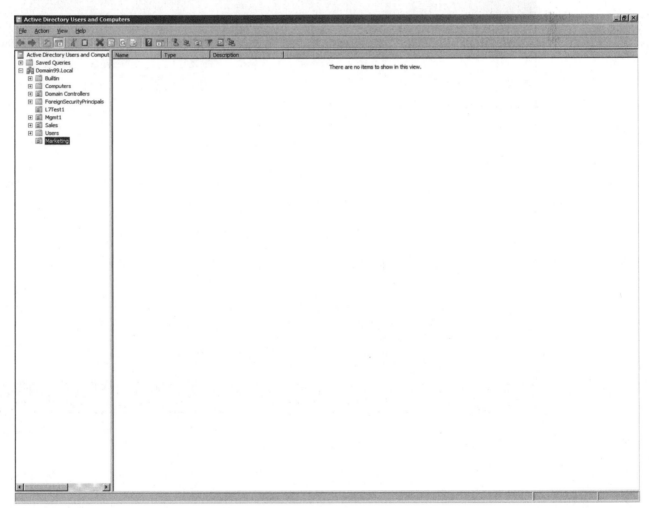

2. Use the Group Policy Management console to create and link a new GPO to the Marketing OU named PwdPol1. Right-click the PwdPol1 GPO and click Edit.

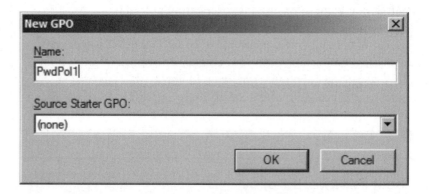

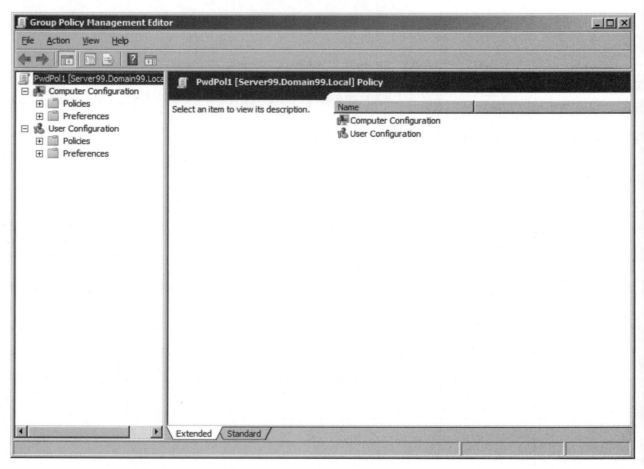

3. Browse to Computer Configuration, click Policies, click Windows Settings, click Security Settings, click Account Policies, and then click Password Policy.

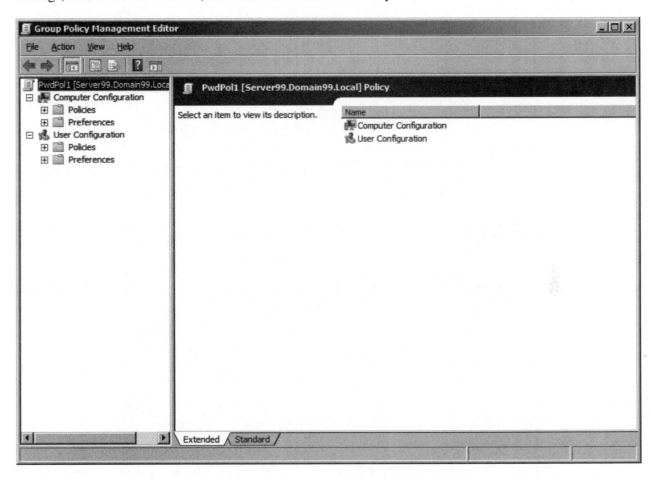

4. Double-click Minimum Password Length. The Minimum Password Length Properties dialog box will be displayed.

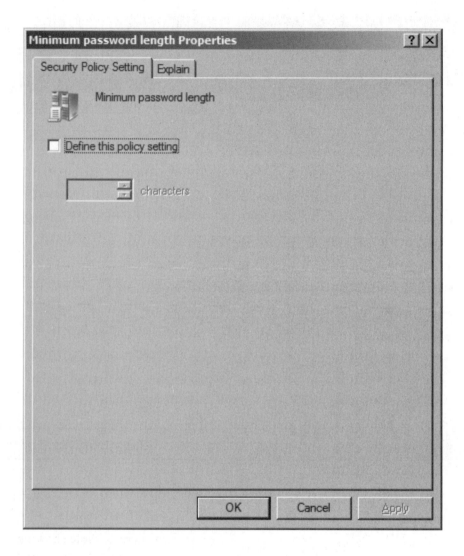

5. Place a checkmark next to Define This Policy Setting. Configure the minimum password length to Password Must Be At Least 14 Characters, and then click OK.

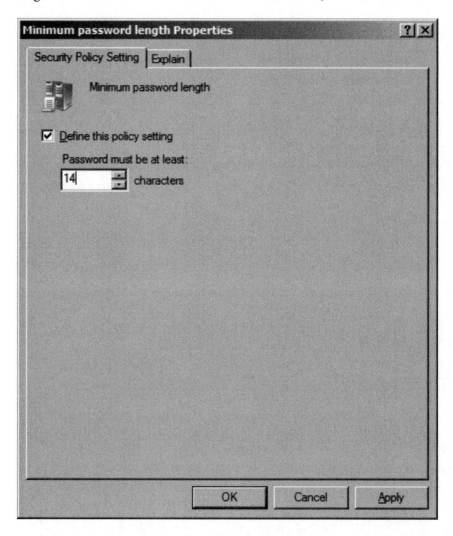

6. Press Ctrl+Prt Scr to take a screen shot of the Group Policy Management console showing that the Minimum password length Properties has been set to 14 characters, and then press Ctrl+V to paste the resulting image into the lab08_worksheet file in the page provided.

7. Close the Group Policy Management Editor.

8. Create a user named Lab8User1 in the Marketing OU with a password of P@ssw0rd and clear the User Must Change Password At Next Logon checkbox.

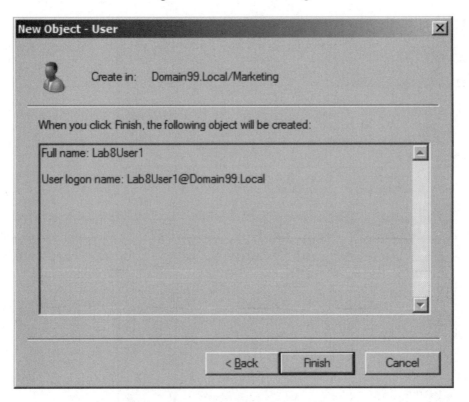

Question 15	P@ssw0rd is an eight-character password. Why are you not required to use a 14-character password?

9. In the Group Policy Management snap-in, right-click the Domain##.Local node and select
    Link An Existing GPO. The Select GPO window is displayed. Click PwdPol1 and click
    OK.

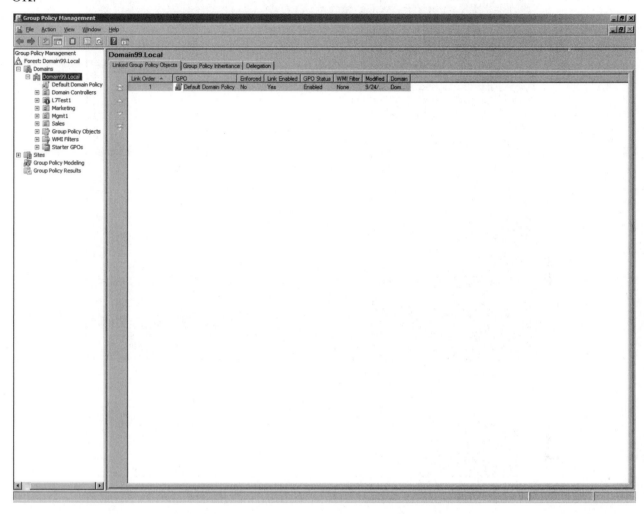

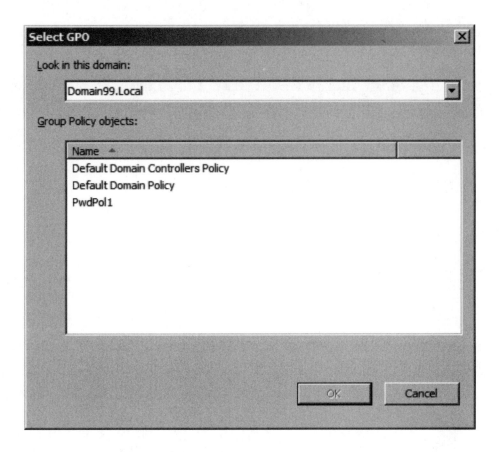

10. On the Linked Group Policy Objects tab, select the GPO link to PwdPol1. Click the Up arrow until the link to PwdPol1 is first in the Link Order.

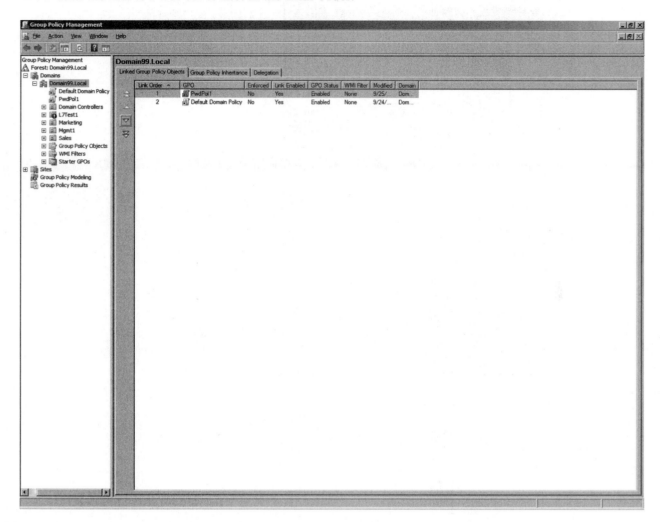

11. Remove the GPO link to PwdPol1 from the Marketing OU.

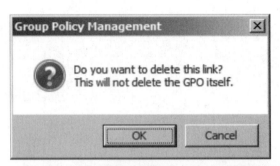

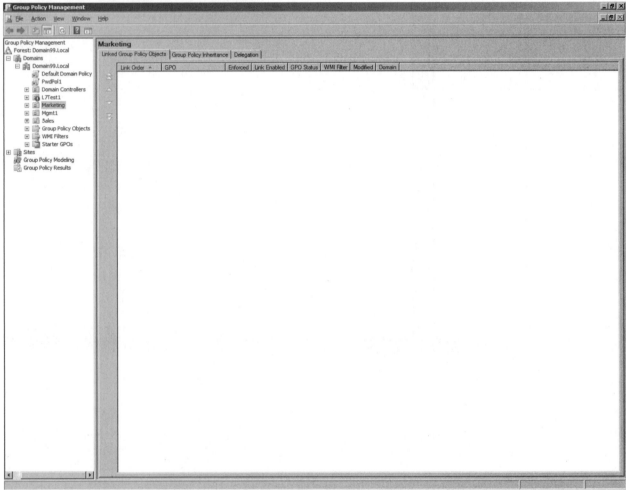

12. Configure Block Policy Inheritance for the Marketing OU. Refer to exercise 8.4, if necessary.

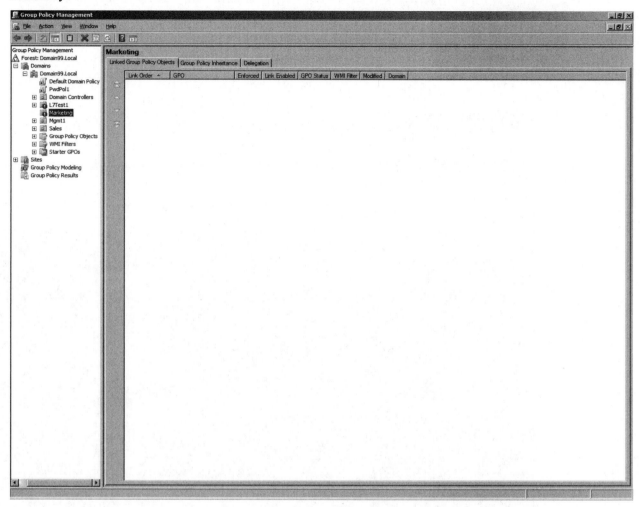

13. On the Workstation## computer, log on as Lab8User1 on the Domain##.Local domain.

NOTE	*In order to log using another account click switch user, then other user and enter the username of the account.*

Question 16	*Are you able to log on with a password that has fewer than 14 characters?*

14. Open a command-prompt window, key **gpupdate /force**, and press Enter.

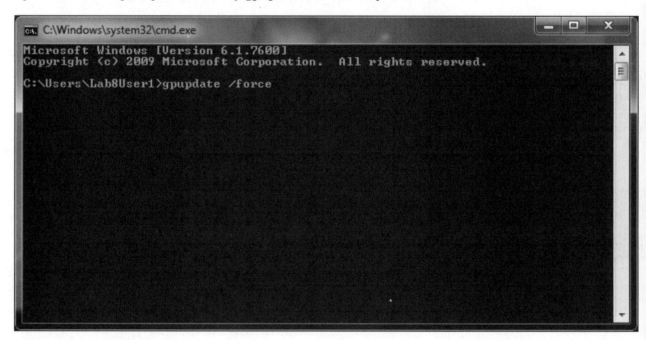

15. On the Server## computer, create a user account in the Marketing OU named Lab8User2 and try to configure the password as P@ssw0rd. An Active Directory message box is displayed. Read the message and click OK.

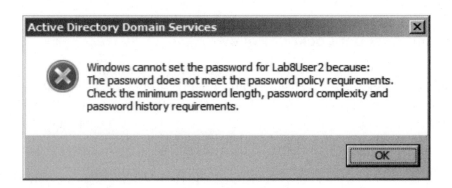

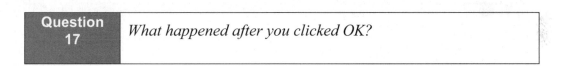

Question 17	*What happened after you clicked OK?*

16. Click Back. Key **P@ssw0rdP@ssw0rd** into the Password text box and the Confirm Password text box.

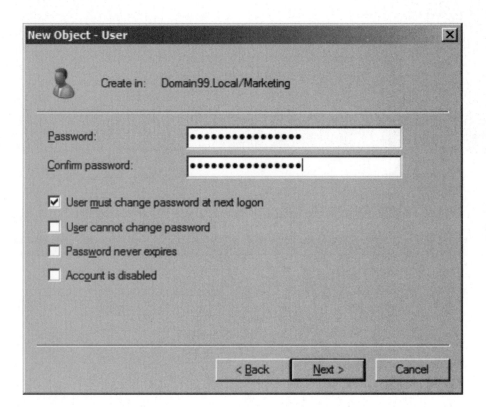

17. Click Next and then click Finish.

Question 18	*Does this password work? What does this teach you about password policy inheritance?*

■ PART B: Adjusting the Account Lockout Policy

1. Use the technique you learned in the previous section to edit the PwdPol1 GPO. Click Computer Configuration, click Policies, click Windows Settings, click Security Settings, click Account Policies, click Account Lockout Policy. Configure the Account Lockout Threshold setting for three Invalid Logon Attempts. When you click OK to configure this setting, a Suggested Value Changes message box is displayed. Click OK.

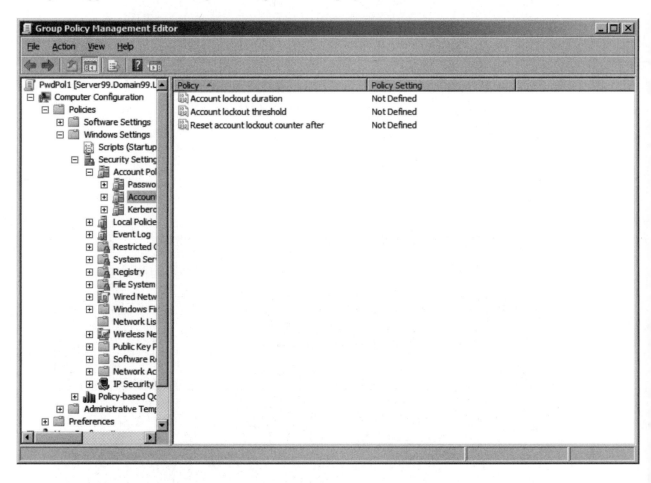

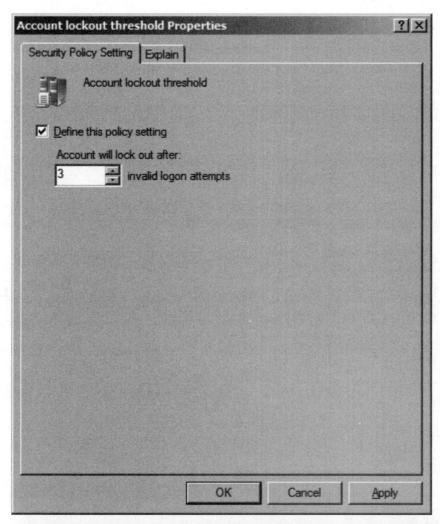

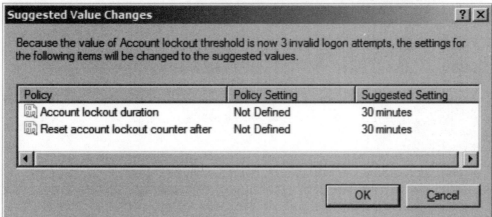

2. Press Ctrl+Prt Scr to take a screen shot of the Group Policy Management console showing that the Account lockout threshold Properties has been set to 3 invalid logon attempts, and then press Ctrl+V to paste the resulting image into the lab08_worksheet file in the page provided.

3. Close the Group Policy Management Editor.

4. On the Workstation## computer, log off and attempt to log on with the Lab8User1 credentials, but when providing the password credentials use the password Pass. Repeat this process three more times.

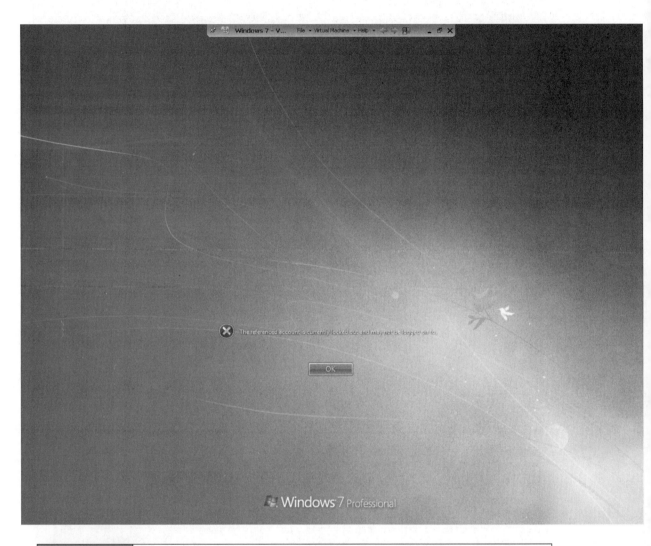

Question 19	*What happens to the Lab8User1 account?*

5. Attempt to log on using the correct password of P@ssw0rd.

Question 20	*Are you able to log on using the correct password?*

6. On the Server## computer, unlock the user account. Open the Active Directory Users And Computers console and drill down to the Marketing OU in the left pane. Right-click Lab8User1 and click Properties. The Lab8User1 Properties dialog box is displayed. Click the Account tab and then place a check mark in the "Unlock account. The account is currently locked out on this Active Direectory Domain Controller" checkbox. Click OK.

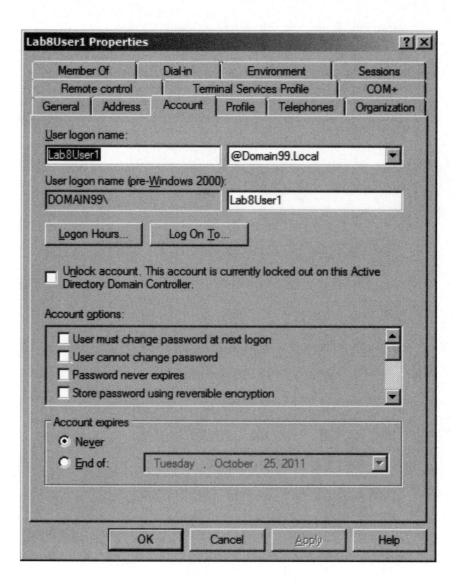

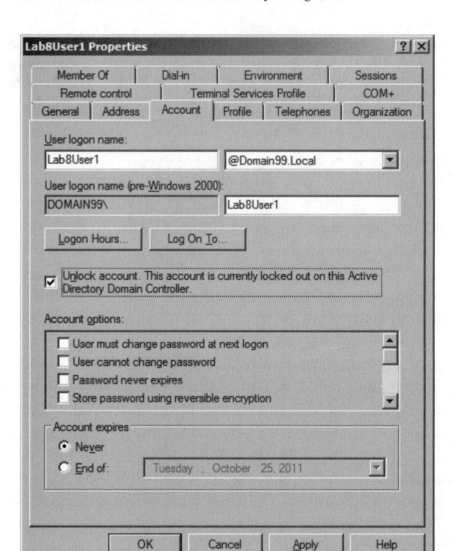

7. On the Workstation## computer, verify that you can log on as Lab8User1 with a password of P@ssw0rd. Log off.

POST-LAB CLEANUP

Overview	The following cleanup activities must be performed before moving on to Lab 8.
Completion time	5 minutes

1. On the Server## computer, log on as the default administrator of the Domain##.Local domain and open the Group Policy Management Console.

2. Permanently remove all GPOs that you created in this lab. This includes PwdPol1, Redirect1 any other GPOs created.

> **NOTE**
>
> *Do not delete the Default Domain Policy or the Default Domain Controllers Policy.*

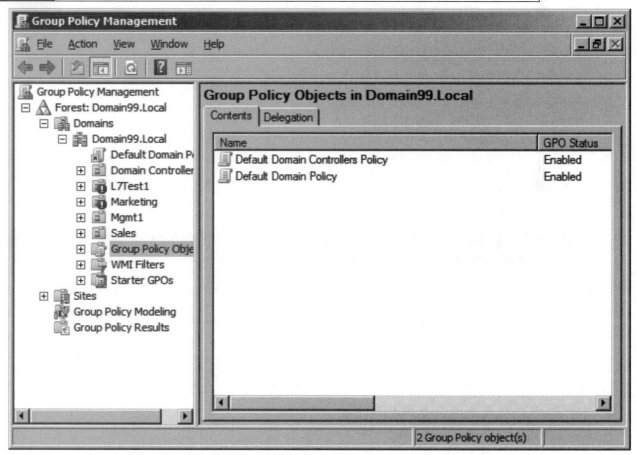

3. Log off of both computers.

LAB 9
SOFTWARE DISTRIBUTION AND CONTROLLING GROUP POLICY

This lab contains the following exercises:

Exercise 9.1   Deploying Software to Users

Exercise 9.2   Using Software Restriction Policies

Exercise 9.3   Controlling Group Policy

Exercise 9.4   Using Security Filtering

Post-Lab Cleanup

Estimated lab time: 95 minutes

Exercise 9.1	Deploying Software to Users
Overview	You need to prepare your test lab for your upcoming experiments. First, remove a child domain that you have configured. Then, configure a member server as a member of the remaining forest root domain. Finally, test the implementation of a Local GPO before you move on to testing Group Policy Objects (GPOs.)
Completion time	25 minutes

■ PART A: Preparing the Distribution Share

1. Turn on the Server## computer and log on using your Administrator account and the password P@ssw0rd.

2. On the Server## computer, insert the Windows Server 2008 installation CD-ROM into the CD-ROM drive. Close any Welcome screen that appears.

NOTE

Remember to use your domain adminstrator account and not the local administrator account.

3. Create a folder named C:\MSI. Right-click the folder and click Share. The File Sharing Window appears. In the Choose People On Your Network dialog box, key **Everyone** and click Add.

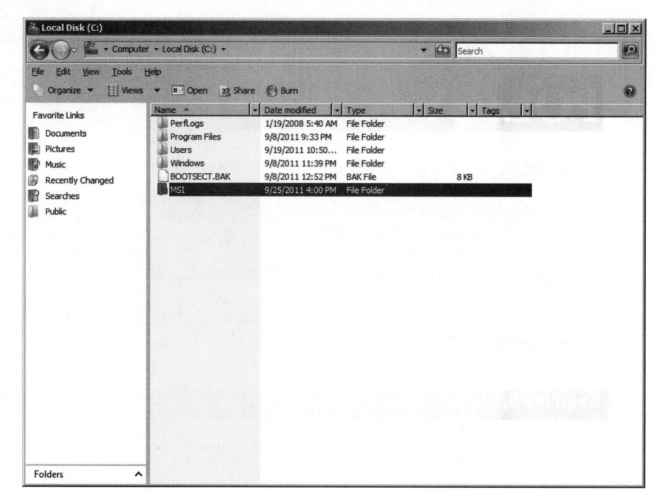

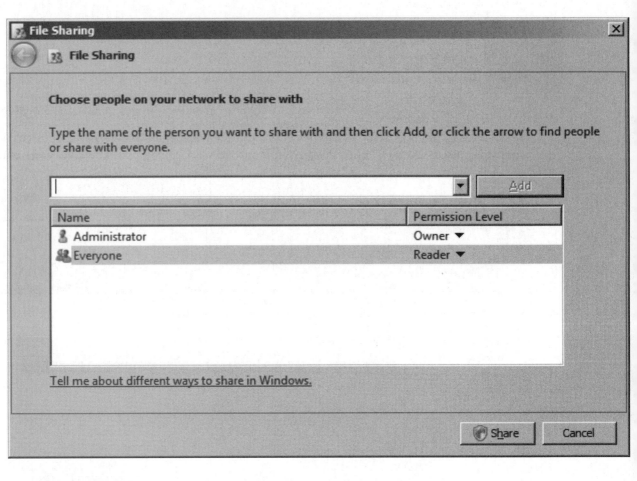

Question 1	*What permission level is assigned to the Everyone group by default?*

4. Click Share, and then click Done.

5. Copy the contents of the the \upgrade\netfx folder on the Windows Server 2008 CD-ROM into the MSI folder.

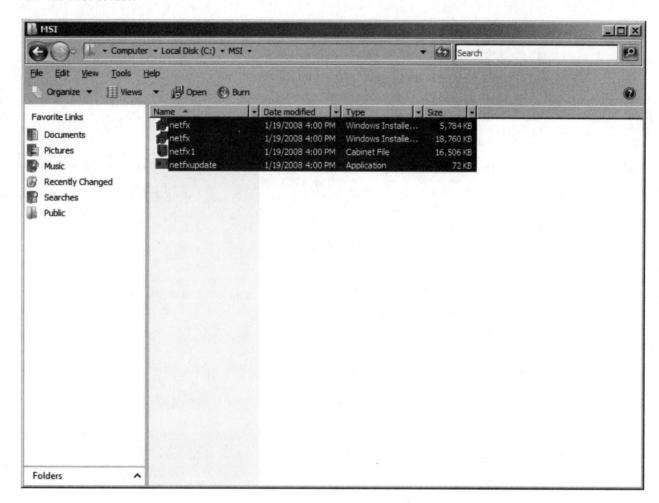

■ Part B: Publishing Software

1. On the Server## computer, open the Group Policy Management Console from the Administrative Tools folder. Drill down to the Domain## node.

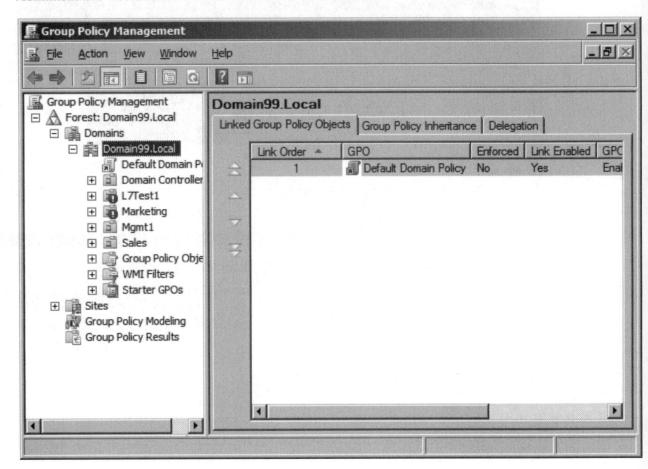

2. Right-click the Domain## node and select Create A GPO In This Domain, And Link It Here. In the Name field, key SoftDist1. Click OK.

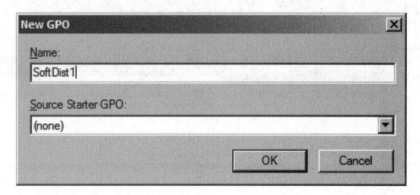

3. Navigate to the Group Policy Objects node. Right-click the RemoveHelp1 GPO and click Edit. The Group Policy Management Editor is displayed.

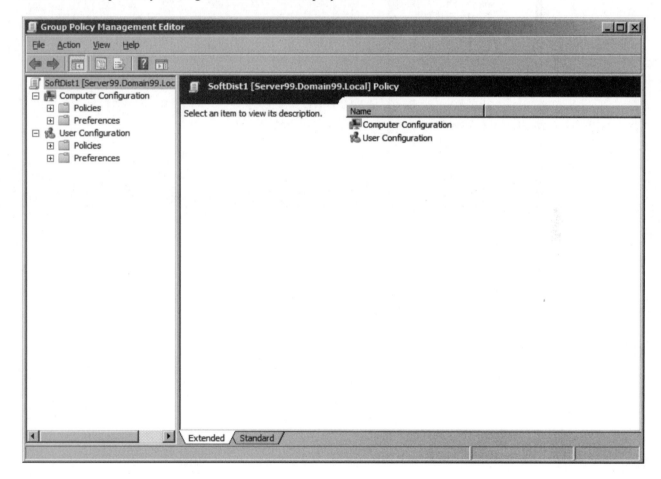

4.   Browse to User Configuration, click Policies, and then click the Software Settings node.

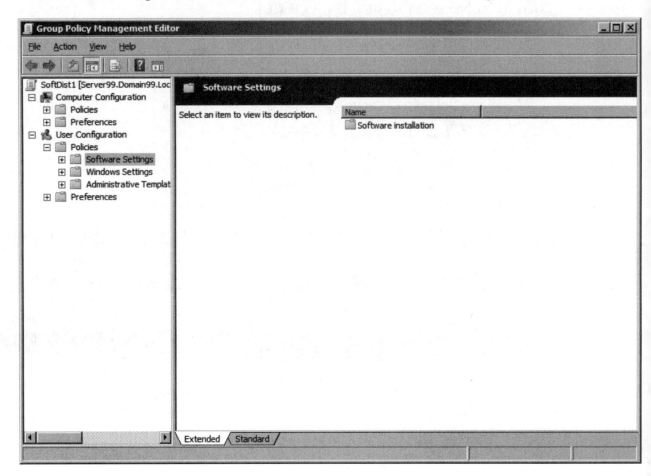

5. Right-click Software installation and click Properties. The Software Installation Properties dialog box is displayed.

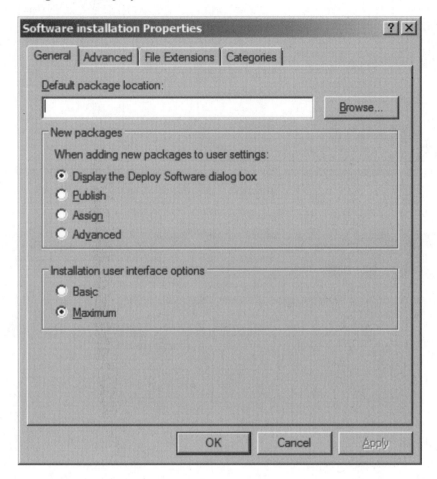

6. Click the Categories tab. Click Add. The Enter New Category screen is displayed. Key **Development Tools**. Click OK twice.

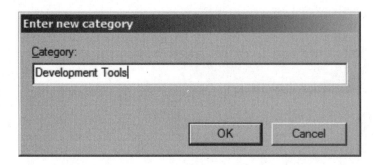

7. Right-click Software Installation, click New, and then click Package. The Open dialog box is displayed.

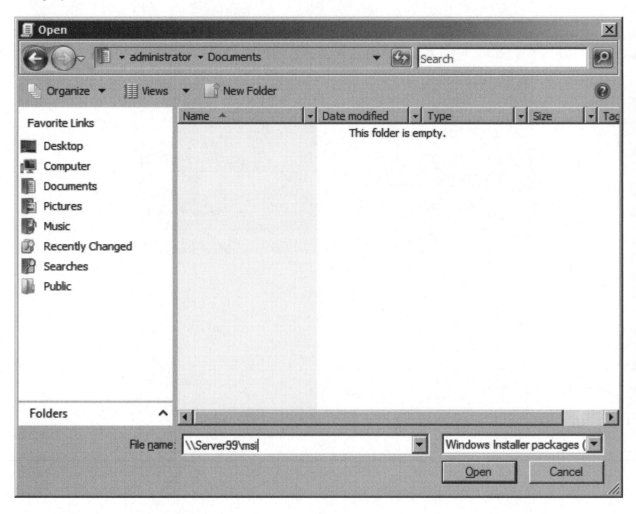

8. In the File Name dialog box, key **\\Server##\msi** and press Enter. Click Netfx and click Open. The Deploy Software dialog box appears.

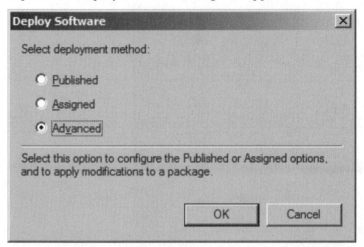

9. Click Advanced and click OK. After a few moments, the Microsoft .NET Framework 1.1 Properties dialog box appears.

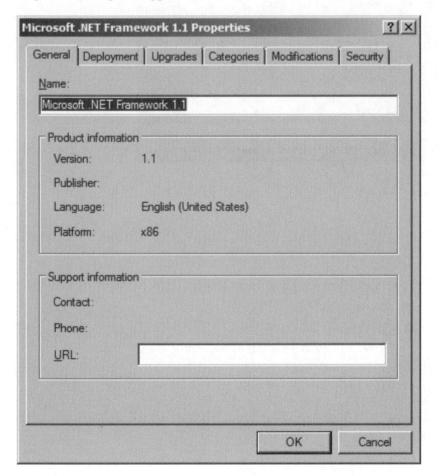

10. Click the Deployment tab. Verify that the Published radio button is selected.

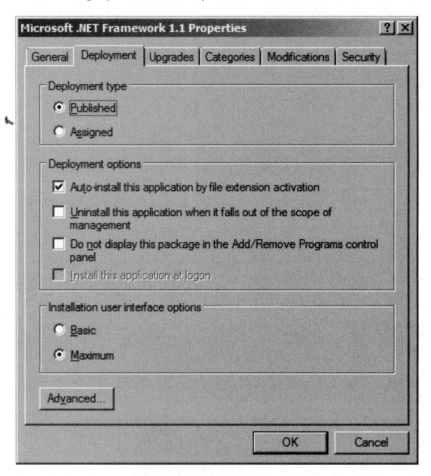

11. Click the Categories tab. Click Select to move the Development Tools category into the Selected Categories column. Click OK.

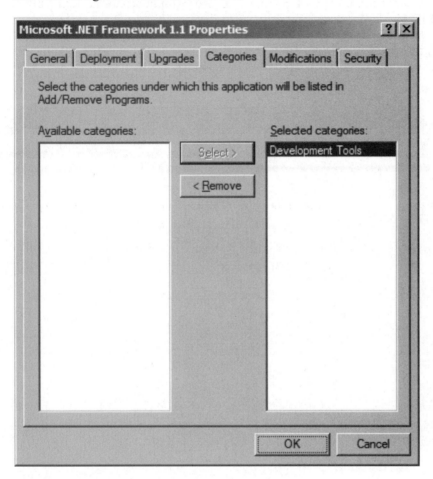

12. Close the Group Policy Management Editor.

13. Close the Group Policy Management MMC console.

■ Part C: Checking for Published Software

1. Turn on the Workstation## computer and log on using your Administrator account and the password P@ssw0rd.

2. Click the Start button, click Control Panel, then Programs and then click Uninstall a program. The Uninstall Or Change A Program window is displayed.

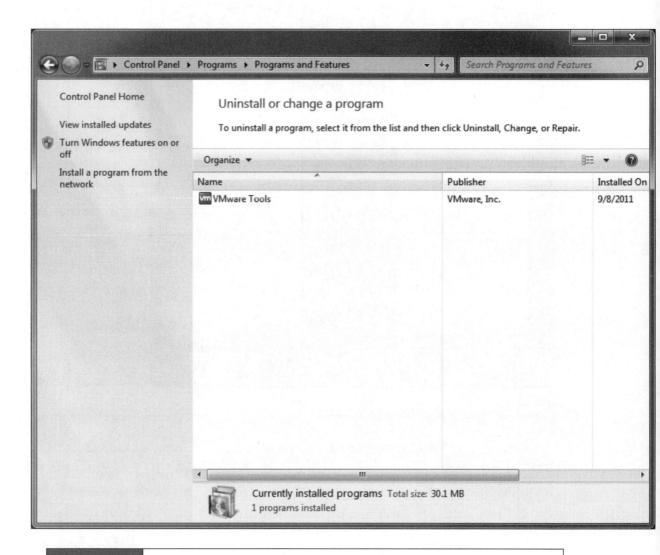

Question 2	*Is the Microsoft .Net Framework 1.1 installed?*

3. Click Install A Program From The Network.

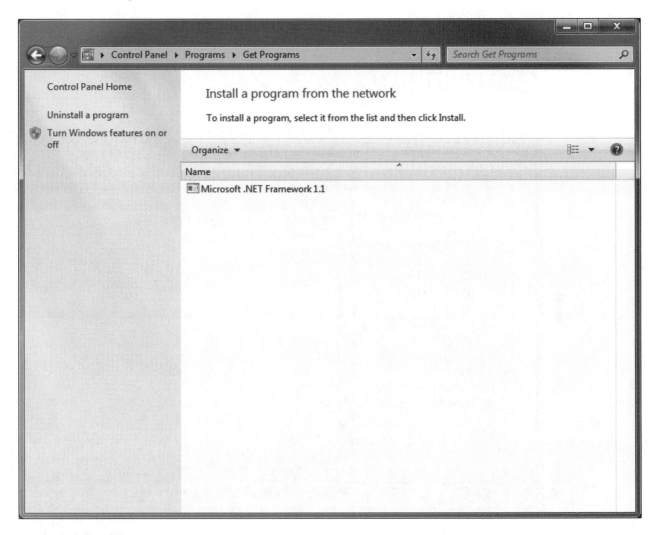

Question 3	*Do you see the Microsoft .Net Framework 1.1 listed?*

4. Press Ctrl+Prt Scr to take a screen shot of the Install a program from the Network screen showing the Microsoft .Net Framework 1.1 listed, and then press Ctrl+V to paste the resulting image into the lab09_worksheet file in the page provided.

5. Close the Programs And Features window.

6. Log off of the Workstation## computer.

■ Part D: Assigning Software

1. On the Server## computer, open the Group Policy Management Console from the Administrative Tools folder. Drill down to the Group Policy Objects node.

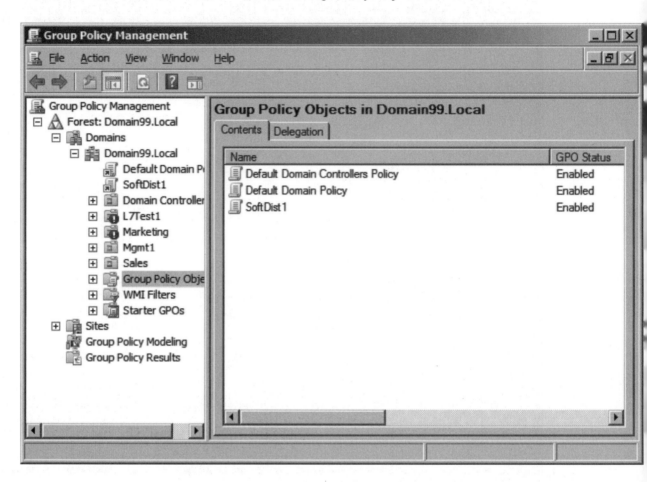

2. Right-click the SoftDist1 GPO and click Edit. Browse to User Configuration, click Policies, click Software Settings, then click the Software installation node.

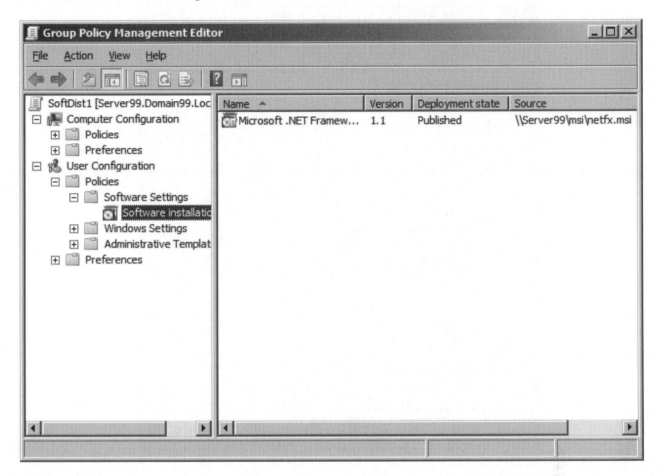

3. Right-click Microsoft .NET Framework 1.1 and click Properties.

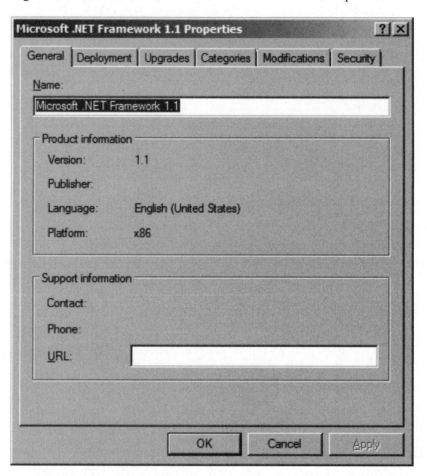

4. Click the Deployment tab. Under the Deployment Type section, click Assigned. In the Deployment Options section, place a checkmark next to Install This Application At Logon. Click OK.

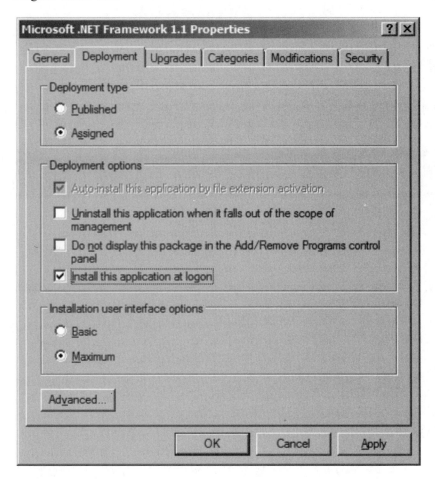

5. Close the Group Policy Management Editor.

6. Close the Group Policy Management MMC snap-in.

■ Part E: Checking for Assigned Software

1. On the Workstation## computer, log on as the default administrator of the Domain## domain.

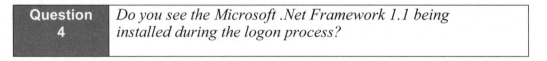

Question 4	*Do you see the Microsoft .Net Framework 1.1 being installed during the logon process?*

2. Click the Start button, click Control Panel, then Programs and then click Uninstall a program. The Uninstall Or Change A Program window is displayed.

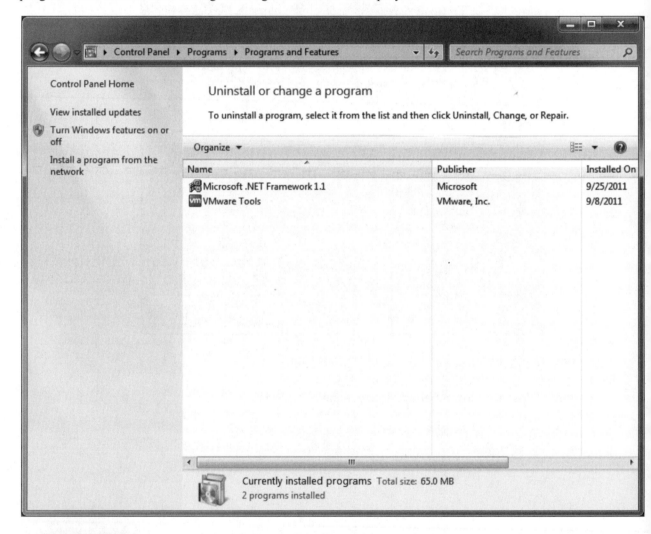

Question 5	*Is the Microsoft .Net Framework 1.1 installed?*

3. Press Ctrl+Prt Scr to take a screen shot of the Uninstall or change a program screen showing the Microsoft .Net Framework 1.1 is installed, and then press Ctrl+V to paste the resulting image into the lab09_worksheet file in the page provided.

4. Close the Programs And Features window.

5. Log off of the Workstation## computer.

Exercise 9.2	Using Software Restriction Policies
Overview	Corporate management decided that too many users spend time browsing the Internet when they should be working. You need to prevent users from accessing Microsoft Internet Explorer. You decide to accomplish this by using Software Restriction Policies.
Completion time	35 minutes

■ PART A: Create a Software Restriction Policy Path Rule

1. On the Server## computer, open the Group Policy Management Console from the Administrative Tools folder. Drill down to the Drill down to the Domain## node.

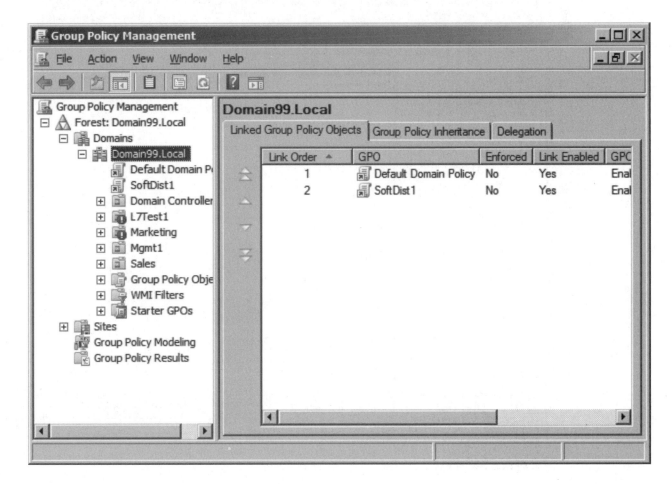

2. Right-click the Domain## node and select Create A GPO In This Domain, And Link It Here. In the Name field, key SRP1. Click OK.

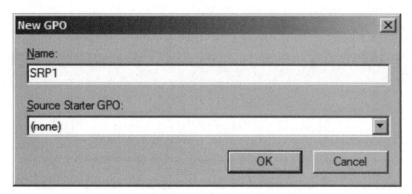

3. Navigate to the Group Policy Objects node. Right-click the SRP1 GPO and click Edit. The Group Policy Management Editor is displayed.

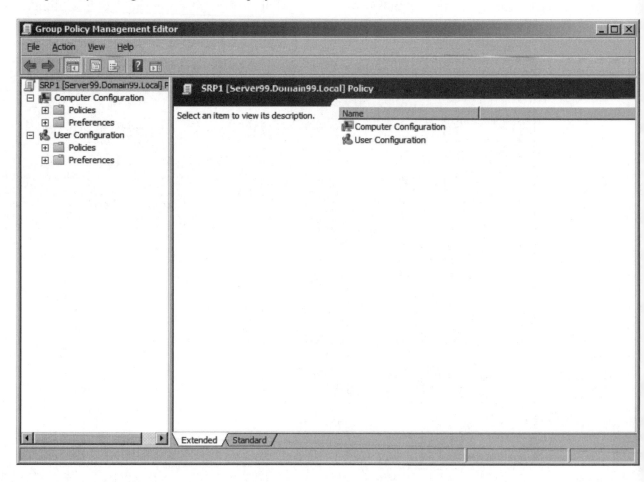

4. Browse to User Configuration, click Policies, click Windows Settings, click Security Settings, and then click the Software Restriction Policies node.

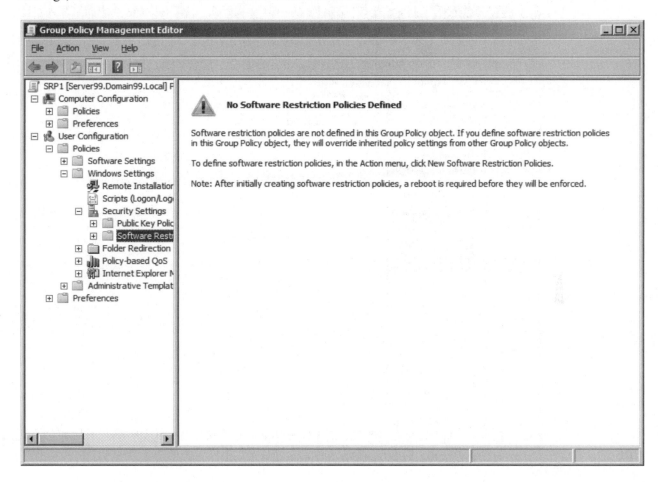

5. Right-click Software Restriction Policies and click New Software Restriction Policies.

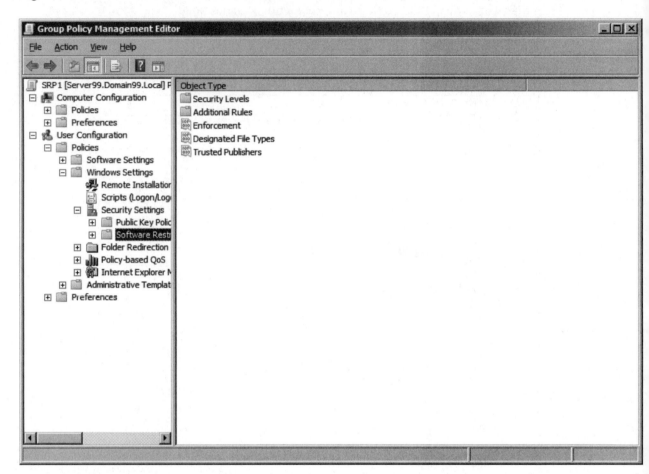

6. In the left pane, click Additional Rules. The default rules are displayed in the right pane. Right-click the Additional Rules object and click New Path Rule. The New Path Rule window is displayed.

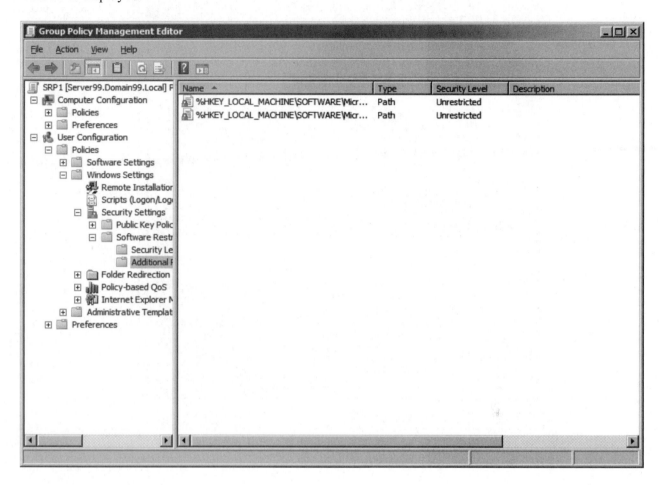

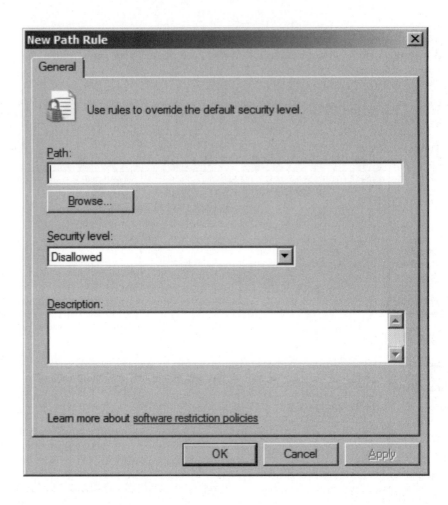

7. In the Path dialog box, click Browse. The Browse For File Or Folder window is displayed. Browse to the following path and click OK:

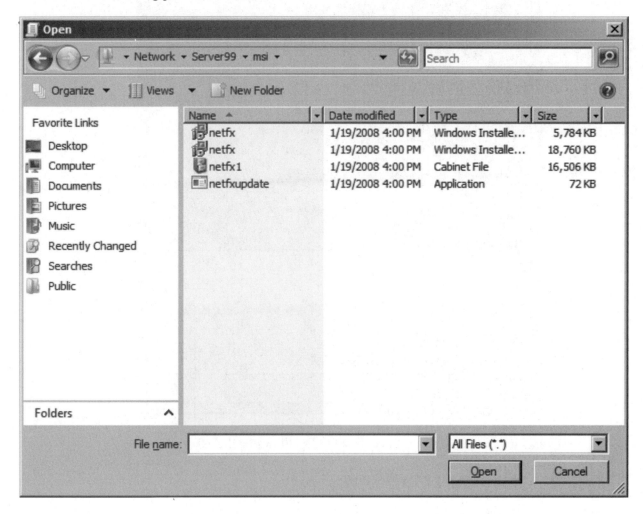

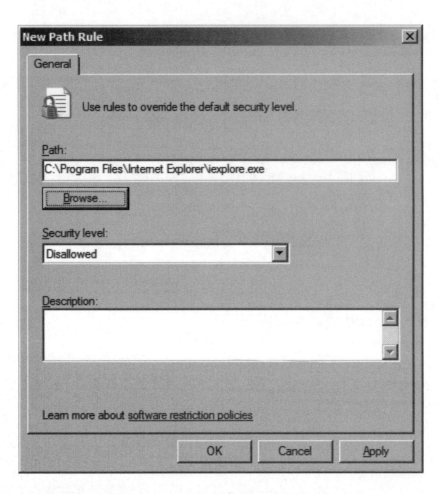

8. Ensure that the Security Level is set to Disallowed. Click OK.

9. Close the Group Policy Management Editor.

10. Close the Group Policy Management MMC snap-in.

■ PART B: Test the Software Restriction Policy Path Rule

1. On the Workstation## computer, log on as the default administrator of the Domain##.local domain.

2. Click the Start button, click All Programs, and then click Internet Explorer. A message box may displayed. If so, read the message and click OK.

Question 6	*Why did the computer fail to open iexplore.exe?*
Question 7	*Can you find a way around this rule that would enable users to run iexplore.exe?*

3. Using the command prompt or Windows Explorer, copy the iexplore.exe executable from C:\Program Files\Internet Explorer to your desktop.

4. Double-click the Internet Explorer icon on your desktop.

Question 8	*What happens after completing step 5?*

5. Log off of the Workstation## computer.

Exercise 9.3	Controlling Group Policy
Overview	In addition to managing Group Policy, you must often trace the application of GPOs to specific computers or users. Use the GPRESULT and RSOP.MSC tools to troubleshoot GPO deployment issues.
Completion time	10 minutes

In this lab, you will use the Organizational Units (OUs), user accounts, and Group Policy Objects listed in Table 9-1. Your first task is to create this structure.

Table 9-1
Organizational Unit Structure

OU	Users	GPO	GPO Settings	GPO Links
10A	10AUser1 10AUser2	GPOA	Remove Run Enabled	10A
10B	10BUser1 10BUser2	GPOB	Remove Help menu Enabled	10B
10C	10CUser1 10CUser2	GPOC	Remove Search Enabled	10C

■ PART A: Creating the OU Structure

1. On the Server## computer using Active Directory Users And Computers, create three OUs, as listed in Table 9-1. (Reference Exercise 7.3 for information about creating OUs.) Create OU 10A and OU 10B as top-level OUs in the Domain##.Local domain. Create OU 10C as a child OU to OU 10B.

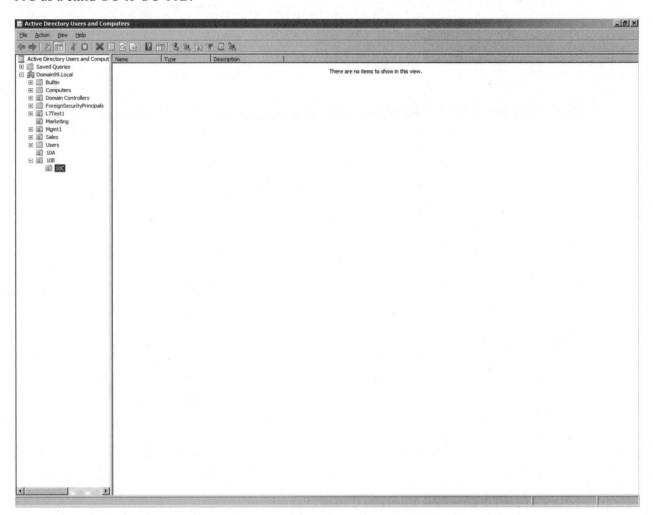

2. Create six user accounts in the appropriate OUs as listed in Table 9-1 (reference exercise 6.1.) Set all user passwords to P@ssw0rd and clear the User Must Change Password At Next Logon checkbox.

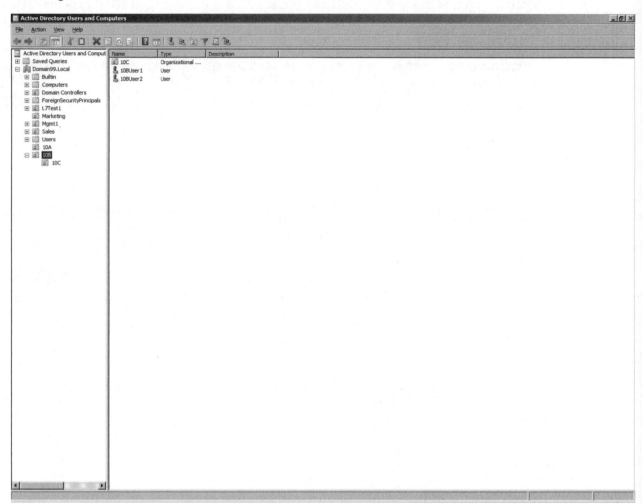

3. Use the Group Policy Management console to create and link a new GPO to the 10A OU named GPOA. Right-click the GPOA GPO and click Edit.

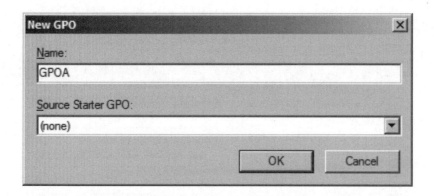

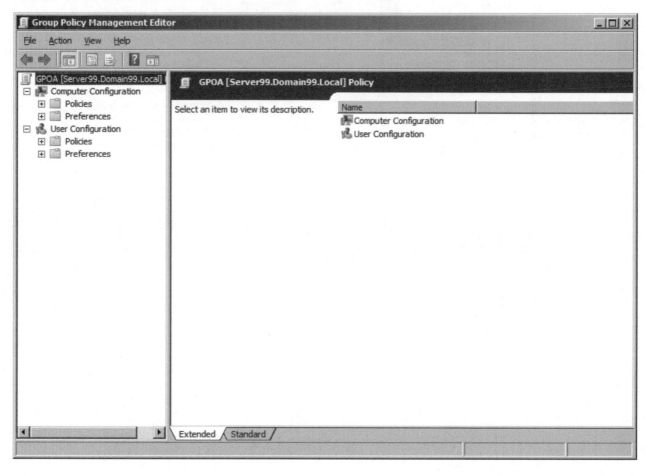

4. Browse to User Configuration, click Policies, click Administrative Templates, and then click Start Menu and Taskbar.

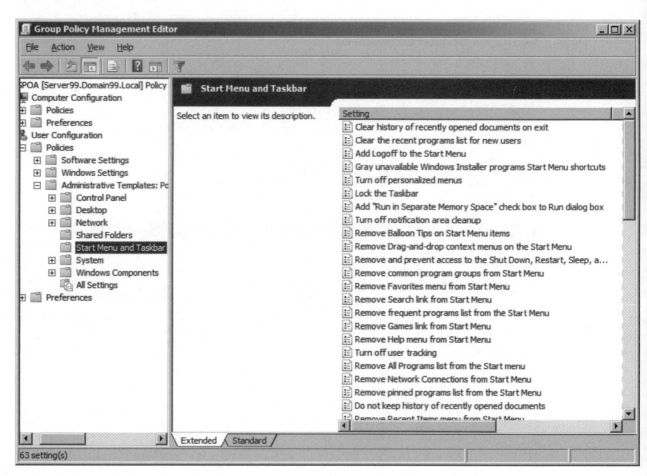

5. In the right pane, double-click Remove Music icon from Start Menu. The Remove Music
    icon from Start Menu. Properties dialog box is displayed.

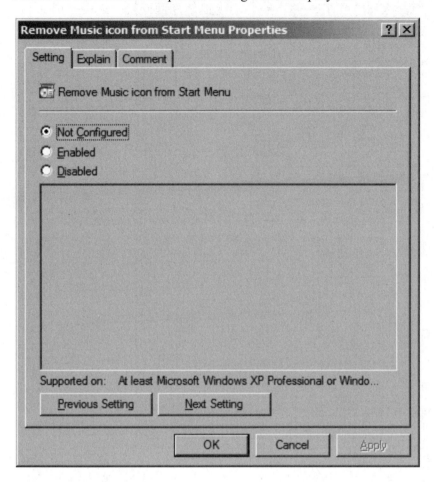

6. Select the Enabled radio button and click OK.

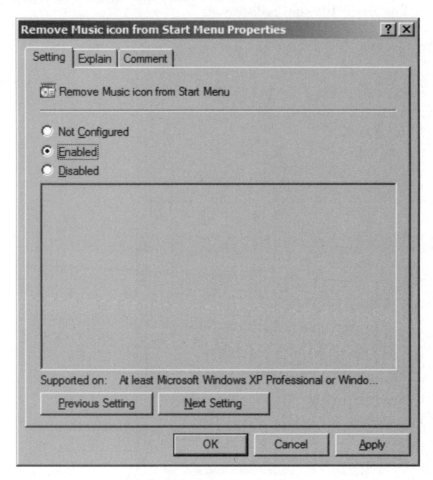

7. Close the Group Policy Management Editor, but do not close the Group Policy Management MMC.

8. Use the Group Policy Management MMC to create and link GPOB to the 10B OU. Edit GPOB and enable the Remove Help Menu From Start Menu setting.

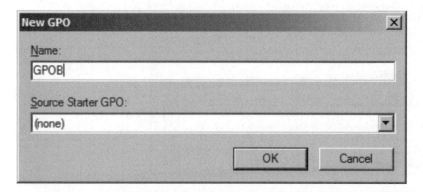

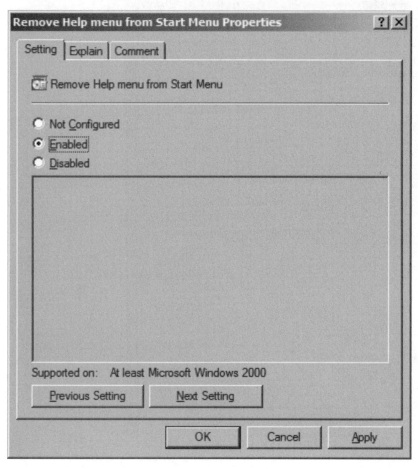

9. Use the Group Policy Management MMC to create and link GPOC to the 10C OU. Edit GPOC and enable the Remove Pictures icon from Start Menu setting.

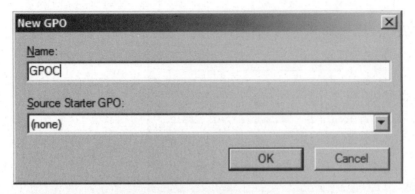

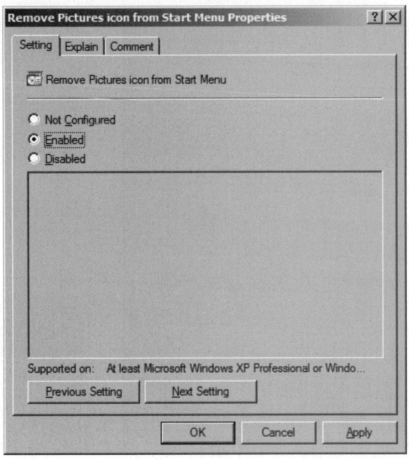

■ PART B: Using GPRESULT to Troubleshoot Deployment

1. On your Server## computer, open a command-prompt window. Key **gpupdate /force** and press Enter.

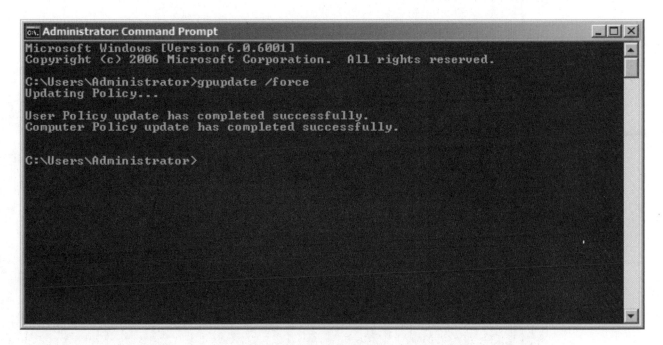

2. Log off of the Server## computer and then log on as 10AUser1 of the Domain## domain.

3. Open a command-prompt window and key **gpresult /r** and then press Enter. After a few minutes, output will be displayed in the command-prompt window.

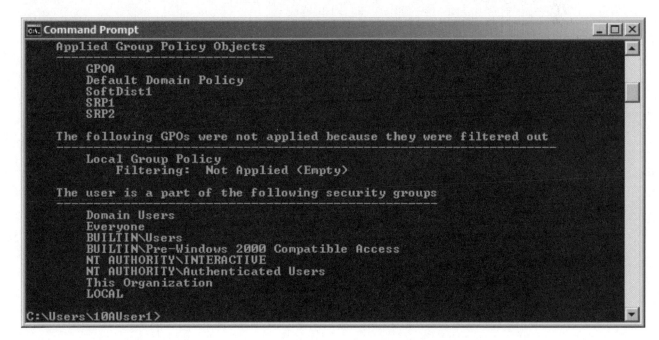

4. Look at the Applied Group Policy Objects section and verify that GPOA is listed.

5. Press Ctrl+Prt Scr to take a screen shot of the gpresult /r results, and then press Ctrl+V to paste the resulting image into the lab09_worksheet file in the page provided.

6. Close the command-prompt window.

7. On the Workstation## computer, log on as 10AUser2 of the Domain## domain. Repeat steps 2 through 4.

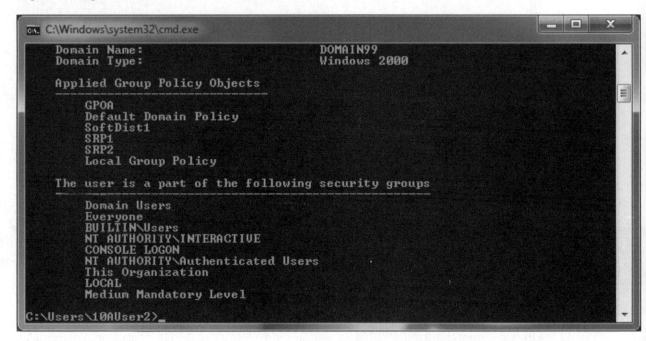

■ Part C: Use RSoP to Troubleshoot Deployment

1. On the Server## computer, log off and log on as 10CUser1 of the Domain## domain.

2. Click the Start button, key **rsop.msc,** and then click OK. When prompted, reenter the password for the 10CUser1 user account. A Group Policy error message is displayed, indicating that the user does not have the administrative permissions to see the security settings applied to the computer. However, this user is allowed to see the settings applying to the user account.

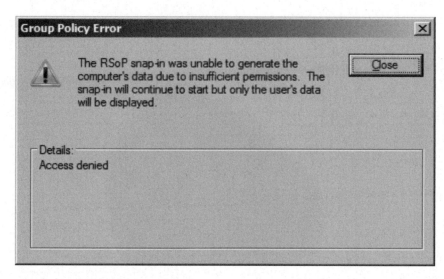

3. Read the error message and click Close. The Resultant Set Of Policy console is displayed.

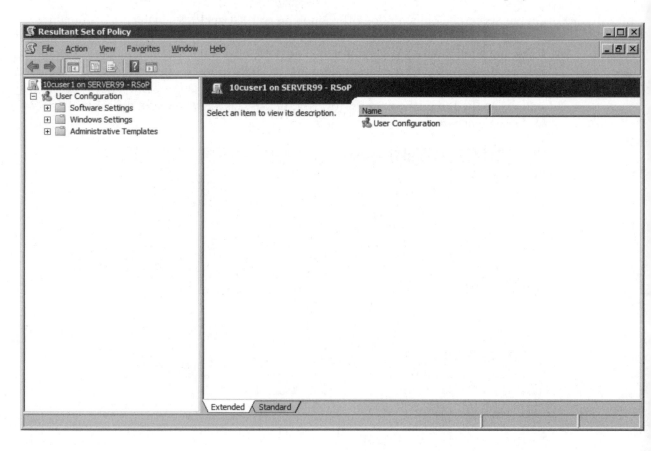

4. In the left window pane, expand Administrative Templates and click Start Menu And Taskbar.

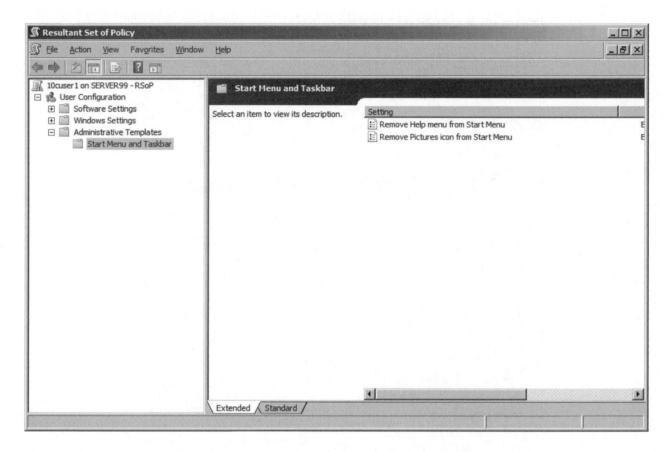

5. Read the contents in the right pane. You should see only the GPO settings that apply to this user account.

Question 9	*What are the names of the settings that apply to this user account?*

6. In the right pane, double-click Remove Help menu from Start Menu. The Remove Help Menu from Start Menu Properties dialog box is displayed.

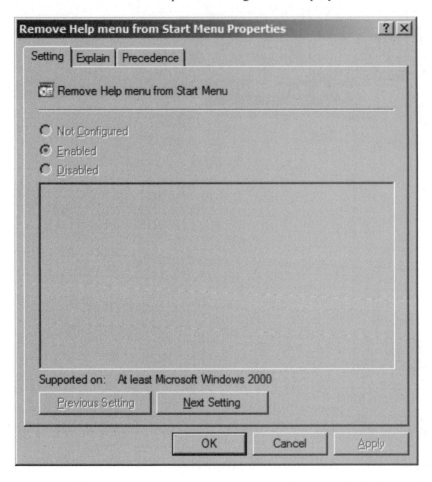

7.   Click the Precedence tab.

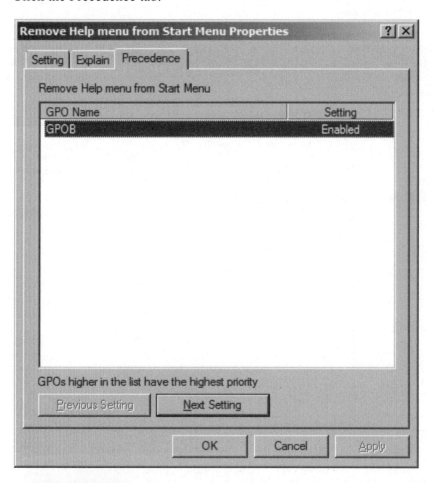

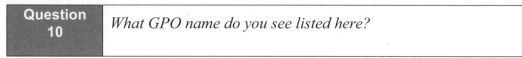

Question 10   *What GPO name do you see listed here?*

8.   Press Ctrl+Prt Scr to take a screen shot of the Remove Help menu from Start Menu Properties page with the Precedence tab selected, and then press Ctrl+V to paste the resulting image into the lab09_worksheet file in the page provided.

9.   Click OK to close the Remove Help Menu From Start Menu Properties dialog box.

10. Close the Resultant Set Of Policy console.

11. On the Workstation## computer, log off and log on as 10CUser2 of the Domain## domain. Repeat steps 2 through 9.

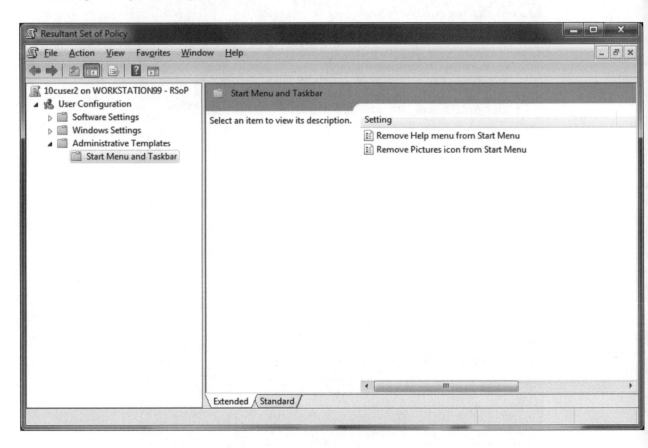

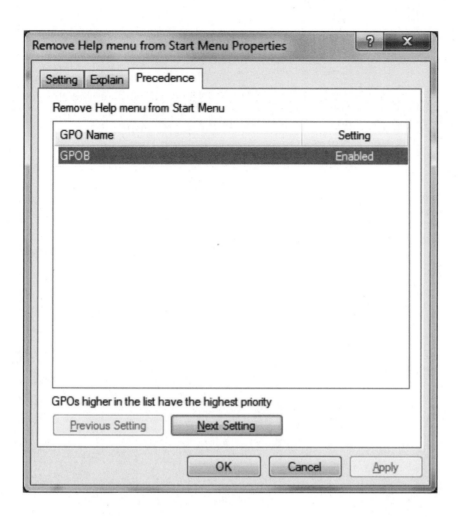

12. On the Server## computer, log off and log on as the default administrator of the Domain## domain.

13. Run RSoP.MSC.

Question 11	*Do you see the error message that the normal user accounts received?*

14. Close the Resultant Set Of Policy console.

Exercise 9.4	Using Security Filtering
Overview	You have a GPO that you want to apply to only members of the 10BGroup1 in the 10B OU. You want to try security filtering to prevent this GPO from applying to other users.
Completion time	20 minutes

■PART A: Configuring Security Group Filtering

1. On the Server## computer, open Active Directory Users And Computers and expand Domain##.Local in the left pane.

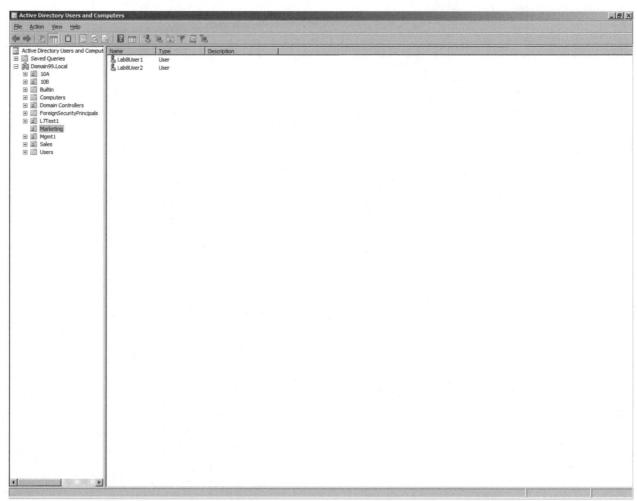

2. Right-click the 10B OU, click New, and then click Group. The New Object – Group
    dialog box is displayed. In the Group Name text box, key **10BGroup1** and click OK.

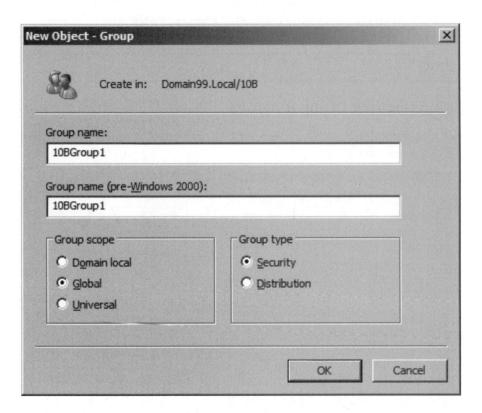

3. Right-click the group you just created and select Properties. Click the Members tab. Add 10BUser1 to the 10BGroup1 group object and click OK.

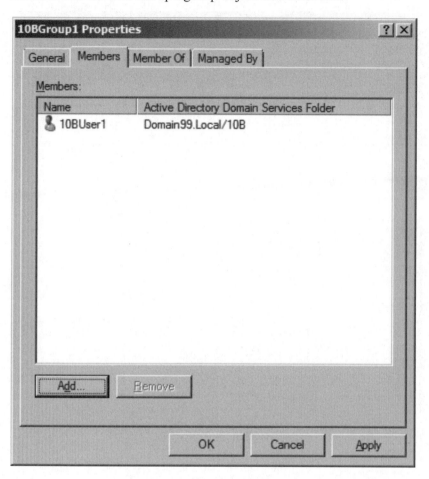

4. Open the Group Policy Management Console from the Administrative Tools folder. Drill down to the Drill down to the Domain## node.

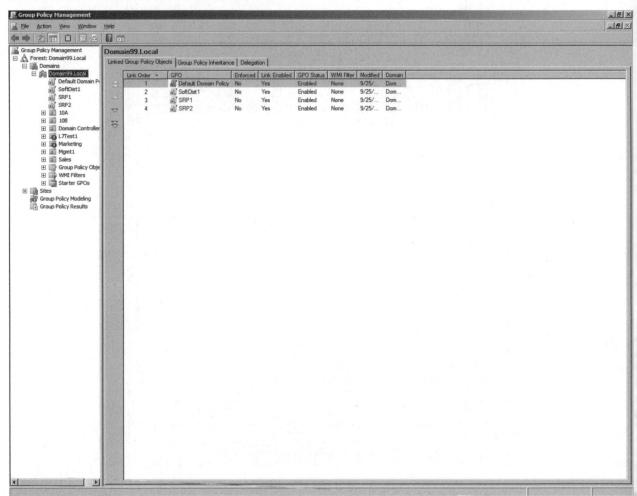

5. Navigate to the Group Policy Objects node. Select the GPOB GPO. In the Security Filtering section, highlight Authenticated Users and click Remove. Click OK to confirm the removal.

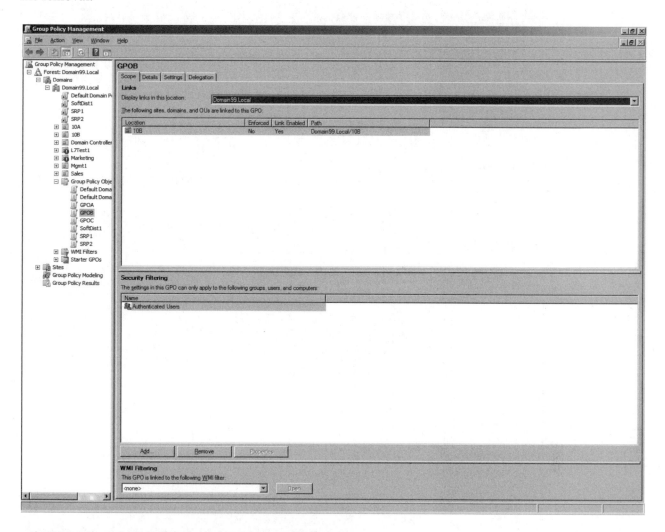

6. Click Add. The Select Computer, User, Or Group dialog box is displayed. Key **10BGroup1** and click OK.

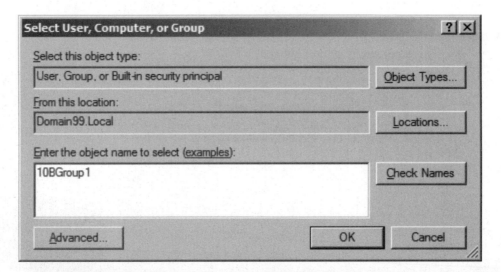

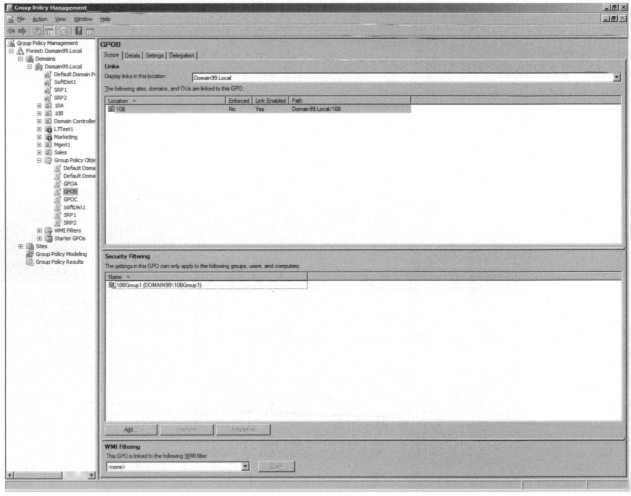

7. Close the Group Policy Management MMC snap-in.

- ## PART B: Testing Security Filtering

  1. On the Server## computer, open a command-prompt window and Key **gpupdate /force** and press Enter. Log off of the Server## computer and log back on as 10BUser1.

  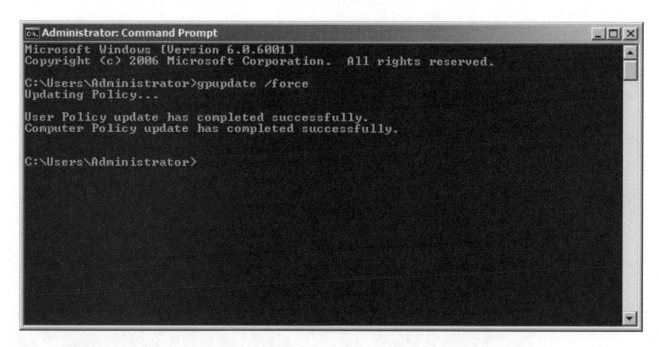

  2. Run GPRESULT /r from a command-prompt window and review the objects listed in the Applied Group Policy Objects section. (Refer to Project 9.3 for additional information about GPRESULT.)

  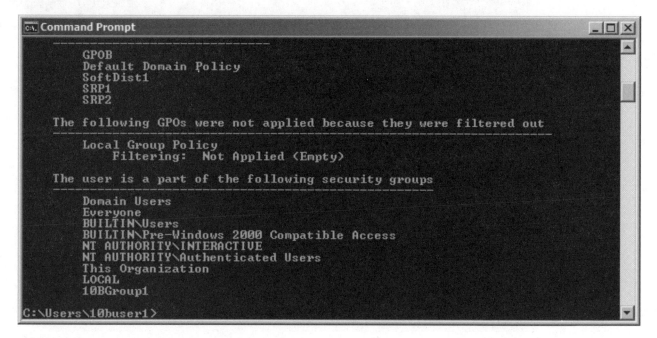

  3. Press Ctrl+Prt Scr to take a screen shot of the gpresult /r results, and then press Ctrl+V to paste the resulting image into the lab09_worksheet file in the page provided.

  4. Click the Start button.

Question 12	*Is the Help And Support menu available?*

5. On the Workstation## computer, log on as 10BUser2 of the Domain## domain.

6. Run GPRESULT /r from a command-prompt window and review the objects listed in the Applied Group Policy Objects section. (Refer to Project 9.3 for additional information about GPRESULT.)

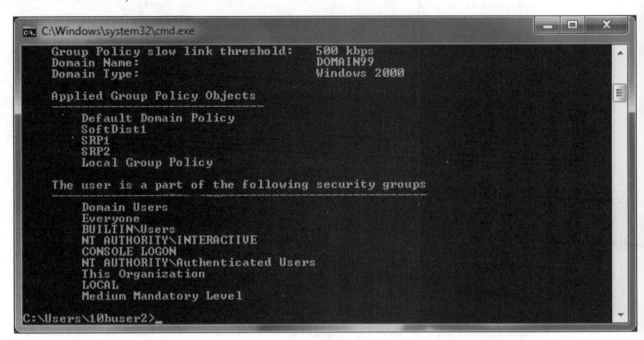

7. Run RSoP.MSC to validate which configuration settings affect 10BUser2. (Refer to Project 9.3 for additional information about RSoP.MSC.)

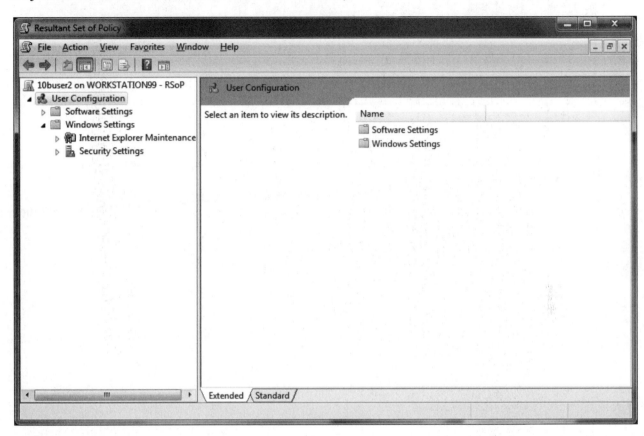

Question 13	*Why does 10BUser2 have a Help And Support menu in the Start menu, but 10BUser1 does not?*
Question 14	*If you want the GPO to apply to all Authenticated Users in the 10B OU and subordinate OUs except the members of 10BGroup1, what must you do differently?*

POST-LAB CLEANUP

Overview	Remove all Group Policy Objects that you configured in this lab.
Completion time	5 minutes

1. On Server## log on using your Administrator account and the password P@ssw0rd. Open the Group Policy Management Console from the Administrative Tools folder. Drill down to the Domain## node.

2. Navigate to the Group Policy Objects node and delete the link the following Group Policy Objects:

   - SoftDist1

   - SRP1

   - SRP2

   - GPOA

   - GPOB

   - GPOC

> **NOTE**
>
> *Do not delete the Default Domain Policy or the Default Domain Controllers Policy.*

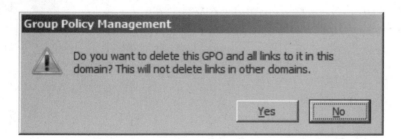

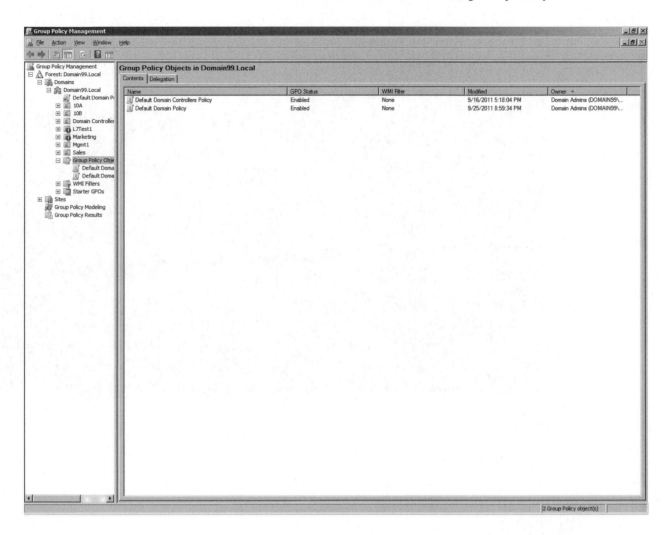

3. Delete the c:\MSI folder that you created in Exercise 9.1.

4. On Server##, open a command-prompt window, key **gpupdate /force**, and then press Enter.

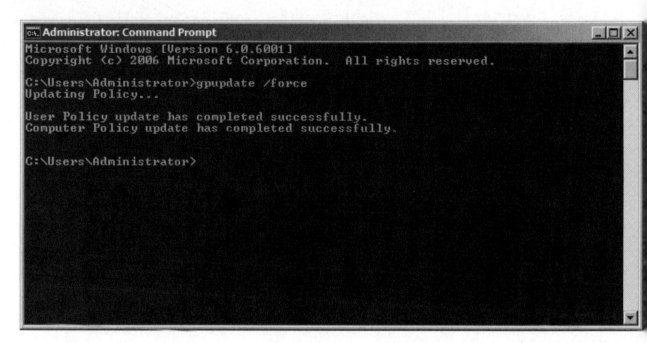

5. Reboot the Server## computer.

LAB 10
DISASTER RECOVERY AND MAINTENANCE

This lab contains the following exercises:

Exercise 10.1 Resolving Replication Issues

Exercise 10.2 Performing a System State Data Backup

Exercise 10.3 Compacting the Database

Exercise 10.4 Performing an Authoritative Restore

Estimated lab time: 110 minutes

Exercise 10.1	Resolving Replication Issues
Overview	Your manager sends instructions to two different administrators to perform conflicting tasks. These administrators perform the tasks on two different domain controllers in two different sites. After replication occurs, you notice odd results in the Active Directory Users And Computers node.
Completion time	30 minutes

■ PART A: Simulate the Issue

1. Turn on the Server## computer and log on using your Administrator account and the password P@ssw0rd.

2. Turn on the Server##A computer and log on using your Administrator account and the password P@ssw0rd.

NOTE	*Remember to use your domain adminstrator account and not the local administrator account.*

3. Verify that you are connected to the Server##A computer within the Active Directory Users and Computers console. To do so, right-click the Active Directory Users And Computers node in the left pane and then click Change Domain Controller. Verify that Current Directory Server is set to Server##A.Domain##.Local. If it is not, you should select Server##A.Domain##.Local in the Change To This Domain Controller or AD LDS instance box. Click OK.

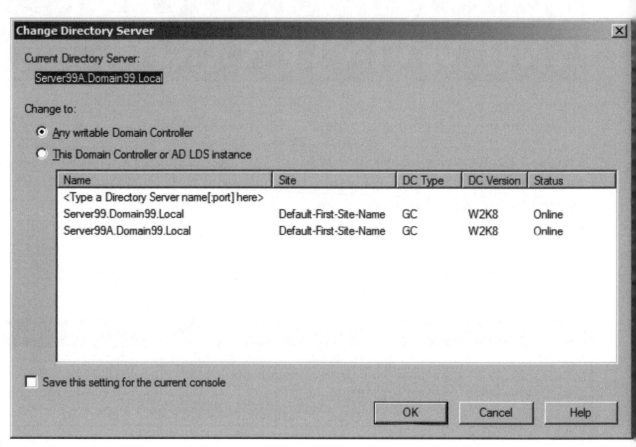

4. Create a new OU named Administration in the Domain##.Local domain.

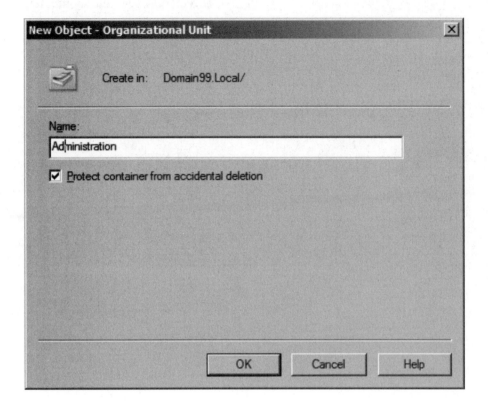

5. On Server## Open the Active Directory Users And Computers node and ensure that you are connected to the Server## computer within the Active Directory Users and Computers console. To do so, right-click the Active Directory Users And Computers node in the left pane and then click Change Domain Controller. Verify that Current Domain Controller is set to Server##.Domain##.Local. If it is not, you should select Server##.Domain##.Local in the Change To This Domain Controller box. Click OK.

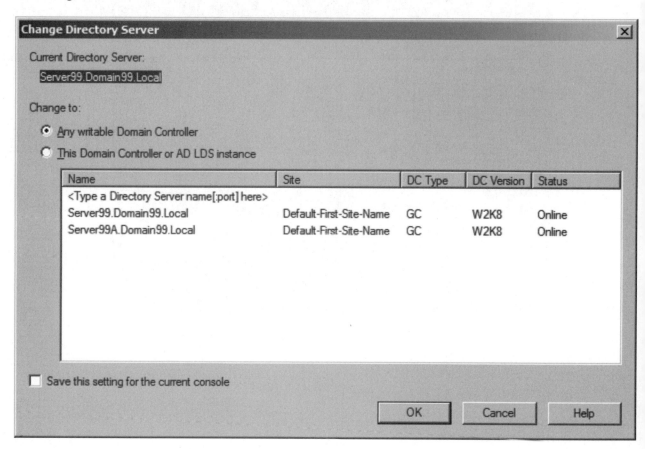

6. Ensure that the Administration OU has replicated to the Server## computer. If you do not want to wait for replication to occur, then force replication using the steps in exercise 4.1.

7. On the Server##A computer, simulate a replication delay by disabling the network connection. To disable the network connection, click Start, and then click Control Panel. Double-click Network And Sharing Center. In the left pane, click Manage Network Connections. Right-click the Local Area Connection icon and click Disable. This prevents the two domain controllers from replicating.

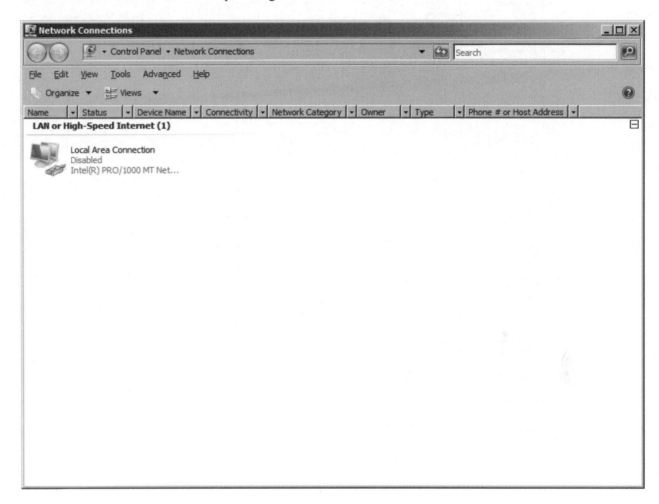

8. On the Server## computer, create three new user accounts inside the Administration OU. Name the user accounts Misty, Samantha, and Denise. For all of these accounts, use P@ssw0rd as the password and clear the User Must Change Password At Next Logon checkbox.

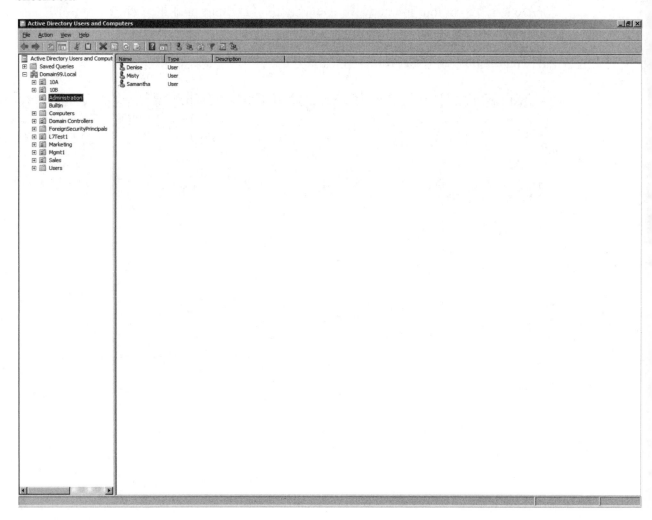

9. On the Server## computer, create a new OU named Accounting in the Domain##.Local domain.

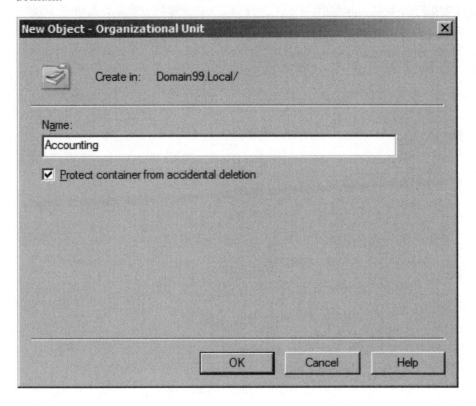

10. Disable the network connection on the Server## computer.

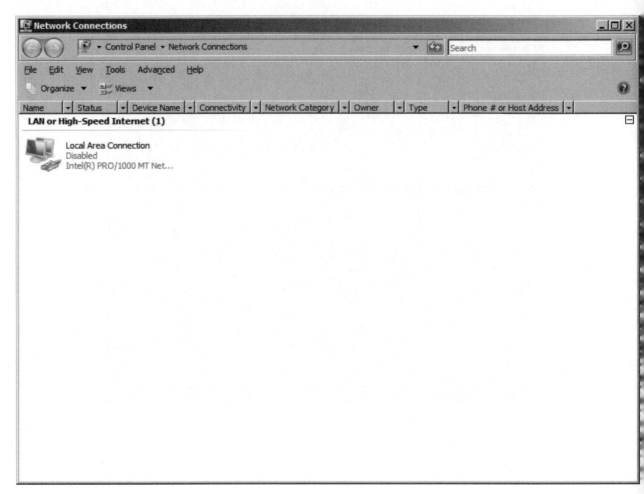

11. Enable the Server##A computer's network connection. To enable the network connection, click Start, and then click Control Panel. Double-click Network And Sharing Center. In the left pane, click Manage Network Connections. Right-click the Local Area Connection icon and click Enable.

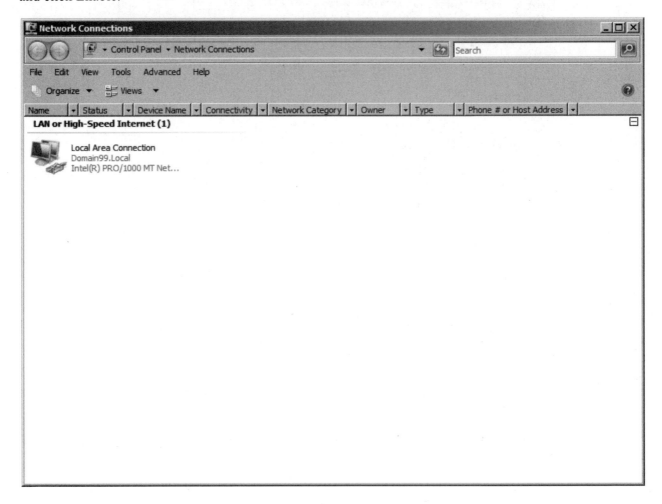

12. On the Server##A computer, create a new OU named Accounting in the Domain##.local domain.

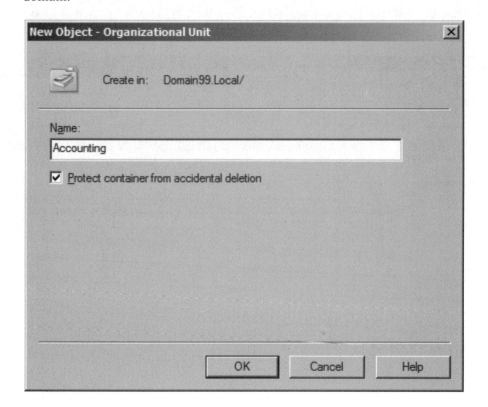

13. Create two new user accounts inside the Accounting OU. Name the user accounts Wedge and Wood. For both of these accounts, use P@ssw0rd as the password and clear the User Must Change Password At Next Logon checkbox.

> **NOTE**
> *You may experience slow performance when creating the users on the Server##A computer while the Server## computer's network connection is disabled, if the Server## computer is the only domain controller that is running the DNS Server service.*

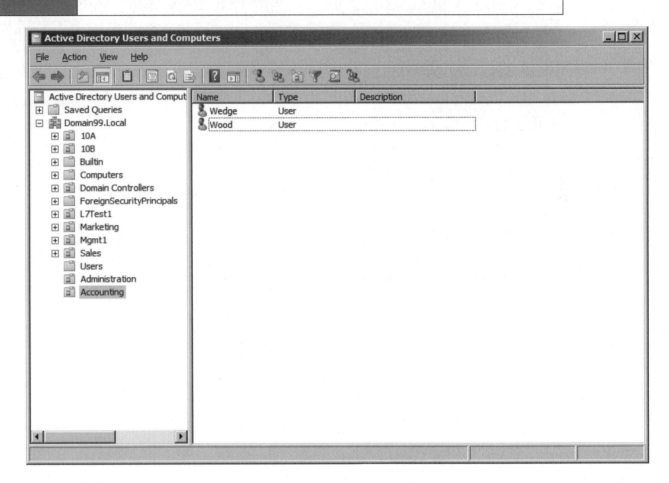

14. In the Active Directory Users And Computers console, ensure that the Advanced Features view option is enabled. To verify that this option is enabled, click the View menu and confirm that a checkmark is displayed next to Advanced Features.

15. Enable the network connection on the Server## computer to allow the two domain controllers to replicate their changes. If you do not want to wait, force replication.

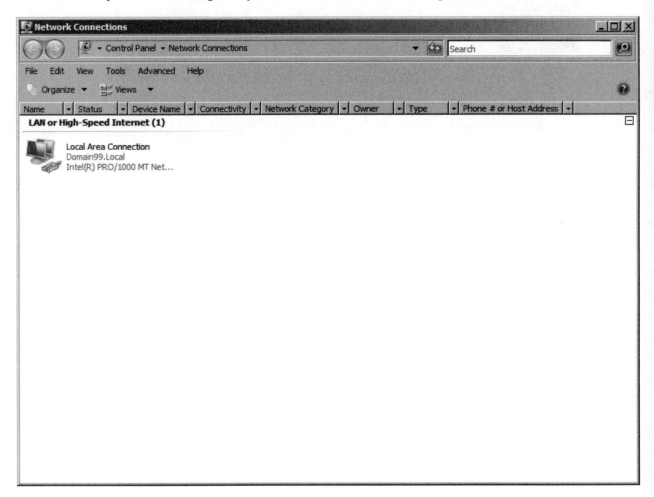

■ **PART B: Discovering and Resolving the Issue**

You learn that the other administrator created an OU named Accounting at nearly the same time that you did. You know there is a replication delay between the two domain controllers, so you think there may be two Accounting OUs.

To view the replication issue:

1. On the Server## computer, close the Active Directory User And Computers node and then open it again. When the console reappears, you should see that the Administration OU is gone. The console displays two Accounting OUs, one of which has additional characters.

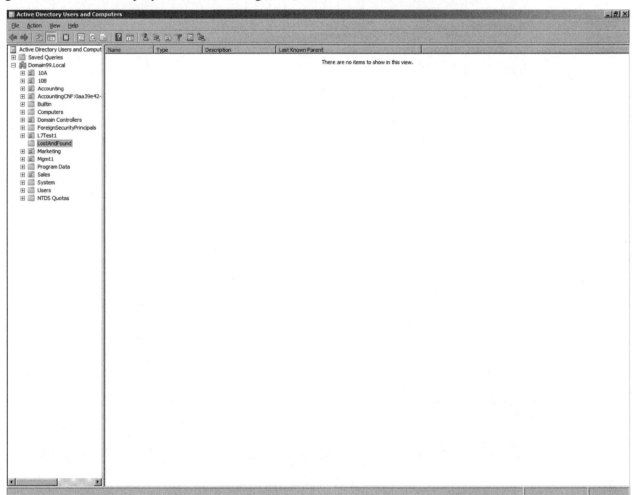

Question 1	*What does the alphanumeric string appended to the Accounting OU name represent?*

2. Press Ctrl+Prt Scr to take a screen shot of the Active Directory Users and Computers console showing the Accounting OUs, and then press Ctrl+V to paste the resulting image into the lab10_worksheet file in the page provided.

3. To resolve the Accounting OU problem, you should first determine if either OU contains any objects. If the Accounting OU with the alphanumeric string appended to the name has unique objects, such as users Wedge and Wood, move all of the objects to the Accounting OU. Then, delete the Accounting OU conflict object with the CNF string appended.

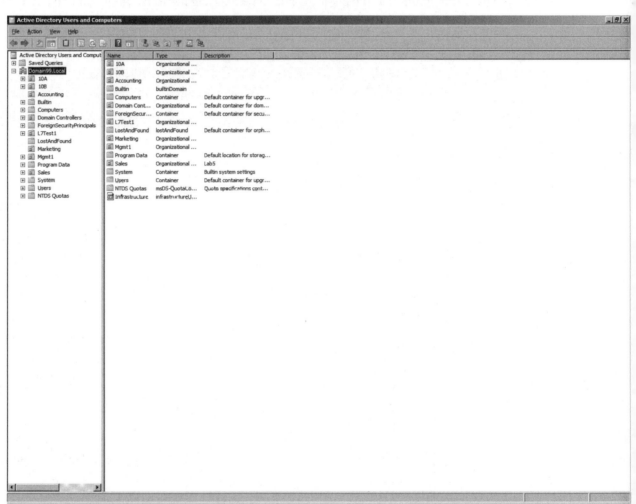

4. Close Active Directory Users And Computers on both domain controllers.

Exercise 10.2	Performing a System State Data Backup
Overview	You are about to make some configuration changes to your Active Directory database. You want to have a current System State data backup before you proceed.
Completion time	30 minutes

■ PART A: Installing the Windows Server Backup Feature

1. On the Server## computer, if the Server Manager window is not already open, click Start, and then click Server Manager.

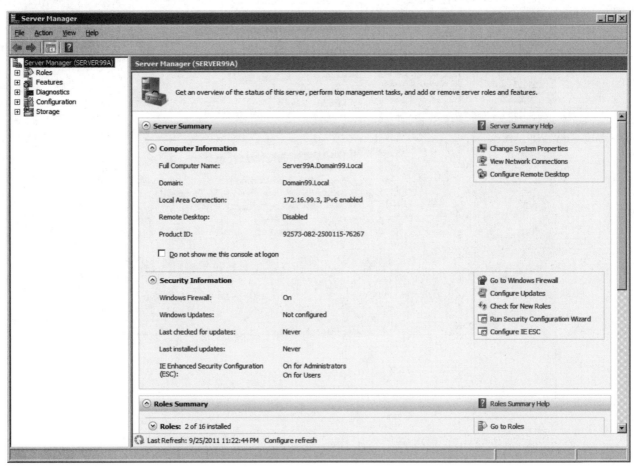

2. In the left pane, browse to Features. In the right pane, click Add Features. The Select Features window is displayed.

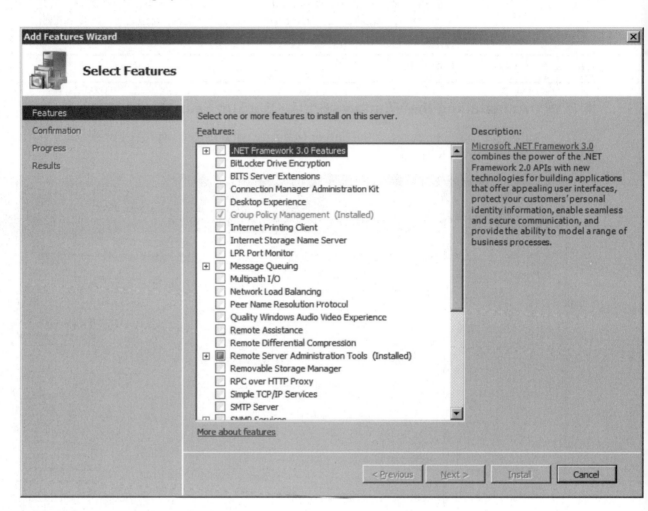

3. Place a checkmark next to the following features:

- Windows Powershell

- Windows Server Backup Features→Windows Server Backup

- Windows Server Backup Features→Command-line tools

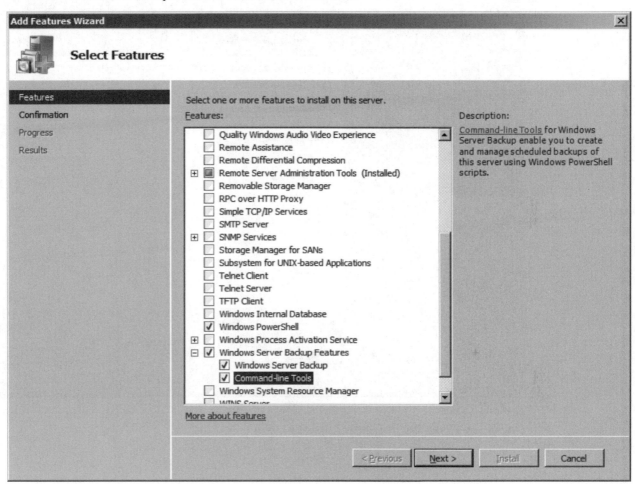

4. Click Next, and then click Install to add the Windows Server Backup feature.

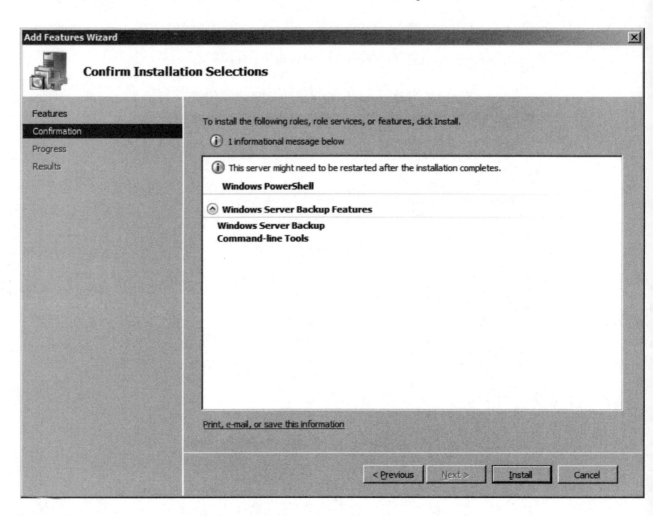

5. Click Close when the installation has completed.

■ PART B: Perform the System State Backup

1. Click Start, click Administrative Tools, and then click Windows Server Backup.

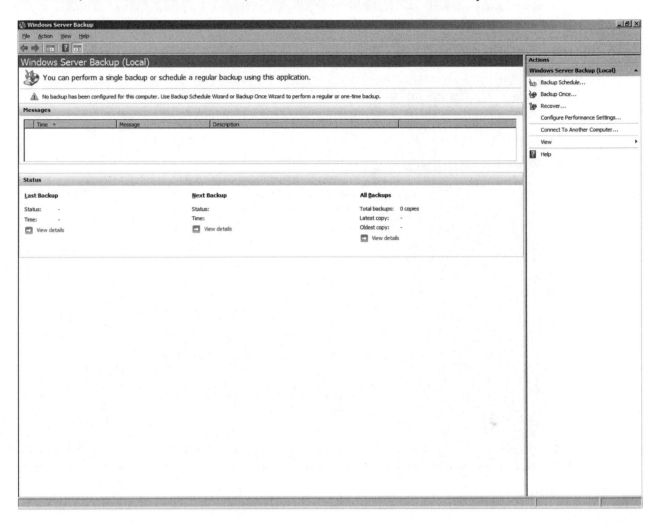

2. Click Action, and then click Backup Once. The Backup Options Wizard is displayed.

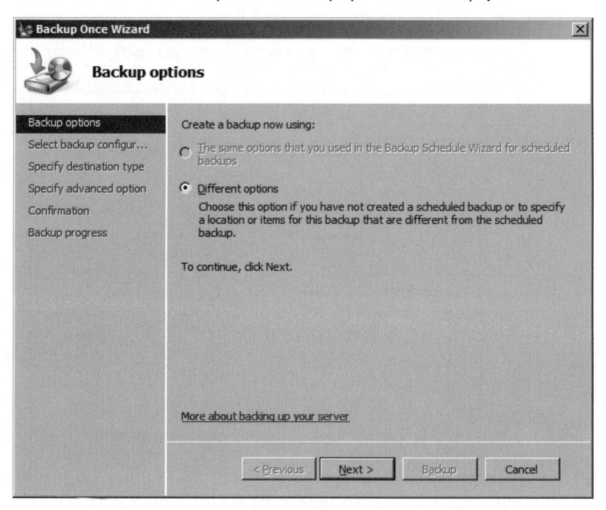

3. Click Next to begin performing a one-time backup. If this is the first backup you have performed, you might see a warning.

4. Click Yes to acknowledge the warning and continue. The Select Backup Configuration screen is displayed.

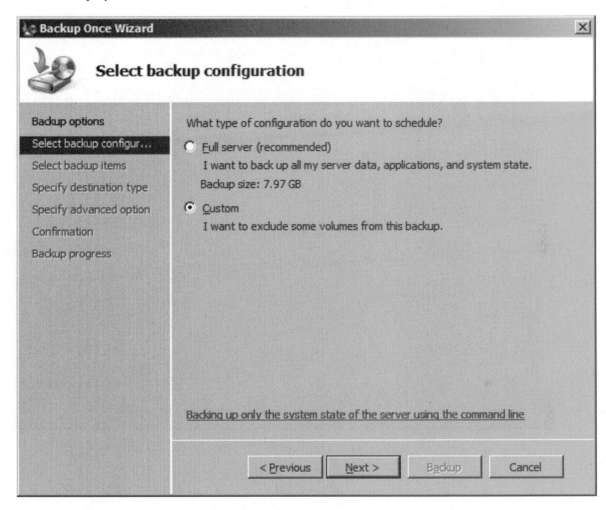

5. Click Custom and then click Next. The Select Backup Items window is displayed.

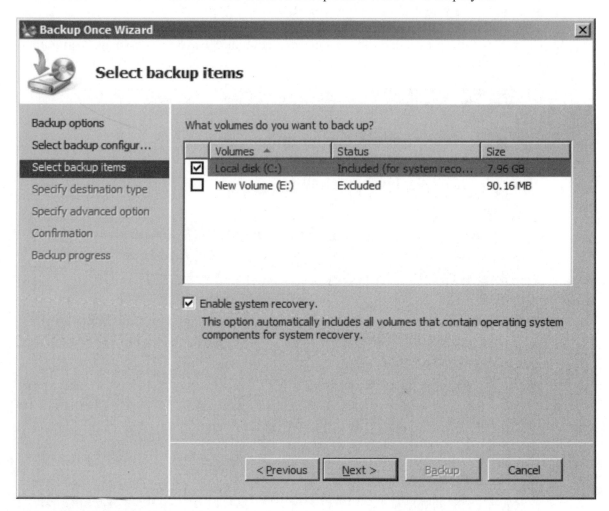

6. Verify that the second hard drive on the Server## computer has been deselected and then click Next. The Specify Destination Type window is displayed.

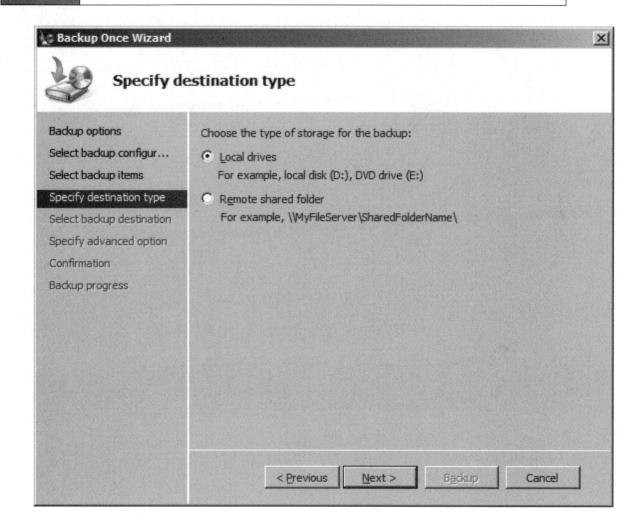

7. Click Local Drives and then click Next. The *Select Backup Destination* window is displayed.

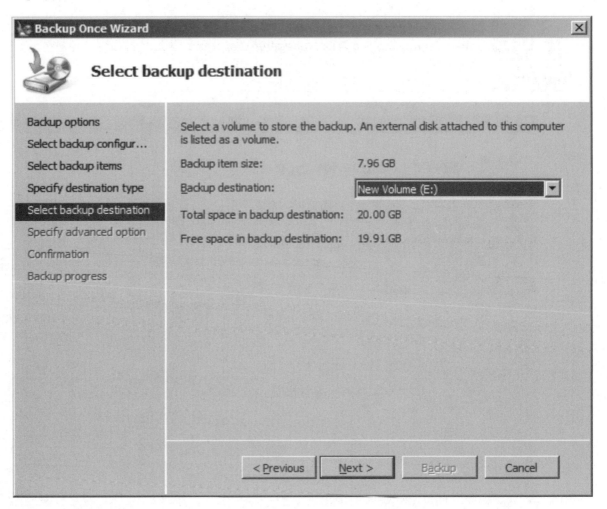

8. In the Backup Destination dropdown list, confirm that the second hard drive on the Server## computer is selected, and then click Next. The Specify Advanced Option window is displayed.

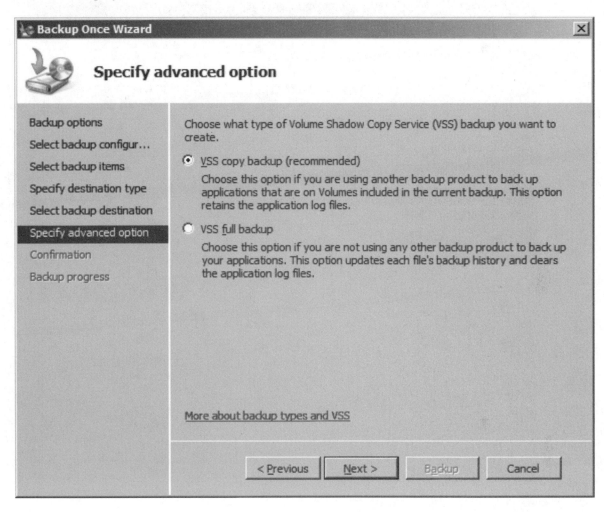

9. Read the description of the VSS copy backup and click Next. The Confirmation screen is displayed.

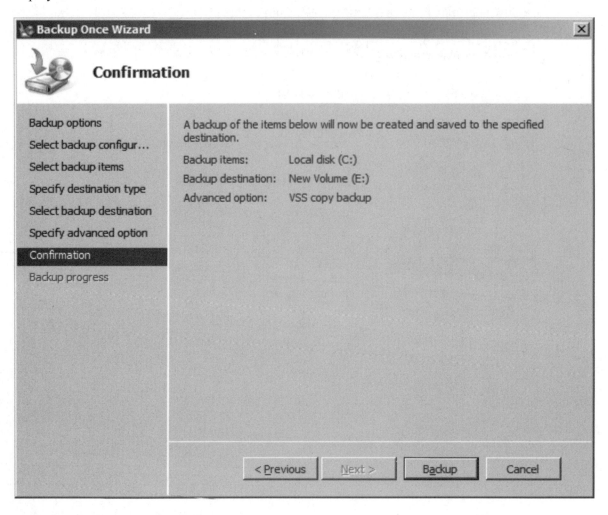

10. Click Backup to begin the backup process.

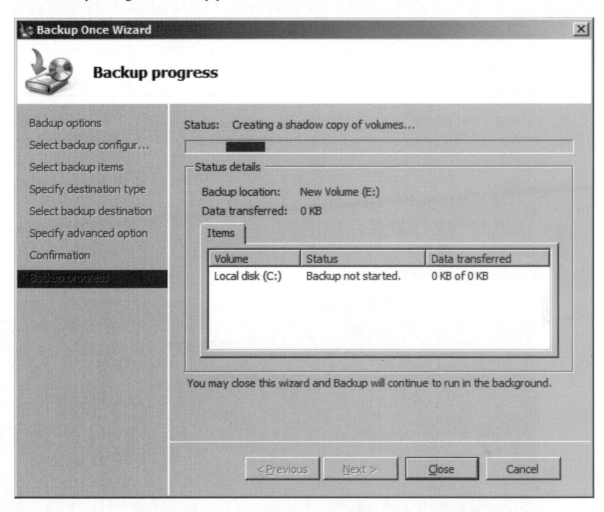

11. Press Ctrl+Prt Scr to take a screen shot of the Backup Once Wizard indicating that the backup was completed, and then press Ctrl+V to paste the resulting image into the lab10_worksheet file in the page provided.

12. Click Close when the backup completes. Close the Windows Server Backup console.

Exercise 10.3   Compacting the Database

Overview	You want to reduce the space that Active Directory occupies on your domain controller.
Completion time	30 minutes

1. On Server## or Server##A open a command-prompt window. To enable Directory Services Restore Mode on the next reboot, key **bcdedit /set safeboot dsrepair**, and then press Enter.

> **NOTE**
> *You can perform this exercise on Server##A, while Server## completes the backup from the last exercise.*

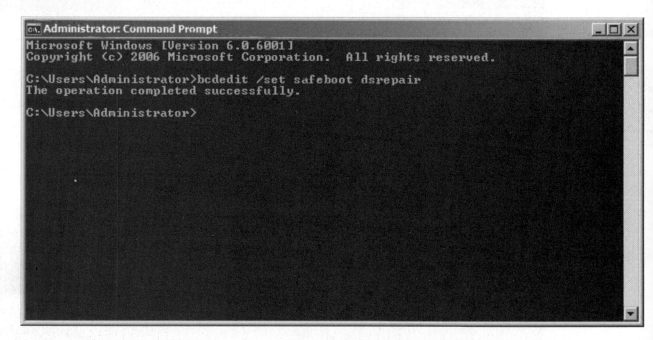

2. Close the command-prompt window and restart the computer.

3. When the computer restarts, log onto the computer using the Directory Services Restore Mode username and password. The username should be Administrator and the password should be P@ssw0rd. The Windows Desktop should indicate that the domain controller is operating in Safe Mode.

> **NOTE**
> *In order to log using a local machine account click switch user, then other user and enter Server##\Administrator as the username.*

4. Open a command-prompt window, key **NTDSUTIL**, and press Enter.

5. Key **activate instance ntds** and press Enter.

6. Key **files** and press Enter. The File Maintenance prompt is displayed.

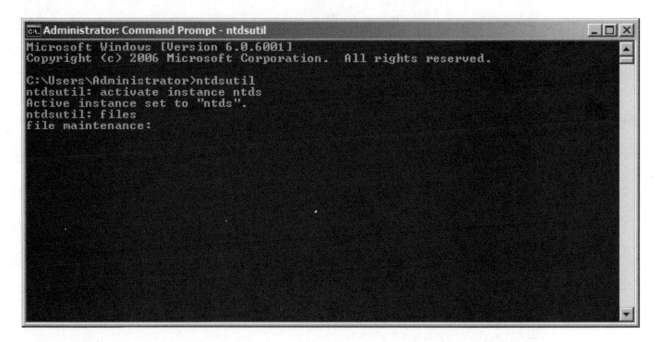

7. Key **?** and press Enter. Notice that you have several options at this prompt. You can check the Active Directory database integrity, move the database, and move the database log files.

8. Key **info** and press Enter. This command displays the current location of the Active Directory database (ntds.dit), the backup directory, and the log files directory.

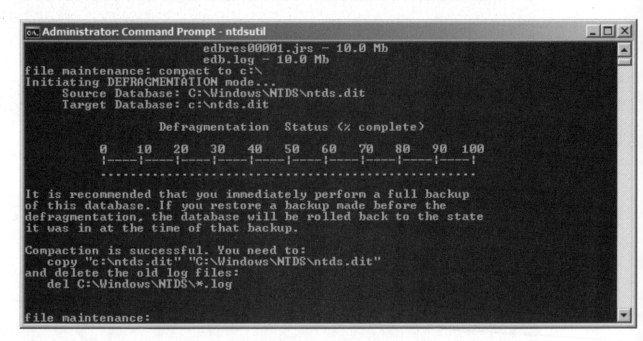

9. To perform offline compaction of the database, key **compact to c:** and press Enter. The database is compacted and you are given directions to replace the existing database.

10. Key **quit** and press Enter. The ntdsutil prompt is displayed.

11. Key **quit** again and press Enter. You are returned to the command prompt.

12. Key **move %systemroot%\ntds\ntds.dit c:\ntds.old** and press Enter. This saves your old Active Directory database in case you have trouble with the newly compacted database. You can delete this copy after you verify that the newly compacted database loads correctly after you restart the computer. Otherwise, you can use the ntds.old file to replace the compacted database.

13. Key **move %systemroot%\ntds*.log c:** and press Enter. This command moves the former Active Directory database log files to the c:\ drive.

14. Key **move c:\ntds.dit %systemroot%\ntds\ntds.dit** and press Enter. This command places the newly compacted database in the appropriate location to load when you restart the computer.

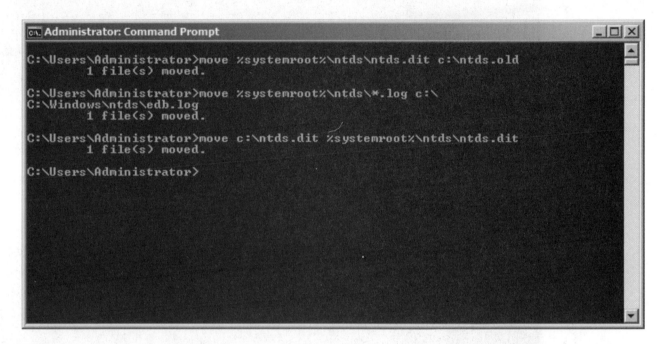

15. Key **dir c:\ntds.old** and press Enter. Statistics for the previous copy of the Active Directory database are displayed.

16. Key **dir %systemroot%\ntds\ntds.dit** and press Enter. The Active Directory database is compacted. Statistics for the newly compacted Active Directory database are displayed. Compare the size of the ntds.old file to the size of the ntds.dit file. You might not see a size difference between the compacted file and the original file, because the database in the lab has not had a chance to become fragmented. On a computer that hosts an Active Directory database that experiences a large number of changes, you could reduce the amount of space that the Active Directory database occupied with the compacting process.

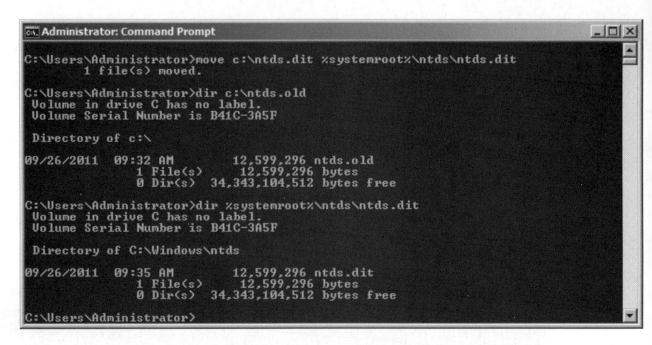

17. Press Ctrl+Prt Scr to take a screen shot of the command prompt window showing the statistics for the newly compacted database and then press Ctrl+V to paste the resulting image into the lab10_worksheet file in the page provided.

18. To remove the Directory Services Restore Mode boot option, key **bcdedit /deletevalue safeboot** and press Enter. Restart the domain controller.

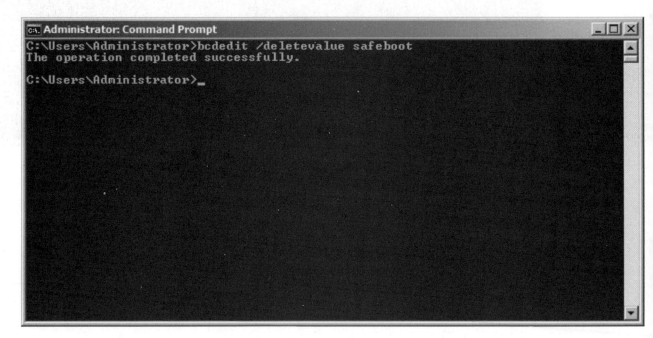

19. If the computer starts properly without errors, log on as the default administrator of the Domain## domain. Open a command-prompt window. Key **del c:\ntds.old c:\res*.log c:\edb*.log** and press Enter. This will delete the old Active Directory database and log files. Close the command-prompt window.

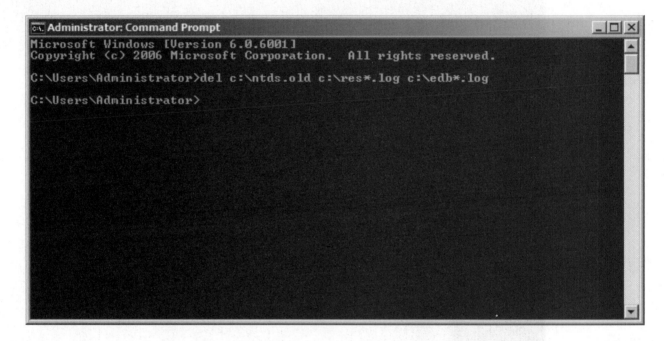

Exercise 10.4   Performing an Authoritative Restore

Overview	You accidentally delete an OU and all of its user accounts. You want to restore the OU using an authoritative restore.
Completion time	20 minutes

1. On the Server## computer open Active Directory Users And Computers.

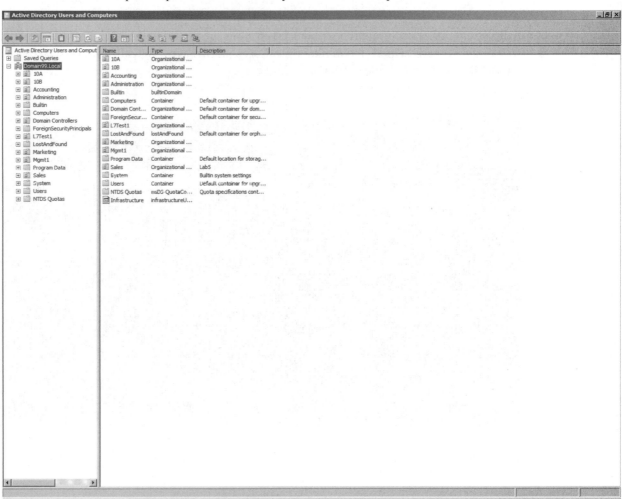

2. In the Active Directory Users And Computers console, ensure that the Advanced Features view option is enabled. To verify that this option is enabled, click the View menu and confirm that a checkmark is displayed next to Advanced Features.

3. Right-click the Administration OU, select properties, when the Administration Properties
    sheet opens select the Object tab and uncheck the Protect object from accidental deletion
    checkbox.

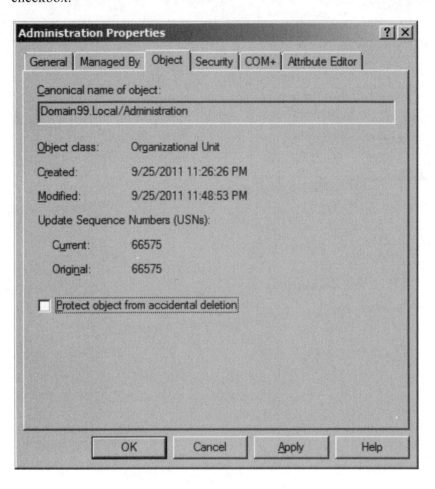

4. Delete the Administration OU and all of its contents. Close Active Directory Users And Computers.

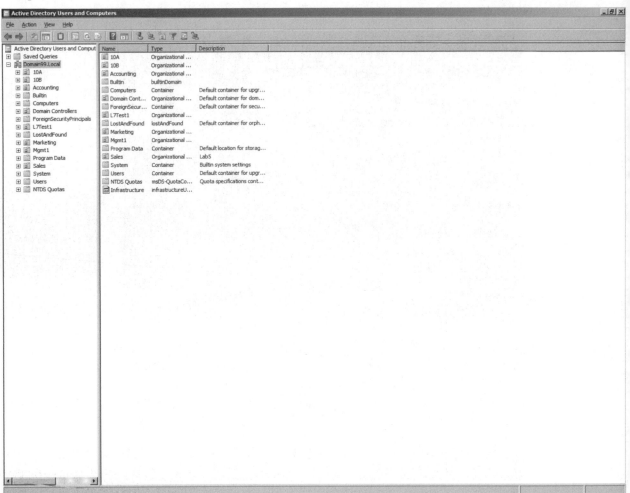

5. Restart the computer in Directory Services Restore Mode.

> **NOTE**
>
> *Remember in order to start in Directory Services Restore Mode you must enter **bcdedit /set safeboot dsrepair** at the command prompt.*

6. When the computer restarts, log onto the computer using the Directory Services Restore Mode username and password. The username should be Administrator and the password should be P@ssw0rd. The Windows Desktop should indicate that the domain controller is operating in Safe Mode.

7. Open a command-prompt window. Key **wbadmin get versions** to obtain the date and timestamp of the backup that you performed in Project 10.3.

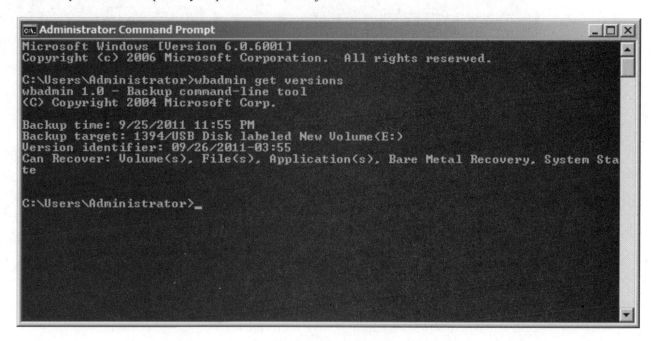

8. Key **wbadmin start systemstaterecovery –version:mm/dd/yyyy-hh:ss**, substituting the month, day, year, hour and second of the backup that you performed.

9. Key **Y** and press Enter to begin the restore process. You might see a warning message before the restore begins. Key **Y** again and press Enter.

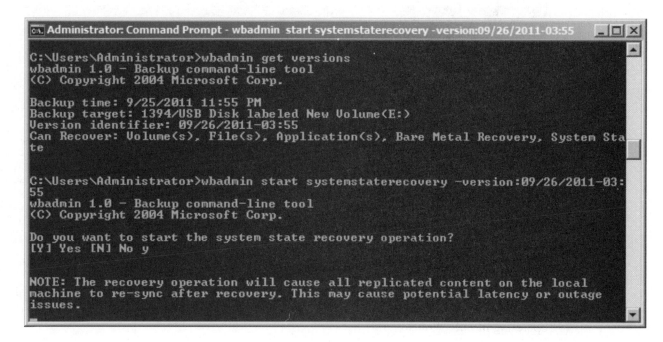

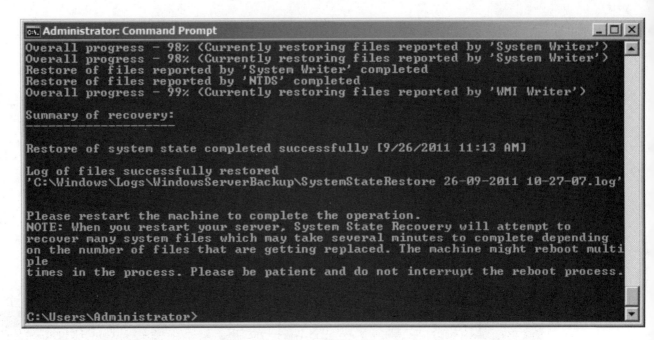

10. Allow several minutes for the restore to complete. After the restore is completed, you will see a message instructing you to restart your system. You must perform the authoritative restore before restarting. Key **ntdsutil** and press Enter.

11. Key **activate instance ntds** and press Enter.

12. Key **authoritative restore** and press Enter.

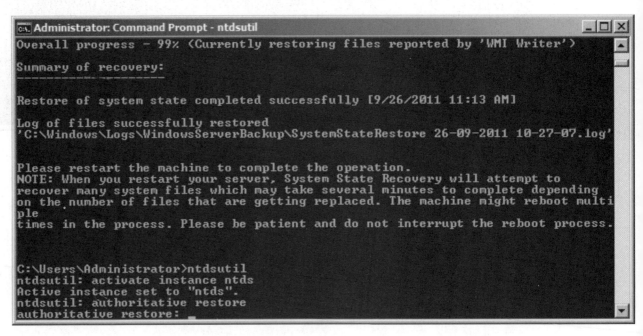

13. Key **restore subtree ou=Administration,dc=Domain##,dc=Local** and press Enter. An Authoritative Restore Confirmation dialog box is displayed.

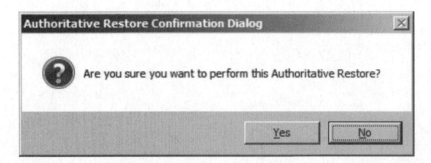

14. Click Yes. The operation may take a few minutes to complete. You will see a message stating that the authoritative restore has been completed successfully.

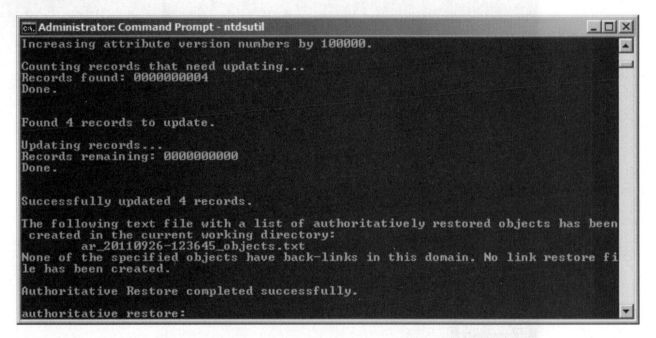

15. Key **quit** and press Enter. Key **quit** again and press Enter. You are returned to the command prompt.

16. To remove the Directory Services Restore Mode boot option, key **bcdedit /deletevalue safeboot** and press Enter. Restart the domain controller and log onto the computer as the default administrator of the Domain##.Local domain.

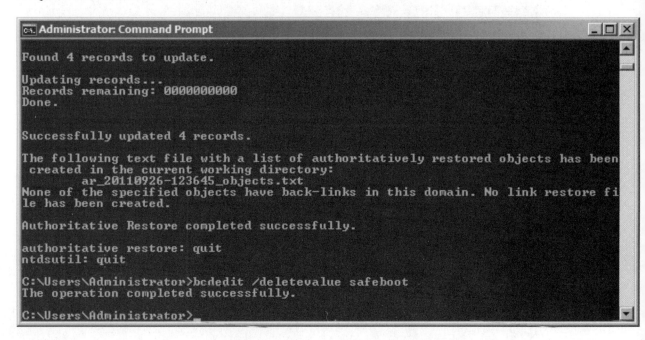

17. Open Active Directory Users And Computers. The Administration OU should be visible in the console. Click the Administration OU to display its contents.

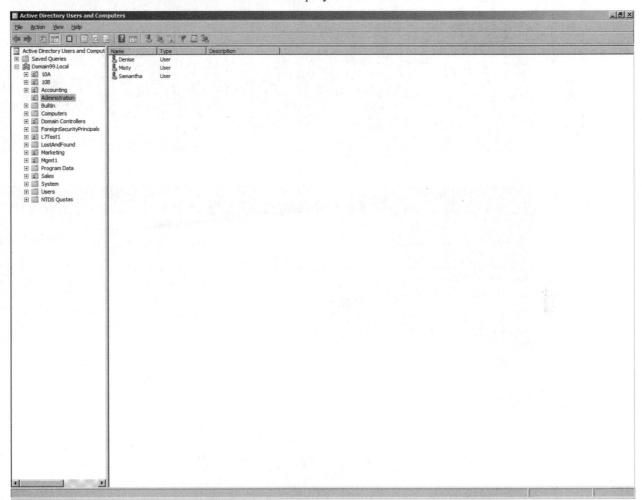

Question 2	*Were the Denise, Misty, and Samantha user accounts restored with the Administration OU?*

18. Press Ctrl+Prt Scr to take a screen shot of Active Directory Users and Computers console showing the contents of the Administration OU, and then press Ctrl+V to paste the resulting image into the lab10_worksheet file in the page provided.

19. Close the Active Directory Users And Computers console.

APPENDIX
REARMING YOUR VIRTUAL MACHINES

Exercise 1.1	Rearming your Virtual Machines
Overview	The following are the steps for rearming a Windows 7 Workstation or Windows 2008 Server machine to extend your evaluation period.
Completion time	10 minutes

> **NOTE**
>
> *This process should be done a few days prior to expiration. You can only perform this process a total of four times and it does not accumulate. Therefore, only use this process just before the expiration date.*

1. Click Start, click All Programs, and then click Accessories.

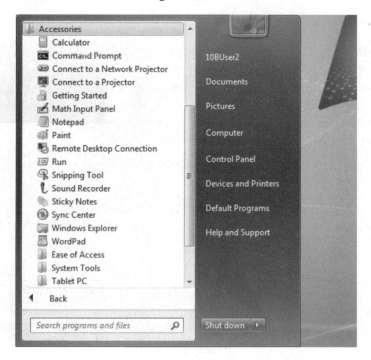

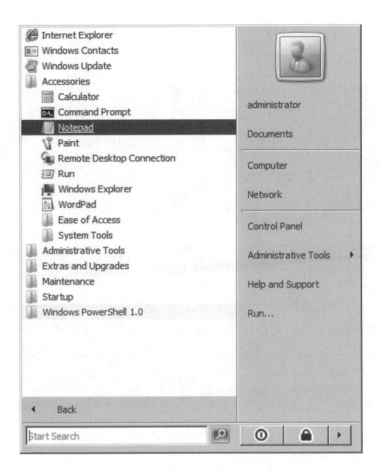

2. Right-click Command Prompt and select Run As Administrator.

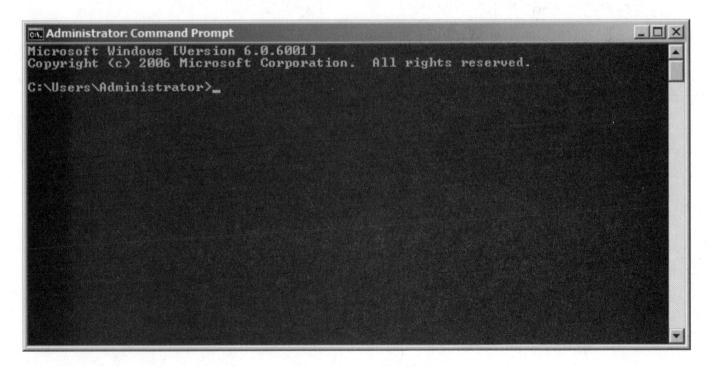

3. At the Command Prompt key: slmgr –rearm   Wait for the following window to appear and reboot your system.

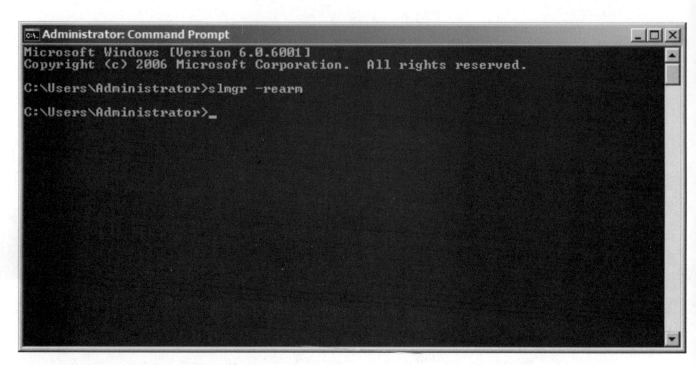

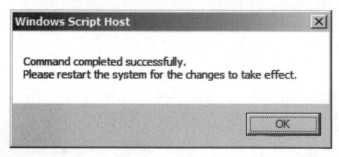